RENDEZVOUS IN PARIS
PICASSO, CHAGALL, MODIGLIANI & CO.
(1900–1939)

RENDEZVOUS IN PARIS
PICASSO, CHAGALL, MODIGLIANI & CO.
(1900–1939)

RENDEZVOUS IN PARIS
PICASSO, CHAGALL, MODIGLIANI & CO.
(1900–1939)

Edited by Christian Briend

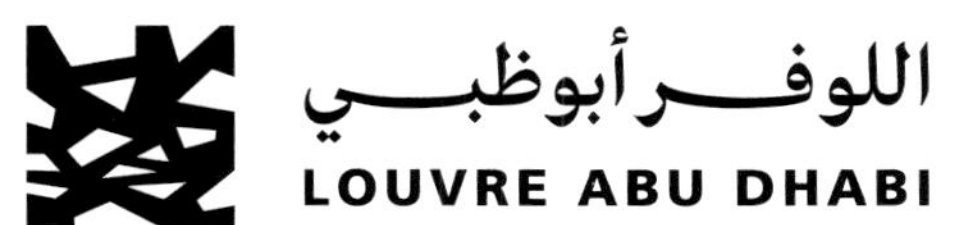

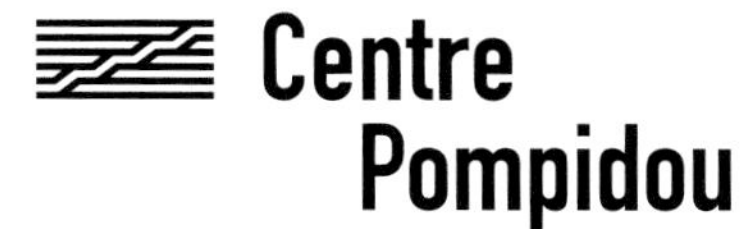

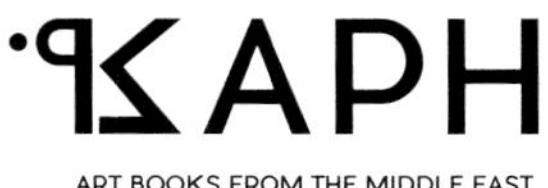

This catalogue is published on the occasion of the exhibition "Rendezvous in Paris: Picasso, Chagall, Modigliani & Co. (1900–1939)", organised by Louvre Abu Dhabi, the Centre national d'art et de culture Georges Pompidou and Agence France-Muséums, and held at Louvre Abu Dhabi from 18 September to 7 December 2019.

CURATORSHIP

Christian Briend, Chief Curator, Head of Modern Art Collection, MNAM-CCI
Assisted by **Anna Hiddleston-Galloni**, Assistant Curator, Modern Art Collection, MNAM-CCI

DEPARTMENT OF CULTURE AND TOURISM – ABU DHABI

H.E. Mohamed Khalifa Al Mubarak, Chairman
H.E. Saif Saeed Ghobash, Undersecretary
H.E. Nawal R. Al Hassani, Executive Director of Strategy and Planning Sector
H.E. Saood Abdulaziz Al Hosani, Executive Director of Support Services Sector
Rita Aoun-Abdo, Executive Director of Culture Sector
Ali Hassan Al Shaiba, Acting Executive Director of Marketing and Communications Sector
Mohammad Al Frehat, General Counsel

LOUVRE ABU DHABI

Manuel Rabaté, Museum Director

Marwa Rubayee Al Menhali, Business Support Director
Lamya Al Nuaimi, Development and Partnerships Manager
Ugo Bertoni, Head of International and Institutional Affairs
Emma Cantwell, Acting Director of Marketing and Communications
Flora Castillon, Visitor Experience & Sales Director
Heros Leask, Legal Counsel
Douglas Masuku, Technical Operations Director
Catherine Monlouis-Félicité, Education and Cultural Engagement Director
Dr. Souraya Noujaim, Scientific, Curatorial and Collections Management Director

EXHIBITION

Dr. Souraya Noujaim, Scientific, Curatorial and Collections Management Director
Juliette Singer, Chief Curator – Modern and Contemporary Art

Virginia Fienga, Museography & Collection Management Manager
Garrett James Donnelly, Museographic Exhibition Unit Head
Maria Papadimitriou, Preventive Conservation Unit Head
Loïc Prat, Acting Registrars Unit Head
Amine Kharcharch, Museography and Multimedia Interpretation Manager

PUBLICATION

Catherine Monlouis-Félicité, Education and Cultural Engagement Director
Laurent Germeau, Publications Manager
Amanda Nicole Smith, Project Manager
Mohamed Zaggar, Publications Senior Editor
Céline Millinder, Senior Visual and Images Officer
Ugo Bertoni, Institutional and forewords coordination

AGENCE FRANCE-MUSÉUMS

BOARD

Sandra Lagumina, Chairperson
Laurence des Cars, President, Établissement Public des Musées d'Orsay et de l'Orangerie
Laurence Engel, President, Bibliothèque Nationale de France
Christian Giacomotto, President of Auditing Committee
Jean Guéguinou, President of Remuneration Committee
Chris Dercon, President, Établissement Public de la Réunion des Musées Nationaux et du Grand Palais
Serge Lasvignes, President, Centre Pompidou
Sophie Makariou, President, Musée National des Arts Asiatiques – Guimet
Stéphane Martin, President, Musée du Quai Branly – Jacques Chirac
Jean-Luc Martinez, President-Director, Musée du Louvre
Maxence Langlois-Berthelot, Managing Director, Musée du Louvre
Alberto Vial, Diplomatic Advisor, Musée du Louvre
Laurence Auer, Director of Culture, Education, Research and Network, Ministry of Europe and Foreign Affairs
Monique Schwartz-Autissier, Comptroller General, Economics and Finance, Ministry of the Economy
Éric Lefèbvre, KPMG Auditor

Anne Mény-Horn, Chief Executive Officer
Stéphane Roisin, General Secretary
Jean-Valère Arifont, Director of Architectural and Technical Affairs
Olivia Bourrat, Scientific Director
Katia Cartacheff, Chief Operating Officer
Olivia Davidson, Head of Exhibitions and Publications

EXHIBITION
Claire Monneraye, Exhibition Manager
Marie Knidler and Véronique Declercq, Exhibition Registrars
Clémence Derrien, Operations – Project Coordinator
Paule Mourani, Interpretation Manager
Mathilde Etot, Interpretation and Education Officer
Beverly Galdamez, Interpretation Officer

PUBLICATION
David Lestringant and Céline Moulard, Freelance Editors
for Agence France-Muséums

CENTRE NATIONAL D'ART ET DE CULTURE GEORGES POMPIDOU

Serge Lasvignes, President
Julie Narbey, Managing Director
Julia Beurton, Deputy Managing Director

MUSÉE NATIONAL D'ART MODERNE – CENTRE DE CRÉATION INDUSTRIELLE (MNAM-CCI)

Bernard Blistène, Director
Xavier Bredin, Administrator
Brigitte Leal, Deputy Director in charge of collections
Catherine David, Deputy Director in charge of research and globalisation
Didier Ottinger, Deputy Director in charge of cultural programming
Frédéric Migayrou, Deputy Director in charge of industrial creation

Mathieu Potte-Bonneville, Director of Cultural Development
Agnès Benayer, Director of Communication and Partnerships
Catherine Guillou, Director of Cutural Engagement

EXHIBITION
Claire Both, Collections Manager
Lucille Royan and Sophie Spalek, Conservators
Émilie Lormée, Charlotte Despagne and Véronique Roca, External Registrars
Éric Galliache and José da Silva, Frame Makers
Laurent de Saint-Maurice, External Frame Maker
Melissa Etave, Art Registrar
Xavier Isaïa and Eric L'Hospitalier, Storage Registrars
Raphaele Bianchi, Olga Makhroff and Saïda Hérida, Loans and Deposits Division
Victor Guégan, Manager of Oral and Written Interpretation Unit

SCENOGRAPHY
bGc studio

GRAPHICS
Atelier Bastien Morin

LIGHTING
Abraxas Concept

AUDIOVISUAL AND MULTIMEDIA INTERPRETATION
Drôle de Trame

The exhibition organisers wish to express their heartfelt gratitude to the Musée de l'Orangerie that supported this exhibition by lending major artworks from its collection as well as the depositary museums:
Musée des Années 30, Boulogne-Billancourt
Musée des Beaux-Arts, Chartres
Musée des Beaux-Arts, Dijon
Musée d'Art Moderne Richard-Anacréon, Granville
Musée de Grenoble, Grenoble
Musée Fabre, Montpellier
Musée National Picasso, Paris
Musée d'Art et d'Histoire du Judaïsme, Paris
Musée d'Art Moderne, Troyes

The exhibition Curator wishes to thank Véronique Borgeaud, Isabelle Daire, Carole Hubert, Doïna Lemny, Jean-Gabriel Massardier and Camille Morando who were also involved in preparing this exhibition at Centre Pompidou. He also expresses his gratitude to Christian Derouet and Anita Hopmans, as well as to the catalogue authors, Sophie Krebs and Yves Chevrefils Desbiolles, for the quality of their scientific contribution.

CATALOGUE AUTHORS

Christian Briend, Curator and Publication Director, Chief Curator and Head of Modern Art Collection, MNAM-CCI
Yves Chevrefils-Desbiolles, Head of Collections, Institute for Contemporary Publishing Archives
Nathalie Ernoult, Assistant Curator, Modern Art Collection, MNAM-CCI
Anna Hiddleston-Galloni, Assistant Curator, Modern Art Collection, MNAM-CCI
Julie Jones, Assistant Curator, Photography Collection, MNAM-CCI
Sophie Krebs, Chief Curator, Musée d'Art Moderne de la Ville de Paris
Inès Lassale, Intern, Modern Art Collection, MNAM-CCI
Anne Lemonnier, Assistant Curator, Modern Art Collection, MNAM-CCI

TABLE OF CONTENTS

FOREWORD

During the early decades of the twentieth century, Paris witnessed the birth of modern art. Here in the Gulf we are enjoying another cultural renaissance, as new creative hubs develop away from the traditional centres in Europe or the United States. A century separates the Paris explored in this new exhibition and contemporary Abu Dhabi, yet parallels can be drawn between the two cities.

Paris was undergoing a period of rapid development at the time, one with an emphasis on cross-cultural exchange and artistic expression. The city welcomed foreigners into its studios, academies and cafés, becoming a true melting pot. Indeed, the artists who formed the École de Paris were mostly expatriates. This is echoed by the United Arab Emirates today; as the country celebrates the Year of Tolerance in 2019, it is recognised as a cosmopolitan place of tremendous diversity and creativity, where all nationalities are welcome and come together to share and innovate.

Abu Dhabi in particular has always had a special relationship with France and its capital, Paris, ultimately leading to collaborations including the foundation of Louvre Abu Dhabi. It is therefore fitting that Louvre Abu Dhabi presents the first global celebration of the École de Paris, bringing many masterpieces for the first time by such legendary names as Pablo Picasso, Marc Chagall and Kees van Dongen from the Centre Pompidou to the UAE. These artists made Paris their home early in their careers, initiating key avant-garde movements such as Fauvism, Cubism and Expressionism and producing era-defining works of art.

It was the critic André Warnod who first brought this group together, writing, "the École de Paris exists. Later art historians will be able, better than we, to define its character and study the elements of its makeup, but we can still affirm its existence and its power of attraction, which brings to us artists from all around the world."[1]

Thanks are due to the curators of the exhibition: Christian Briend, Chief Curator and Head of Modern Art Collection at Centre Pompidou, assisted by Anna Hiddleston-Galloni, Assitant Curator of Modern Art Collection, Centre Pompidou; as well as to Centre Pompidou and Musée de l'Orangerie, as this exhibition presents significant works from their collections. Centre Pompidou is a key partner for Louvre Abu Dhabi, as made evident not only by this exhibition, but also by the major loans of modern and contemporary artworks from the Musée National d'Art Moderne collections displayed in the permanent galleries of Louvre Abu Dhabi.

I invite you to make the most of this wonderful opportunity to see the best of Paris and, indeed, all the world, here in Louvre Abu Dhabi.

MOHAMED KHALIFA AL MUBARAK

Chairman of the Department of Culture and Tourism – Abu Dhabi

1 André Warnod, "L'École de Paris," *Comœdia*, 27 January 1925 [the original French is as follows: "L'École de Paris existe. Plus tard, les historiens d'art pourront, mieux que nous, en définir le caractère et étudier les éléments qui la composent, mais nous pouvons toujours affirmer son existence et sa force attractive qui fait venir chez nous les artistes du monde entier."]

FOREWORD

The 2007 intergovernmental agreement between France and the United Arab Emirates is the cornerstone of an unparalleled partnership between the great national museums of France, under the umbrella of Agence France-Muséums, and Louvre Abu Dhabi, whose ambitions we are proud to support. Jointly organised with the French museums, Louvre Abu Dhabi's temporary exhibitions are fascinating illustrations of the story of cultural globalisation told throughout its permanent galleries, while at the same time highlighting the best of the French collections.

Conceived in conjunction with the Centre Pompidou, a stakeholder in Agence France-Muséums from the outset and already a lender of artworks to the museum's galleries, the exhibition "Rendezvous in Paris: Picasso, Chagall, Modigliani & Co. (1900–1939)" marks the start of Louvre Abu Dhabi's second season devoted to "Changing Societies". It offers a new look at the decisive role played by foreign artists in the artistic laboratory that was Paris in the first four decades of the 20th century. In bringing to Abu Dhabi some of the finest works in the collections of the Centre Pompidou, together with others from the Musée de l'Orangerie, the exhibition reveals the unique dynamism of Paris, "Capital of the Arts", which saw the emergence of the major modern art movements at this time. The great diversity of the public that will encounter these in Abu Dhabi, since the United Arab Emirates is home to over two hundred nationalities, was an invitation to rethink our own way of looking at these masterpieces, making this joint exhibition the fruit of a fascinating cooperation with a shift in focus.

We join together in acclaiming the remarkable commitment of exhibition curator Christian Briend, who has risen to the challenge in developing, with the assistance of Anna Hiddleston-Galloni, a new and revealing account of the period for the museum's varied public. We also wish to express our thanks to the staff of the Centre Pompidou, its president, Serge Lasvignes, and Bernard Blistène, director of the Musée National d'Art Moderne, as well as the staff of Louvre Abu Dhabi and Agence France-Muséums whose work has made this exhibition possible.

We hope that the vibrant cosmopolitanism of this exhibition, which coincides with Abu Dhabi's international contemporary art fair, will resonate with a public drawn from every quarter of the globe, reflecting the vitality of Abu Dhabi, now more than ever a crossroads of cultures and place of artistic encounter.

SANDRA LAGUMINA
President of the Board of Directors, Agence France-Muséums

JEAN-LUC MARTINEZ
President of the Scientific Council, Agence France-Muséums

FOREWORD

The poet and art critic Guillaume Apollinaire famously wrote that without artists everything would fall into chaos, that poets and artists together determine the features of their age.[1] At Louvre Abu Dhabi, as we investigate significant moments in our universal human history, the achievements of artists and their societies are what form our narrative. As we launch our new season of exhibitions and cultural programmes under the theme "Changing Societies", it is a pleasure to introduce, in an exhibition organised in conjunction with the Centre Pompidou, seminal works by artists from around the world who were based in Paris between 1900 and 1939. It explores the wider movements with which individual artists were associated (ranging from Fauvism to Abstraction and Art Deco), along with the places in the city where they congregated and interacted, looking, for example, at the shift from Montmartre to Montparnasse during the 1910s.

The exhibition features major artists such as Picasso, Chagall, Modigliani and Brancusi, but also other mediums like photography, where the visitor 'sees' the urban landscape of Paris through iconic images by Brassaï, Marianne Breslauer, Florence Henri, François Kollar, Germaine Krull, Man Ray and others. In the final section, devoted to portraiture and the career of Chaïm Soutine, Tamara de Lempicka's powerful female forms are commanding, as are earlier works by Sonia Delaunay. Relationships with writers were vital to their success. Some of the most important portraits in the exhibition are of art critics, such as Picasso's portrait of Gustave Coquiot (1901), painted soon after the Spaniard arrived in Paris, and Giorgio de Chirico's mysterious and premonitory portrait of Guillaume Apollinaire (1914), who like many others, weakened by war wounds, would die of influenza during the Spanish flu pandemic of 1918.

Echoing the new exhibitions, Ruth Mackenzie, CBE, Artistic Director of the Théâtre du Châtelet curated a cultural programme including performances inspired by Picasso's Cubist artworks and the poetry of Jean Cocteau and Guillaume Apollinaire, and illustrated through "living machines", choreography and electronic music associated with Cubist-inspired images projected onto the museum buildings.

We are grateful to Christian Briend, Chief Curator and Head of Modern Art Collection who curated this exhibition with Anna Hiddleston-Galloni, Assitant Curator of Modern Art Collection, both from the Centre Pompidou. I would like to thank Serge Lasvignes, President of the Centre Pompidou, Bernard Blistène, Director of the Musée National d'Art Moderne, Laurence des Cars, President of the Musées d'Orsay et de l'Orangerie and Cécile Debray, Director of the Musée de l'Orangerie for the artworks on loan for this exhibition. Finally, I would like to thank Anne Mény-Horn, CEO of Agence France-Muséums, and her team who worked on the production of this exhibition and Louvre Abu Dhabi team, especially Souraya Noujaim and Juliette Singer who lent it a unique dimension, placing it at the opening of the new cultural season.

MANUEL RABATÉ

Director of Louvre Abu Dhabi

1   Guillaume Apollinaire, *Selected Writings*, New York, New Directions Books, 1971.

FOREWORD

From the outset, the Centre Pompidou has played its part in the extraordinary intellectual and artistic venture that is Louvre Abu Dhabi. Until now, its contribution has chiefly been the loan of the many masterpieces from the holdings of the Musée National d'Art Moderne that have regularly complemented Louvre Abu Dhabi's own collections, which already include important works by the great 20th-century Western artists.

When the time came to decide on what was to be the first of the temporary exhibitions curated by the Centre Pompidou, it was the Louvre Abu Dhabi team who came up with the idea. This is worth underlining, so greatly does the theme of this exhibition resonate with the social and political preoccupations that inform the universal museum designed by Jean Nouvel. For in focusing on a highly distinctive period in French art – one when young painters, sculptors and photographers flocked to early-20th-century Paris from all over the world to make a decisive contribution to the city's art scene – the exhibition raises, in particular, the question of cosmopolitanism. Most notably from Germany, Spain, Italy, the Netherlands, Russia and even Japan, these artists — Constantin Brancusi, Marc Chagall, Kees van Dongen, Tsuguharu Foujita, Amedeo Modigliani and Pablo Picasso among them — rivalled in formal invention the greatest French artists of the time (Georges Braque, André Derain, Henri Matisse …). As eloquent testimony to this are the paintings, sculptures and photographs assembled by Christian Briend, curator of the exhibition. He sought to display works by universally recognised artists alongside others less well-known figures, an acquaintance with which will help us better understand, in all its complexity, this crucial period in the history of France, brought to an end by the Second World War.

Today, it seems odd to make such a distinction between French and foreign artists, one which has no relevance to our modern-day appreciation of the international art scene. Yet in redeploying within a strictly historical framework the categories of another age, the exhibition underlines the fundamental contribution of the so-called "Other", as it highlights issues raised in the 1920s and 30s by a globalisation still then in its infancy.

This exhibition could not, of course, have been organised without the closest of collaborations between the Centre Pompidou, Louvre Abu Dhabi and Agence France-Muséums. That, in itself, is a measure of how much we value these partnerships, rooted in a common conviction and a shared enthusiasm.

SERGE LASVIGNES
President of the Centre Pompidou

BERNARD BLISTÈNE
Director of the Musée National d'Art Moderne

THE SCHOOL OF PARIS (1901–1939)

Christian Briend

THE LURE OF THE CAPITAL

Since the term "The School of Paris" first appeared in 1925, it has been widely used to refer to the extraordinary artistic flowering that resulted from the presence of many painters and sculptors from all over Europe, Asia and America who came to the French capital from the dawn of the 20th century to the Second World War.

These artists, and the photographers who joined them in the 1920s – many of them women – were often fleeing social and political conditions that were not conducive to artistic freedom, notably in Russia and central Europe. Paris offered them a milieu that lent itself to the exchange of ideas and to creativity.

This spontaneous flow of artists to a foreign city, facilitated by the development of the railways in the second half of the 19th century, was without precedent in the history of art. But what was the appeal of Paris?

Firstly, the artists' desire to travel to the French capital was sparked by the international aura of the city and its art scene at the time, enhanced by the success of the World's Fair (Exhibition Universelle) of 1900. Publications that reached them while they were still in their home countries and exhibitions of French art had made some aware of the series of movements that emerged in Paris before 1900, including Naturalism, Symbolism and, most importantly, Impressionnism and Post-Impressionism, which rapidly became influential worldwide. This aura tended to diminish the roles of other important centres of art such as Berlin, Vienna and Munich, the only cities that could rival the artistic attractions of Paris at that time, notably for German-speaking artists.

Almost all the painters and sculptors now seen as part of the School of Paris arrived in the city before the First World War.[1] Following the Czech artist František Kupka (arrived 1896) and Kees van Dongen from the

---

1   This is true of all those selected for the present exhibition, with the notable exception of the Polish artist Tamara de Lempicka, who did not move to Paris until 1917.

Netherlands (1899), Pablo Picasso from Spain (1900), Amedeo Modigliani from Italy (1906), Diego Rivera from Mexico (1909) and Tsuguharu Foujita from Japan (1913) were all in Paris. They were joined by contingents of then Russian citizens, including the Byelorussians Ossip Zadkine (1909), Marc Chagall (1911) and Chaïm Soutine (1913), the Ukrainians Sonia Terk (who became Sonia Delaunay in 1906 after mariage), Alexandre Archipenko (1908) and Chana Orloff (1910) and the Lithuanian Jacques Lipchitz (1909). Poles, including Kisling (1910), were equally numerous (noting that their country was partitioned from the early 19th century until 1918), as were Hungarians such as Alfred Reth (1905) and Romanians such as Constantin Brancusi (1904).

Even before their arrival and even if their knowledge of French was – and sometimes remained – approximate, all these artists knew that once in Paris they could count on the support of their compatriots and also on a favourable ecosystem. It was said in Warsaw, Vitebsk and Moscow that, in certain quarters of Paris, artists could cheaply rent – or simply improvise – a studio in which to pursue the work they had begun at home. Having often received a solid basic training in their home countries from respectable local representatives of academicism, these artists were aware of the many centres of study which seemed to embody the term "School of Paris", and where they could benefit from advice from established artists and, crucially, have access to free models. More accessible than the venerable École Nationale des Beaux-Arts, which some attended as unenrolled observers,[2] these academies of painting and sculpture were private institutions, often set up by artists in the Montparnasse district, where students could enrol without sitting an entrance exam. Classes at the Académie Julian (founded 1868), Académie Colarossi (1870), Académie de La Palette (1900), Académie Ranson (1908) and Académie de la Grande-Chaumière (1909) offered greater freedom and variety than the offical academic system, which was losing ground at the time, and were also more widely open to women.

Above all, for foreign painters and sculptors, Paris was a centre for all different kinds of art. Where the art of the past was concerned, a visit to the Musée du Louvre was obligatory for most newcomers, even if, like Chagall,[3] they tended to prioritise visits to the large annual exhibitions known as Salons, which were then enjoying their heyday. At the Salons, artists could learn about new trends, leading some to rapidly update their style. For advocates of a modern form of art, the two most important were the Salon d'Automne (founded 1903), site of the Fauvism scandal in 1905, and, more significant still, the Salon des Indépendants (founded 1884), where Cubism was revealed to the general public in 1911 and which had the advantage of operating without a selection panel. Artists who came to Paris often as penniless unknowns could show examples of their work and – why not? – find private buyers, or interest a gallery owner who might even give them a contract. Looking at the catalogues of the Salon des Indépendants from just before the First World War, we are struck by the international nature of the event, which showed works of note by many foreign artists, who may or may not have been present in Paris at the time.

The visibility of art in Paris was also maintained by the many galleries that appeared at the turn of the century and proliferated into the 1930s, often under conditions of financial insecurity. Some gallery owners gave a warm welcome to *émigré* artists, including Berthe Weill, Georges Chéron, Jeanne Bucher and Hedwige Zak. The group and solo exhibitions they organised were frequently reviewed in the press – also expanding in this period – by journalists and critics who were not necessarily positive.[4]

Lastly, the liberal political regime and climate of intellectual openness and moral tolerance that prevailed under the Third Republic helped turn Paris into a mutually stimulating meeting place for many foreign artists – notably those of Jewish origin, who were often subject to demeaning laws and discrimination in

2   *Auditeurs libres* in French. Two such were Eugène Zak and Mané-Katz, who, on arriving in Paris, trained under Léon Gérôme in 1902 and Fernand Cormon in 1913 respectively. In 1909, Jacques Lipchitz studied under Jean-Antoine Injalbert.
3   In his autobiography, first published in 1931, Chagall recalls: "The day after my arrival, I went to the Salon des Indépendants" (*Ma vie*, Paris, Stock, 2003, p. 143).
4   On this, see the article by Yves Chevrefils Desbiolles, p. 26 in the present catalogue.

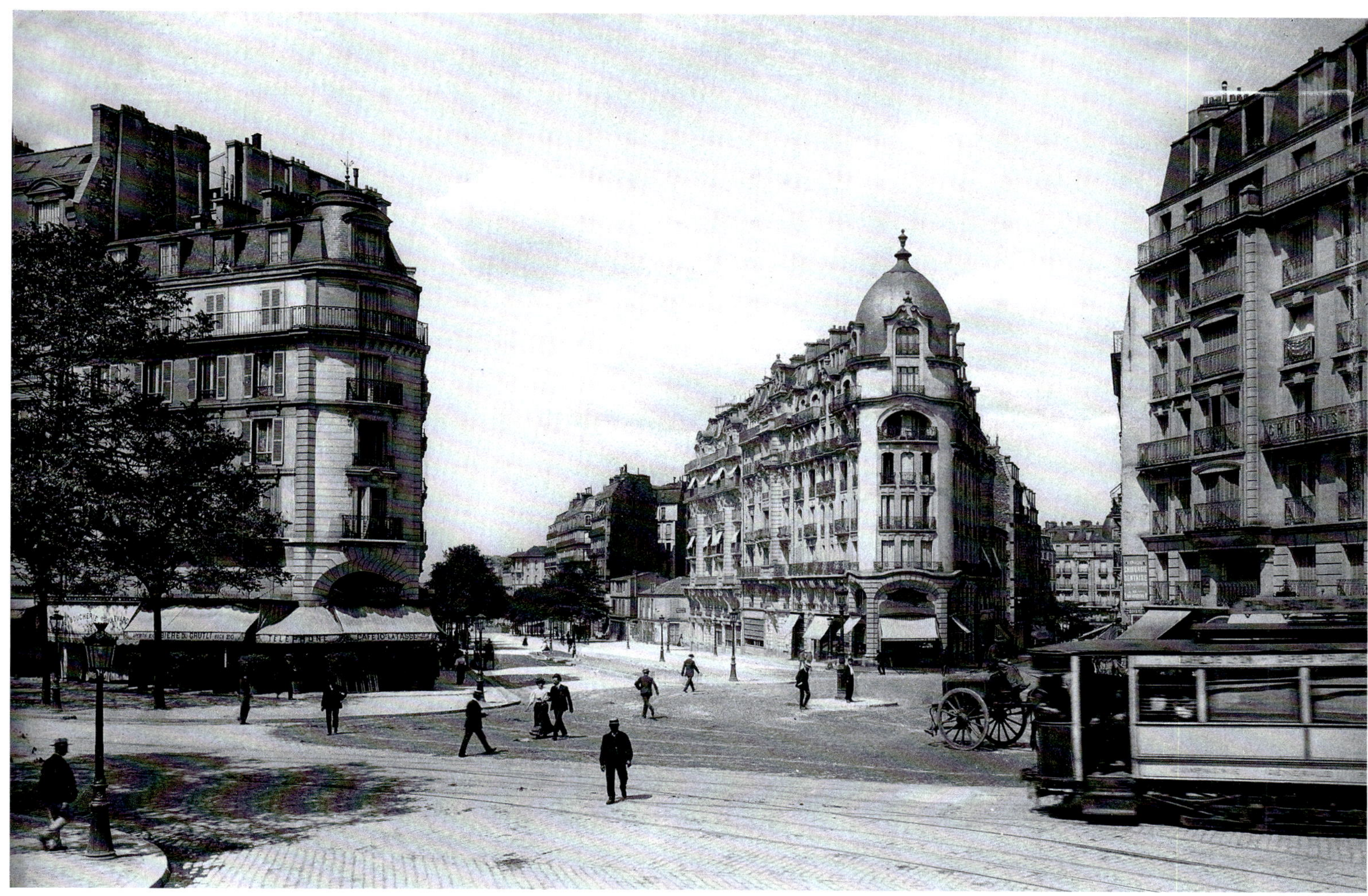

FIG. 1
Boulevard Raspail, at its
intersection with Boulevard du
Montparnasse, around 1910
Photograph by Léon & Lévy
Roger-Viollet, LL-1356 PARIS RES

their home countries. In the early 20th century the abundance of satirical journals in Paris, some with anarchist tendencies, such as *L'Assiette au beurre*, offered an appreciable source of income for artists arriving in the capital. Early in their careers, Juan Gris, Picasso, Kupka, Van Dongen and Marcoussis regularly contributed to these reviews with illustrations that were often remarkable and had a significance for their artists that went beyond simply earning their bread and butter.

The cosmopolitan nature of Paris in this period was reflected in the emergence of bohemian communities of artists, who would meet up in dance halls and large cafés such as Le Dôme, La Rotonde and La Coupole, clustered around the Carrefour Vavin, where Boulevard du Montparnasse crosses Boulevard Raspail [FIG. 1].[5] Following the abandonment of the Butte Montmartre,[6] once the home of Cubism, Montparnasse became the legendary epicentre of art in 1920s' Paris; it was a golden age framed by tragedy with the premature death of Amedeo Modigliani in 1920 and the suicide of Jules Pascin in 1930. Following this period the atmosphere in Paris became increasingly sombre, as economic, social and political crises led to the outbreak of the Second World War.

5   See Billy Klüver and Julie Martin, "Carrefour Vavin", in Kenneth E. Silver and Romy Golan (eds), *The Circle of Montparnasse. Jewish Artists in Paris, 1905–1945*, exh. cat., New York, The Jewish Museum, 1985, pp. 68–79.
6   The relocation of the Académie Ranson in 1911 and, crucially, Picasso's move from his studio in Montmartre to his new address in Montparnasse in 1912, provide a chronological benchmark for this change of place, at a time when the two districts had become linked by the Nord-Sud Métro line, which opened in November 1910.

VAGUE BOUNDARIES

The notion of a School of Paris, popularised by the critic André Warnod, remains unwieldy, firstly due to its lack of precision, and also because it is hard to translate into some languages. The term emerged comparatively late, at a time when most of these foreign artists had been living and working in Paris for some twenty years, and retains a certain air of condescension. There was a prevailing idea among critics of the day that Paris, portrayed as comparable to the "master" of a school, provided the artists with more than they gave it in return, which is an incomplete view of the reality. We should note that, having taken up this idea widely expressed by his colleagues, Warnod did admit that it is "very hard to identify what the foreigners take from us and what we take from them".[7]

The then classic contrast between the School of Paris and the French School sheds little light on the former notion.[8] The term French School related to a conception current in the history of art which saw the large museums identify different national "schools", and was used by critics of the 1930s to refer to French artists. At the time, these were divided into former Nabis (such as Pierre Bonnard and Maurice Denis), post-Fauves (such as Henri Matisse, Raoul Dufy and Albert Marquet, who advocated the dynamic use of plain bright colour) and post-Cubists (notably Georges Braque and Fernand Léger). Some of these artists, including Henri Matisse, the painter André Lhote and the sculptor Antoine Bourdelle [FIG. 2], gave classes at various academies, where their teaching was highly valued by foreigners in Paris. These eminent French artists, to whom we should add André Derain, who was well respected in Montparnasse circles, were seen as a distinct group that contrasted with the School of Paris. However, this binary opposition proved too simple to take account of the variety of aesthetic fields covered by foreign artists living and working in Paris. So it is now generally accepted – and the present exhibition more or less concurs – that neither the Surrealists, including Spanish artists Joan Miró and Salvador Dalí, nor the advocates of abstraction, including Dutch artist Piet Mondrian (who had been in Paris since late 1911 [FIG. 3]), Russian artist Vassily Kandinsky (who settled in the inner suburbs of Paris in December 1933) or, late in the period, the young German Hans Hartung, were part of the School of Paris, as these were two quite separate movements.[9] In reality, the foreign artists identified as belonging to the School of Paris seem to be distinguished from the rest on grounds of aesthetics and iconography, rather any topographic or sociological criteria. These artists, who remained entirely faithful to a primarily figurative form of art, are united by their indifference to developments in abstraction and – Chagall aside – limited recourse to imagination. Even though it is difficult – indeed impossible – to apply the same stylistic label to all the artists of the School of Paris, we can say that their attachment to figuration is often characterised by an emphasis on the specificities of the medium and by a highly expressive approach to creating a painting, epitomised in the work of Soutine. Soutine's dynamic use of the brush, feverishly applying paint in thick layers, helped to naturalise a form of expressionism which, in the work of native French painters of the day, was found only in the work of those less aesthetically engaged, such as André Dunoyer de Segonzac, Henri Le Fauconnier and Maurice de Vlaminck. While the female nude, such as those of Modigliani or Van Dongen, frequently fell foul of the prudery of some contemporaries, it seems portraiture was the genre of choice for artists of the School of Paris, including Modigliani, who had his artist friends sit for him, Kisling and his archetypal figures with large black eyes [CAT. 44] and Pascin, who portrayed the features of women he loved in pearly hues [CAT. 41]. Meanwhile, Soutine restored dignity to people of less means, such as waiters, grooms and cooks, while, at the

7   André Warnod, *Les Berceaux de la jeune peinture. L'École de Paris*, Paris, Albin Michel, 1925, p. 8.
8   See Romy Golan, "The *École Française* vs. The *École de Paris*. The Debate About the Status of Jewish Artists in Paris Between the Wars", in K. E. Silver and R. Golan (eds), *The Circle of Montparnasse…*, op. cit., p. 80.
9   Two exceptions to this among the artists presented here are Sonia Delaunay and František Kupka, who developed a geometrical form of abstraction after the First World War.

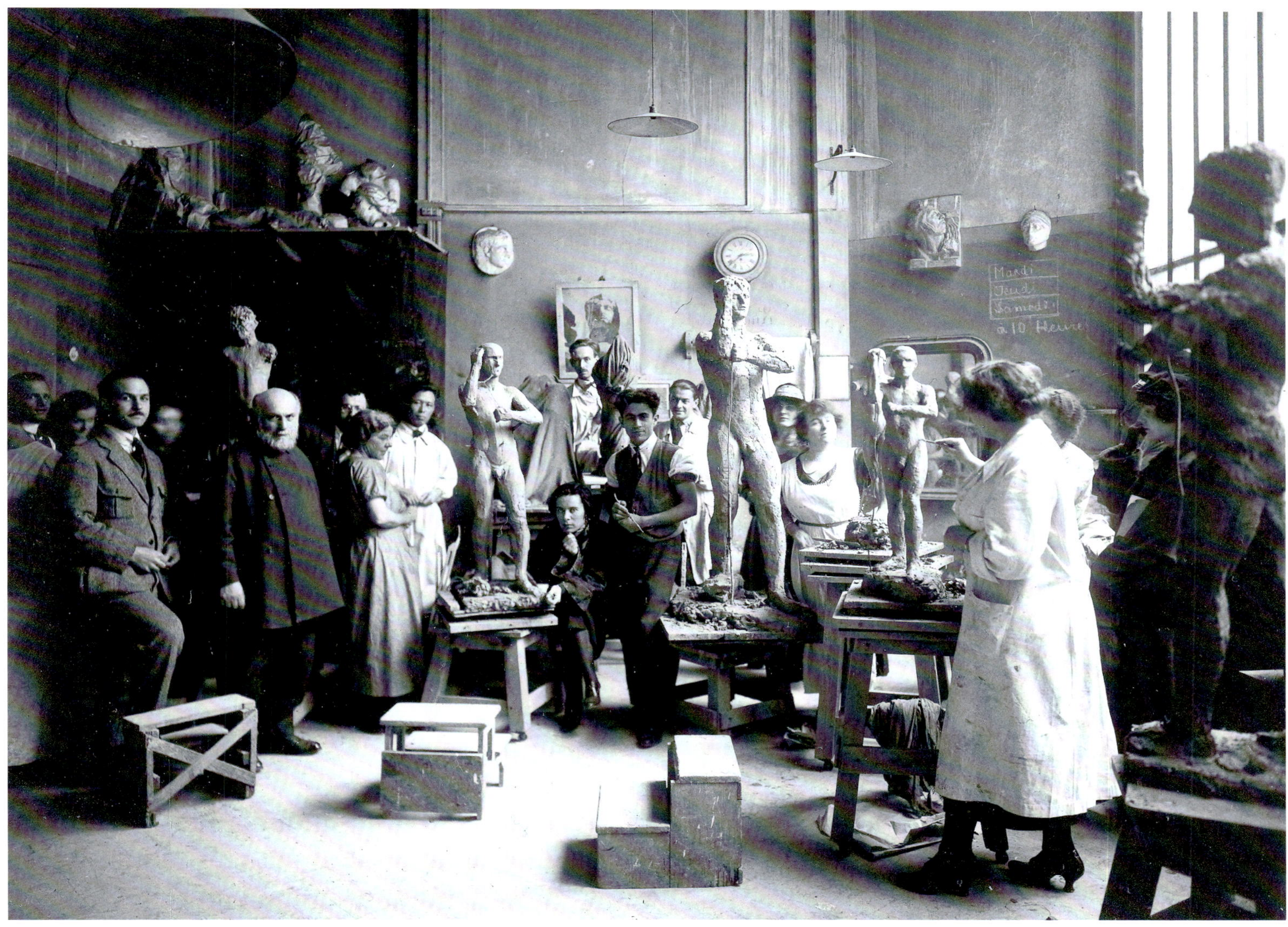

FIG. 2
Antoine Bourdelle and his
pupils at the Académie de la
Grande-Chaumière
Photograph by Henri Manuel
Paris, Musée Bourdelle, MB Ph 2183

opposite extreme, Van Dongen painted society portraits in ever greater numbers following his encounter with the world of haute couture [CAT. 79]. All made important contributions to portraiture. By comparison, Bonnard, Dufy and Matisse, who left Paris for the south in this period, were more drawn to landscape or the depiction of often anonymous models in lavish interiors. This preference among the artists of the School of Paris for a genre that is quintessentially linked to the issue of identity is no doubt connected to the trauma of exile that many of them experienced. Initially reflecting a desire for self-promotion, Foujita's many self-portraits – with or without a cat [CAT. 46] – reflect the uncomfortable position of a painter constantly seen in France through the prism of his far-Eastern origins, while his compatriots regarded him as overly Westernised. Similarly, the costume of the German Jewish dealer Alfred Flechtheim, portrayed as a Spanish torero [CAT. 78], could be interpreted as Pascin's desire to distance himsef from the racial and national labelling to which both painter and model could still fall victim, even in the land of the Declaration of Human Rights.

As confirmation of this interest in portraiture,[10] we should note that portraits formed the majority of the works on show at the only museum of the period dedicated to "foreign schools". The collections of this national institution were subsequently bequeathed to the Centre Pompidou.

---

10   ...which led us to open the exhibition with the portrait of a very Parisian figure painted by Picasso just after he moved to the city [CAT. 1] and to close it with the the caricature-like figure of an anonymous Frenchman whom Max Beckmann met in a train [CAT. 83], as he was leaving Paris to return to his home country.

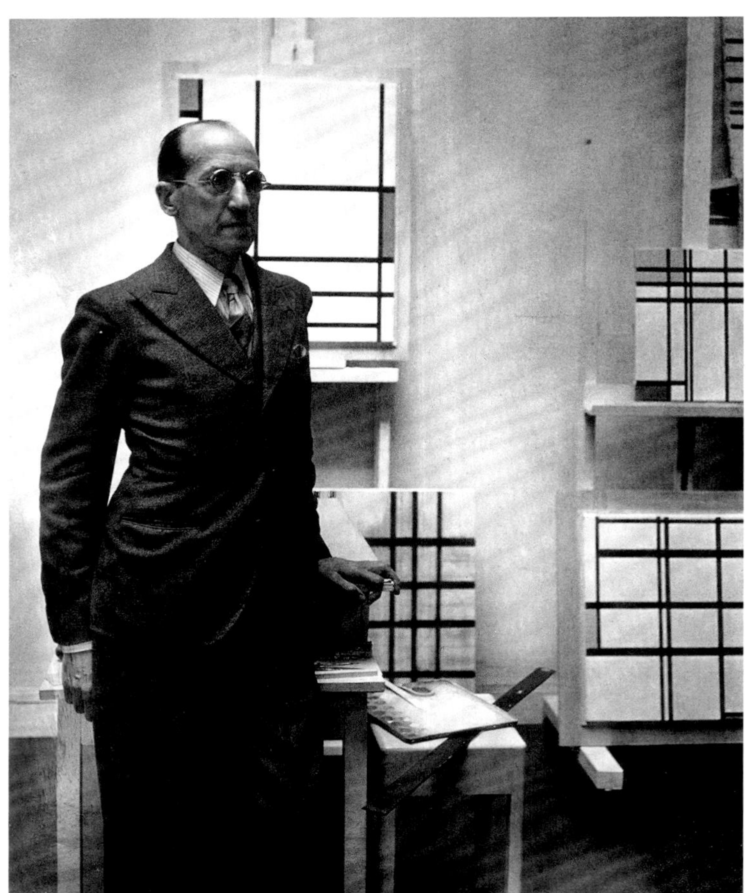

FIG. 3
Piet Mondrian in his studio on
Rue du Départ, Montparnasse, 1937
Photograph by Rogi André
Paris, Centre Pompidou –
Musée National d'Art Moderne,
AM 1982-307

A MUSEUM FOR THE SCHOOL OF PARIS?

"The separation of Art and State is a fait accompli," wrote André Warnod in 1925, not without reason.[11] The national museums' recognition of the contribution of foreigners to an increasingly international Paris art scene came late, but was no less real for that; it was officially recognised in 1932 when the Musée National des Écoles Étrangères Contemporaines (the National Museum of Contemporary Foreign Schools) was opened at Jeu de Paume with an interior redesigned with assistance from an American patron.[12] The most central and spacious room in a building then at the forefront of modern museography was Room XIV, devoted to the School of Paris and much discussed in the press. However, the museum's permanent collection was not yet large enough to cover the walls, so loans were requested from dealers and collectors to enable the likes of Picasso, Van Dongen and Pascin to be represented with important works [FIG. 4]. A lack of both money and, crucially, support from the acquisitions committee due to the policy of André Dezarrois, the museum's curator since 1922, meant that the state collections remained poor in representative works of the School. Where the artists featured in the present exhibition are concerned, paintings by Chagall, Foujita, Mela Muter and Van Dongen were purchased in the 1920s and supplemented by gifts from groups of donors, such as those of the Friends of Living Artists. Purchases increased in the following decade with the first acquisitions of works by Modigliani [CAT. 37], Picasso (his portrait of Gustave Coquiot [CAT. 1] acquired with some difficulty from the sitter's widow in 1933), Tamara de Lempicka [CAT. 81] and Kisling [CAT. 44], all on show here. These were later joined by works by Juan Gris, Eugène Zak, Maria Blanchard and Georges Kars. Meanwhile, Pascin was represented in the collection of the Jeu de Paume through Alfred's Flechtheim's bequest of his portrait in 1938, preceded two years earlier by gifts from Pascin's wife, Hermine David, and mistress, Lucy Krogh [CAT. 41]. Notable by his absence was Soutine, since Dezarrois, to his great regret, was unable to secure the purchase of any of his works for his museum, due to hostility from the acquisitions committee. Similarly, at that time the collection included no sculptures by Archipenko, Lipchitz or Brancusi, no doubt regarded as overly influenced by Cubist aesthetics, although Chana Orloff was represented.

This outline of early acquisitions by the French state shows that institutional recognition of the School of Paris remained limited. Furthermore, when the museum of foreign schools opened in 1932, many challenged the artificial division between French and foreign artists. In fact, as soon as the museum opened its very existence was criticised and a project emerged to bring French and foreign artists together in a new institution. Ultimately, however, it was the outbreak of the Second World War in 1939, followed by the German occupation, that caused foreigners to leave Paris and precipitated the closure of the museum of foreign schools. Automatically suspect in the eyes of the Nazis, who scorned "degenerate art" and whose artistic conceptions were openly

11   A. Warnod, *Les Berceaux de la jeune peinture...*, op. cit., p. 9.
12   Since 1922 this museum, housed in a former real tennis court (Jeu de Paume) at the bottom of the Tuileries gardens, opposite Place de la Concorde, has been an annexe of the Musée National du Luxembourg, the first French museum for living artists, which opened in 1818.

racist and anti-modern, the Jeu de Paume was requisitioned to hold artworks confiscated from dealers and collectors of Jewish origin.

It is striking to note that neither the museum of foreign schools, nor the School of Paris, comprising artists regarded as "undesirables" and "stateless" by the Nazis, survived the dark days of the war. In 1947, when the Musée National d'Art Moderne opened in the Palais de Tokyo – built ten years earlier for the Exposition Internationale des Arts et Techniques dans la Vie Moderne (International Exposition of Art and Technology in Modern Life) – it housed the state's collections of works by both French and foreign artists. At the same time, in an artistic landscape now entirely transformed, the notion of a School of Paris had lost all use and meaning. As proof – should any be needed – of the malleability of this vaguely defined label, it then went on to acquire a new, almost opposite meaning. In an ideological context marked by artistic rivalry between Paris and New York, the term "School of Paris" was now used to describe French artists working within a renewed abstraction movement.

And yet – and the aim of the present exhibition is simply to show this once again – despite its lack of clarity, the label of 1925 remains lastingly associated with a time and place characterised by a stimulating cosmopolitanism, where exceptional figures on the fringes of the avant-garde were together able, in defiance of history, to ensure the survival of figurative art.

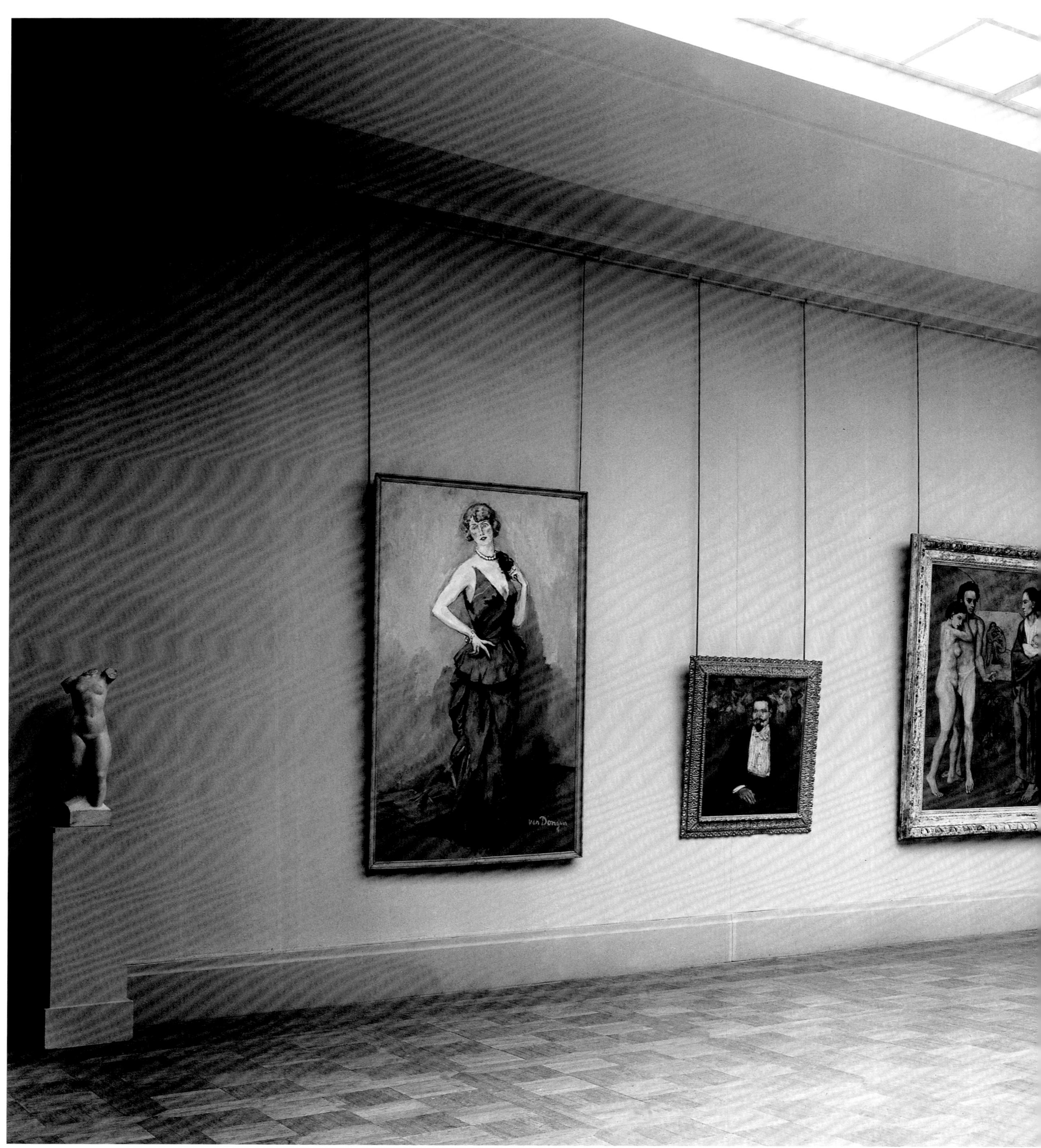

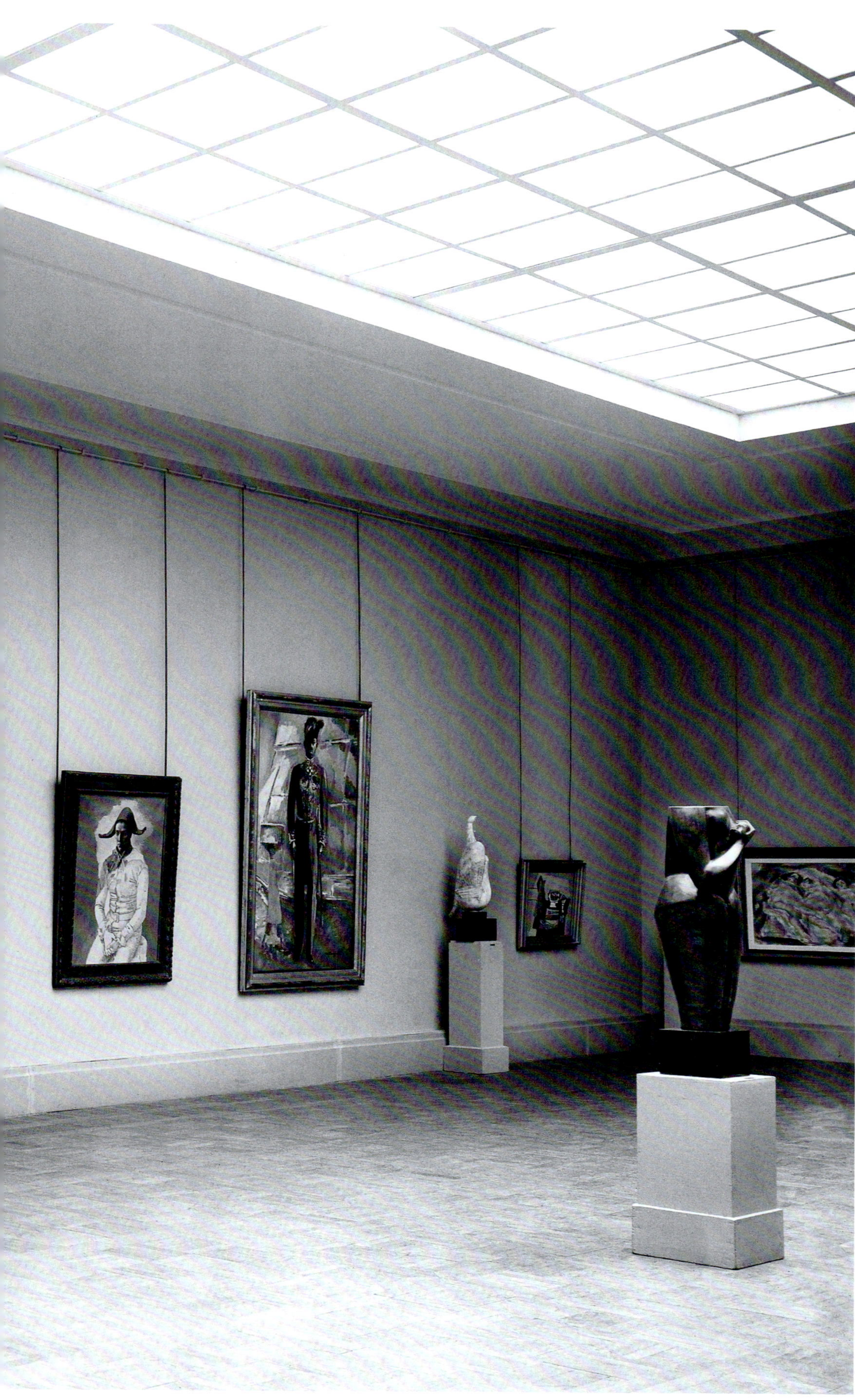

FIG. 4
Room XIV at the Musée
National des Écoles Étrangères
Contemporaines, around 1932,
with works by Pablo Picasso (among
them the portrait of Gustave
Coquiot), Kees van Dongen, Ossip
Zadkine and Jules Pascin
Unknown photographer
Charenton-le-Pont, Médiathèque
de l'Architecture et du Patrimoine,
MNLUG00023

THE SCHOOL OF PARIS IN THE CITY'S PRESS (1914–1925)

Yves Chevrefils Desbiolles

"If I might now offer my recollections of these painters, who, having relieved themselves of their cardboard suitcases, would run from the Gare du Nord, where they had just arrived, to the Louvre, the Petit Palais, to Luxembourg. So it was that one morning … I saw before *A Burial at Ornans* a young man unknown to me, low of brow and shifty of eye … He looked at the works of the masters of old just as believers gaze upon holy images. I was curious enough to follow him through the galleries of the Louvre. A few hours later, apparently sated, he made his way towards the exit, pausing before Ingres' *The Source* before descending the stairs and recovering from the cloakroom a valise that must have contained his travelling things."[1] This was 1912, and the young Waldemar-George (1893–1970), not yet at all the influential art critic he would become, had just encountered Chaïm Soutine.

Upon his arrival in Paris in 1911, Marc Chagall also hurried to the Louvre, and then to the Salon des Indépendants. "No academy could have given me all I discovered by gorging myself on the exhibitions of Paris, on its picture-shop windows, its museums,"[2] he would note in his autobiography. For Soutine and Chagall and so many other artists who arrived in those years from the farthest reaches of Europe and beyond, Paris, before it ever gave its name to a school, was more than anything a dazzling wonder. "There are no longer schools," wrote Guillaume Apollinaire (1880–1918) in the *Paris-Journal* of 16 June 1914, "but painters of different temperaments and talents who endeavour to render in form and colour what it is they feel about life." When, despite this, a decade or two later, the term "School of Paris" was adopted, it designated not some shared style or aesthetic, but rather a collective, deep-rooted desire for being. A desire that had already found its favoured neighbourhood and its most important institution.

1   Waldemar-George, *Les Artistes juifs et l'École de Paris*, Algiers, 1959, pp. 9–10.
2   Marc Chagall, *My Life*, trans. from the French of *Ma Vie* by E. Abbott, New York, Orion Press, 1960, p. 102.

MOUNT PARNASSUS: A WORLD OF ITS OWN

In the mythology of ancient Greece, Mount Parnassus was home to the Muses. It is said, in the spirit of irony, that the students so baptised a hillock just beyond the bounds of 17th-century Paris where they liked to go and recite poetry. According to art critic André Salmon (1881–1969), writing in the appropriately titled magazine *Montparnasse* of 20 June 1914, the Parisian Mount Parnassus of the second half of the 19th century, "whose artistic watering-trough, La Closerie des Lilas, was no more than a wooden hangar", already boasted "three academies, a dozen Scandinavians and four Spaniards". In the years before the Great War, the neighbourhood attracted growing numbers of provincials and foreigners, thanks to its low rents and still almost rustic aspect at a time when Montmartre had already fallen prey to tourists and property speculators. Between the old city walls and the Latin Quarter, the streets were a hive of activity. "It was then", concludes Salmon, "that Mont Parnasse began to take on the air of a foreign landscape."

Towards the end of winter in 1914, the *Mercure de France* noted that the bohemian painters of Montmartre had "emigrated, in the shape of Cubists" to the academies, studios and cafés of Montparnasse. It would seem that it was La Rotonde that first attracted the custom of these arty refugees: "Opposite are the Germans. Here is where the Slavs tend to sit. The Jews go among both." The artists came to form true communities on the café terraces of Montparnasse. In the words of an anonymous contributor writing in the 1 July 1921 issue of the eponymous magazine, it was a "great intellectual crossroads where the sons of every nation rub shoulders, united by a common artistic ideal, where the art of tomorrow is developed, and where, perhaps, the fusion of the peoples of Europe and of the world is being prepared". The closing words of this advocate well evoke the internationalist utopia championed by the publication's editorial board. Yet there already existed a place where such ideas would soon be put to the test: the Salon des Indépendants.

THE SALON DES INDÉPENDANTS –
"REVITALISING ART AND MAKING IT FLOURISH AGAIN"

Intimately linked to the fame of Paris and Montparnasse, the reputation of the Salon des Indépendants had reached the most distant lands. Since 1884, this unconventional annual exhibition, without jury or prizes, had allowed artists – beginners, amateurs or established professionals – to show their works with no more formality than the payment of a membership fee. As Apollinaire simply put it in the *Intransigeant* of 18 March 1910: "The Salon des Indépendants predicts the future of the fine arts every year, the way a barometer predicts the weather." There, observed André Warnod (1885–1960) [FIG. 4], the great chronicler of artistic Montmartre, in the *Avenir* of 28 January 1920, one might dream of glory and success, "with the same freedom as enjoyed by the painters of old [i.e. of the 18th century] when on the feast of Corpus Christi [some two months after Easter] they showed their paintings in the open air on Place Dauphine".

A climate of peace having been more or less re-established in Europe after the long interruption of the Great War, there were calls for the reopening of the peaceable aesthetic battle that had been fought in the exhibition spaces of the Salon des Indépendants. Was it not there, in the shacks and glass exhibition halls made available by the City of Paris [FIG. 1], that the Post-Impressionists, the Fauves and the Cubists had been discovered? Had not many of the paintings exhibited there now acquired "a history", as Apollinaire had prophesied in *L'Intransigeant* of 18 March 1913? And did this not mark, in fact, the victory of free art over the official art represented by the Salon des Artistes Français, whose paintings were hung among the splendours of the Grand Palais? The revival of the exhibition in 1919–20 was thus accompanied by a significant demand: like its rival, the Salon des Artistes Français, the Salon des Indépendants should be awarded the right to take place at the Grand Palais, a dignity the government had the power to confer. This call was universally supported, on both the left and right of the art-critical spectrum, and the request was granted. Officially recognised at long last as a charitable body, in 1920 the Société des Artistes Indépendants was given permission to hold its 31st Salon at the Grand Palais. More than six thousand works were displayed.

What to do with so many paintings and sculptures? Works had hitherto been assigned to broad aesthetic tendencies by exhibition officials who placed them in the relevant spaces. There remained, however, the paintings of those who defied classification, often the objects of acerbic commentary in the press. The canvases of this "army corps of benighted amateurs, cleaning women who paint on Sunday mornings and photo-painters rejected by the 'Artistes Français', the innocent bores who make up eighty-five per cent of the exhibitors" — in the words of Louis Vauxcelles (1870–1943) in *L'Éclair* of 9 February 1923 — were marshalled in what Claude Roger-Marx (1888–1977), even harsher in *L'Humanité* of 28 January 1920, called the "rubbish rooms".

A guardian of French tradition, Roger-Marx had for a long time hoped, like Vauxcelles, that Cubism would prove no more than a passing fad. At the Salon of 1920 he had regretfully to admit that the wartime break had not dried up the springs of this art that seemed to him so alien to the French sense of measure in all things. In that same article in *L'Humanité,* he thundered against "the invasion of foreign elements, of *littérateurs* [art critics] in love with paradox rather than with truth". Hanging on the walls of one room, however, were the works of a certain Francis Picabia, an artist who on occasion practised his own brand of art criticism, but one whose sensibility was directly opposed to that of Vauxcelles and Roger-Marx, even as he shared their contempt for Cubism. His name appears on the blurb for a Dada event held at the Grand Palais on 5 February 1920: "Cubism represents a dearth of ideas. They cubed primitive paintings and African sculptures, cubed violins, cubed guitars, cubed the picture papers, cubed shit and cubed young girls' profiles, and now they want to cube money!!!"

Unsurprisingly, responses to the Dada manifestation itself were amplified and taken to the point of absurdity in certain corners of the press: "Dadaism is madder than Cubism!" exclaimed the writer and literary critic Marcel Pays (1881–1963) in an article of 7 February 1920. "It looks very much like a concerted effort to denature our national genius, an endeavour directed – would you believe it! – by neutrals and a few snobby Frenchmen unashamedly flirting with intellectual Bolshevism." And if it wasn't "intellectual Bolshevism", the bogeyman was "Boche art" – the flimsiest of accusations, but the most effective among a public mostly unfamiliar with the emergence and circulation of aesthetic ideas.

Nevertheless, behind these alas-so-predictable reactions, lay an inarticulate but fundamental anxiety that extended beyond strictly nationalist or populist milieus to trouble conservative critics like Roger-Marx. Anti-academic critics were nonetheless displeased, like Vauxcelles, with recent innovations and even such champions of modernist painting as the writer Roger Allard (1885–1961). Had it come to the point where foreign artists and foreign aesthetic ideas were seen as the best that Paris had to offer?

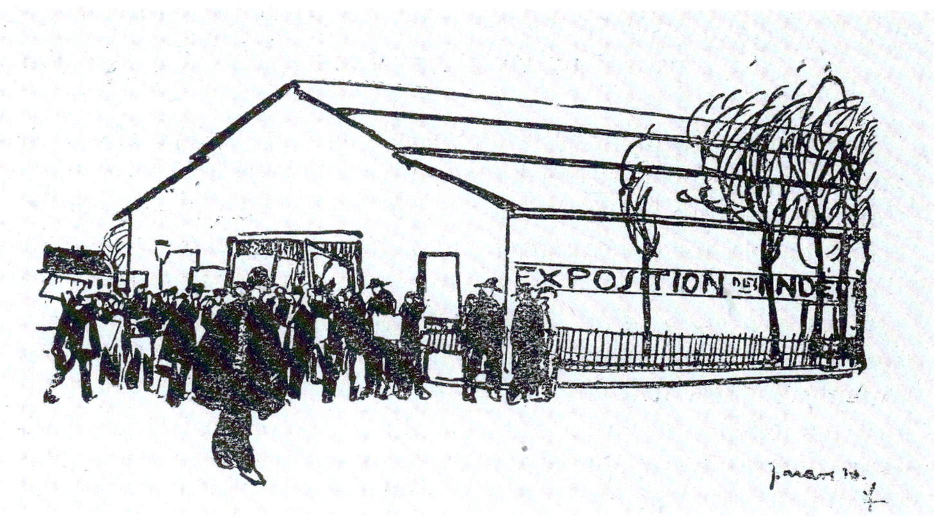

FIG. 1
"À propos du Salon des Indépendants",
drawing published in *La Revue du Palais*, February 1922
Paris, Bibliothèque Nationale de France, Literature and Art Department, 8-Z-15129

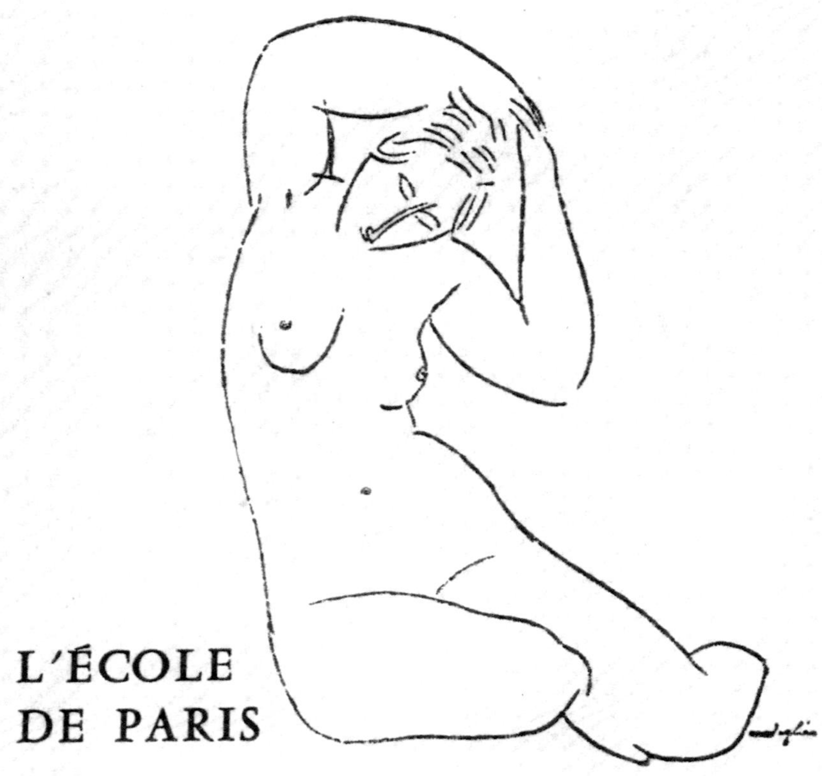

FIG. 2
Cover of *Les Berceaux de la jeune peinture. L'École de Paris* by André Warnod, Paris, Albin Michel, 1925
Private collection

TOO MANY WORKS? TOO MANY ARTISTS? TOO MANY FOREIGNERS?

The first skirmish seemed almost trivial. It was proposed that the Salon des Indépendants exclude those artists who showed at jury-selected exhibitions. To the supporters of this constitutional amendment, to join the Société des Artistes Indépendants was to espouse an ethical position that condemned all prior selection, recognising only the judgment of critics and public. Translated into policy, this virtuous insistence on principle would eliminate the most fortunate of the society's members, who formed an élite of sorts among the exhibitors, those who more than the others had the painterly means or reputation to win over a jury. An agreement was reached: those artists who were faithful to the principles of the society could show four paintings, the less committed only three. This compromise, however, did not solve the problem of excessive numbers, either of artists or of works exhibited; and above all, it did not achieve what had been the unstated object of the original proposal, which was to exclude the big names. So, in the name of the egalitarian ideals of the Société des Artistes Indépendants, it was decided to do away with categorisation by artistic tendency and to organise the exhibition instead on strictly alphabetical lines.

This upset nearly everyone. It was a mode of organisation that verged on the absurd, wrote the future *académicien* Émile Henriot (1889–1961) in *Le Temps* in February 1923, leading only to an incoherent jumble – "a howling hodgepodge of canvases that kill each other dead in an indescribable confusion!" Henriot quoted the painter Fernand Léger, on the losing side on the committee of the Société des Artistes Indépendants: "What is the problem you have with the last of the Cubists ... having a room of their own?" The problem? In *La Revue française* of 17 February 1924, Roger Allard – art editor of *La Nouvelle Revue française* – put it like this: it was "the constitution, within the Salon, of these little affinity groups that seek to monopolise to their own advantage – both visitor attention and publicity in the newspapers". Any isolated work, any artist unassociated with a movement, ended up lost in an endless succession of works in which the *finito* rubbed elbows with the sketch. Whatever their talent or reputation, these members saw themselves consigned to *de facto* anonymity, despite the labels, and despite the catalogue that listed the names of all exhibitors without doing anything to counter the monotony with which the visitor was confronted. In *La Gazette des sept arts* of 10 February 1923, Waldemar-George too lamented the loss of the old system:

> The public were very fond of these groupings in series ... They could find, always in their place, their favourite painters. They could follow their development. They located them within categories and gained a general idea, very simple and very clear, of the state of painting in today's France. At the Salon des Indépendants, they [now] find themselves disarmed.

The unrest that persisted at the Salon des Indépendants flowed from a mindset already criticised before the war by Fernand Léger, in a conference reported by Apollinaire in the *Paris-Journal* of 13 May 1914:

> Rather than complain of the great number of foreign artists, one should thank them for coming here to find their aesthetic ideas and for contributing their efforts and their fresh insights. Paris has

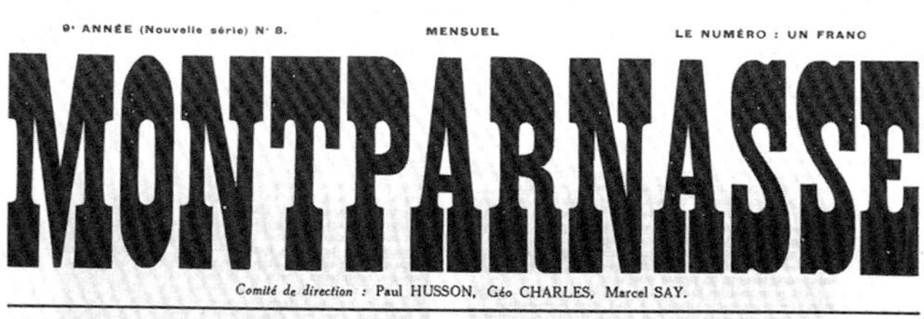

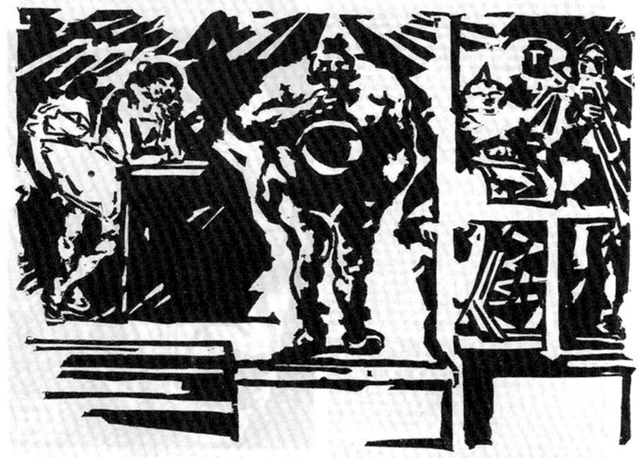

FIG. 3
Cover of *Montparnasse* magazine, Paris, 1 February 1922
Paris, Centre Pompidou, MNAM-CCI, Bibliothèque Kandinsky

become the great fair of painting, and there's nothing wrong with that. The Paris Fair is the Salon des Indépendants. People come from all over the world.

Long discussed *mezza voce* among the Artistes Indépendants as elsewhere, the question of the foreigners now emerged into the daylight. One of the first who dared write of it in the press was Émile Henriot, in an article for the *Temps*: "There is still the matter of the foreigners. This is a more delicate issue … Classification by nationality is nevertheless justified; it would obviously help introduce a little order into the Salon." The idea of putting all the foreign artists together, set apart from the French, seems at this early stage to have been entertained only with reservations: "One might well allow the principle, but without making it obligatory, leaving everyone free to take their paintings elsewhere and have them hang alongside friends of their own choice." Alive to Henriot's arguments, Allard suggested in *La Revue universelle* of 1 March 1923, that one might "every five or six years" group "painters and sculptors by nationality … Certainly, we cannot be too grateful to the foreign artists who have brought us a particular sensibility, a distinctive turn of the imagination, but we must reject any claim by barbarism, whether real or simulated, to direct the development of contemporary art."

"A CERTAIN SCHOOL OF MONTPARNASSE"

It was here, in this article of Allard's in the *Revue universelle,* that the term "School of Paris" appeared for the first time. It is found, however, in a sentence that is highly disparaging of the category of artists of whom Allard speaks: "A certain school of Montparnasse artists seeks to pass itself off abroad as the School of Paris (the term 'French school' being open to accusations of chauvinism)." There followed a long controversy that saw debate turn to polemic, polemic to quarrel and quarrel to confrontation.

On 8 February 1923, the day of the opening of the 34th Salon des Indépendants, Louis Vauxcelles wrote in the daily newspaper *Excelsior*: "The foreigners, Parisianised or not – and by Parisianised I mean those who have submitted to the disciplines fashionable in the studios of Montparnasse – are still numerous among the Indépendants." He paid tribute to Foujita, Per Krogh and Marcoussis as three artists who did "honour to the French school whose virtues they seek to assimilate". This backhanded compliment was intended to do only one thing, revealed the same day, but in another publication, the *Carnet de la semaine*: to establish a qualitative distinction between artists who had arrived, who were now "Parisianised", and the "aliens" who hung about Montparnasse, sometimes "naturalised", but nonetheless "not yet assimilated". Now the far-right press piled into the breach. One example among many is an article published in *Le Ruy Blas* of 15 February 1923, entitled "That so many artists should be strange [étranges] is vexing … But that so many of them should be foreigners [étrangers] is far worse": "In perusing the catalogue we find the key to the mystery. We find names ending only in *-off*, *-ski*, *-bers*, *-sonn* or *-agh*. These 'independents', then, are for the most part foreign. What are such foreigners doing here?" A question followed by others more odious: "What do they live on? … Is there not an interesting and profitable investigation to be carried out by the police, into their true occupations and means of support?"

Early the next year, in his column in the cultural magazine *Comœdia,* André Warnod could only sadly observe that foreign artists were indeed to be segregated from their French fellows at the Salon of 1924, the 35th of the series, going on immediately to explicitly challenge the rationale for the move. Certainly, he wrote, French art sometimes found itself represented at exhibitions by artists who were not themselves French, by nationality, culture or even, sometimes, temperament.

… but is it the role of the Indépendants to organise little groups in their Salon – the Indépendants so driven by a passion for equality that they decided to adopt an organisation by alphabetical order?

We have always protested against an equality from below whose first result is to bring down the level of the whole. This has always been a deplorable idea in art.

As one might expect, Roger Allard fiercely defended the decision of the society's committee. In *La Revue française* of 17 February 1924, he attacked the noisy minorities of La Rotonde and other cafés of Montparnasse, that were skilful in gaining the attention of the press: "Having learned most of what they know from us [the foreign artists] are seeking to gain credence abroad for the idea of a school of Paris in which teachers and originators, on the one hand, and disciples and copyists on the other, are indifferently amalgamated to the advantage of the latter." Consigned to ill-defined status by lower-casing the "school", the term, as used by Allard in 1924, refers to *la part de l'Autre*[3] – the place or side of the Other – from whence came, he believed, the "disciples and copyists". As put by Waldemar-George in *L'Amour de l'art* of February 1924, the painfully unresolved question was this: "Should French art be thought of as an ethnic or as a purely aesthetic concept?"

Louis Vauxcelles had already answered in an article in the *Excelsior* of 26 November 1923: "To deny the ethnic foundation is madness: who more Flemish than Breughel, more Spanish than Goya?" In the same article, the writer suspects a "handful of foreign artists" of having fostered a climate of insurrection with their endless invective and aggressive challenges to the committee: "'The society is ours, it's for you to leave if you don't like it,' they yell somewhat indiscreetly, the countless colourists who have come to our country to make use of Cézanne, Matisse, Derain and Friesz … 'You have no right to demand our papers.'" These people were uncultured, said Vauxcelles; they lacked the discretion called for on entering someone else's home. "It is this vulgarity, this lack of tact, that has finally wearied many whom it would be difficult to tax with jingoism or xenophobia," Vauxcelles then wrote in *L'Ère nouvelle* of 29 November 1923. Admittedly, the streets of Montparnasse could sometimes be rowdy. Behind the creative excitement of academies and studios there was another side of the coin: the partying that blunted the edge of poverty and the drinking and fighting that came with it and, above all, the depression that lay in wait for those disillusioned by lack of success. This aspect of things is described in great detail in works of fiction – contemporary *romans à clef* – such as André Warnod's *Lina de Montparnasse* (1928) or Michel Georges-Michel's *Les Montparnos* (1929).

There was one event in particular that scandalised Vauxcelles. In December 1922 and January 1923, under the guidance of dealer Paul Guillaume, the famous American collector and philanthropist Alfred C. Barnes had bought some fifty paintings by Soutine and other works by Montparnasse artists. This business with Barnes could not be allowed to pass. Waxing indignant in the same 29 November issue of *L'Ère nouvelle,* Vauxcelles denounced more ferociously than ever the hijacking of the designation "French art" by painters from abroad,

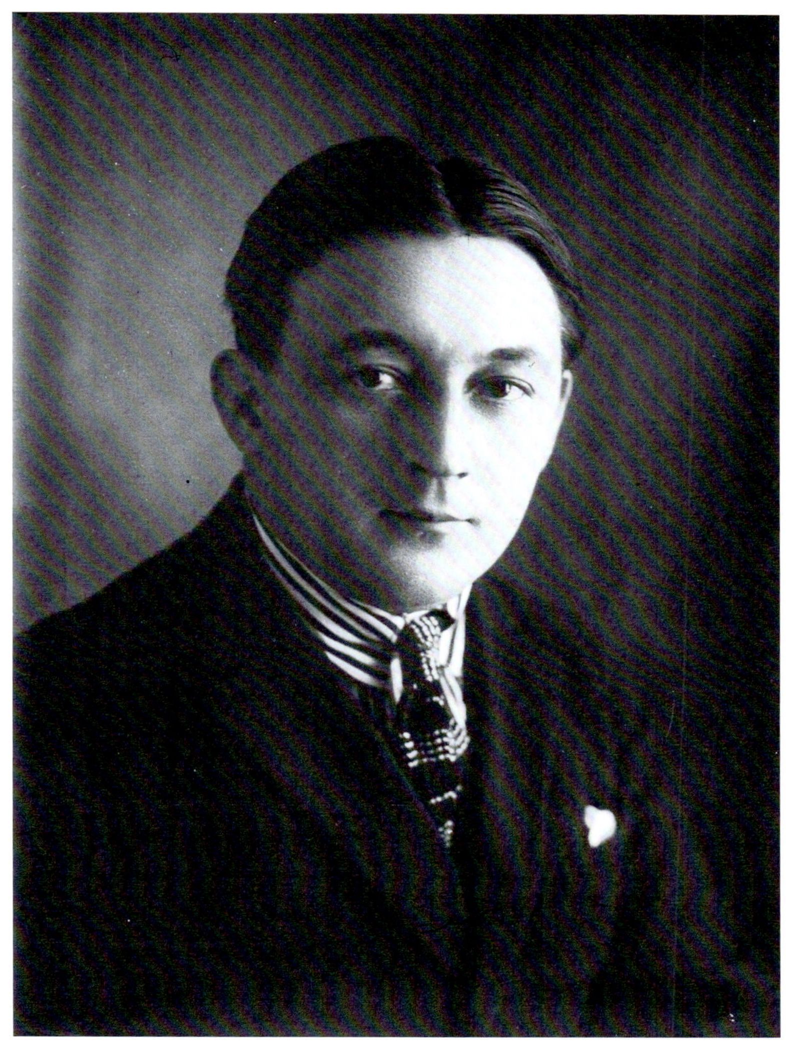

FIG. 4
Portrait of André Warnod, 1923
Agence Meurisse press photo agency
Paris, Bibliothèque Nationale de France, Prints and Photographs Department, EI-13 (2749)

3   Jean-Louis Andral and Sophie Krebs, eds, *L'École de Paris, 1904-1929, la part de l'Autre*, exh. cat., Paris, Musée d'Art Moderne de la Ville de Paris, 2000.

by "Slavs" like "M. Soutine (whom I do not know, and by whom I have only ever seen bad paintings)". Barnes, he went on to say, "has every right … to buy Soutines. Certainly, and even Kikoïnes, Krémègnes and all the other third-raters of the Little Entente.[4] What is important is that, on the other side of the Atlantic, these curious products should by no means be mistaken for French art."

THE SCHOOL OF PARIS, AT LAST

The polemic ran on in the same tone for many months. In *La Revue mondiale* of 1 January 1924, Waldemar-George found it deplorable that "the foreign artists who live in Paris and all the friends of French art in Europe and America should find themselves insulted in this fashion by a decision contrary to the principles of equality and hospitality that were the pride of the Salon des Indépendants". Then deputy editor at *L'Amour de l'art,* a prestigious art magazine, Waldemar-George sent "a terrible letter" to Vauxcelles, his editor-in-chief, which the latter addressed in the long article in *L'Ère nouvelle* cited above. "Your doctrine … of unqualified nationalism is indefensible", Waldemar-George wrote. It was a rift that could not be repaired, and Vauxcelles soon gave up the editorship of *L'Amour de l'art*, leaving it in his junior's hands. However, the older critic warned his younger colleague: "Waldemar, dear Waldemar, do remember this saying: 'You're always a reactionary to someone.' The day will soon come when a desperately young man a thousand times more cubiphile and rotondomaniac than you will call you an establishment hack, a dinosaur, even a champion of French art." In this, Vauxcelles was astonishingly prescient. Between the very end of the 1920s and the *Anschluss*[5] in March 1938, Waldemar-George underwent a spectacular doctrinal conversion that took him to the heart of Italian fascism, reviling the School of Paris he had defended in 1923–24 and relegating even the so-called "French" school to second place behind an "Italian school" that found its inspiration in the long-gone Roman Empire. At the time, Vauxcelles had gone on to let his opponents know that there was worse to be found elsewhere – in Rome, indeed, where an international art exhibition was being held. In *Le Carnet de la semaine* of 21 January 1924, he quoted from an article by Ardengo Soffici that had appeared in the Italian press: "The France that only yesterday possessed the most sincere and vital artists is today prostrate, the victim of excesses she herself encouraged. A host of … 'hyphenated internationals' has sullied her lucid, fresh and harmonious spirit, and today she has gone mad, along with the rest of the world."

Le Bulletin de la vie artistique, the bi-monthly magazine of Galerie Bernheim-Jeune, carried an extended debate that lasted over several issues. One of the opponents of classification by nationality published in the *Bulletin* of 1 February 1924 was the painter Marcel Gromaire, who noted that "by its force of attraction, its spirit of freedom and the interest it provokes", the Salon des Indépendants was "in its own way the most important channel for the diffusion of the French style of thought". And Gilbert Bellan, another painter, offered this insightful analysis: "As for the influence of one nation on another, no one can pretend to certainty; intercourse between nations leads to learning, not borrowing. Such influences are of moment in the history of the world."

In *Comœdia* of 7 May 1924, Warnod reported the resignation of Fernand Léger, viscerally opposed to classification by nationality. And in *L'Ère nouvelle* of 23 October 1924, Florent Fels (1893–1977) mischievously asked Vauxcelles in which national group one should put the painter Jules Pascin: "He is of Balkan origin … born in Vidin, Bulgaria, a town inhabited chiefly by Turks, to a Spanish–Jewish father and an Italian mother born in Serbia. I may add that Pascin is also a naturalised American." That year, at the Grand Palais, one went

---

4   The Little Entente was a diplomatic and military alliance between Czechoslovakia, Yugoslavia and Romania, formed under French auspices in 1920.
5   Anschluss refers to the political union of Austria with Germany achieved through annexation by Adolf Hitler on 12 March 1938.

"Round the World in 55 Rooms" – the title of an article by Warnod in *Comœdia* of 9 February 1924. In those rooms allocated to foreign artists, large placards were hung:

> … bearing the name of a nation, and beneath, one or two paintings. And that is a country … In short, visitors are astonished to see so few foreign paintings on the walls when it is constantly said that Paris has been invaded by painters from all over the world. But it's simply that the foreigners have stayed away from the Salon.

It is worth underlining that it was in this negative context that Warnod made his memorable declaration in *Comœdia* of 27 January 1925: "The School of Paris exists." He adopted the term coined by his colleague Roger Allard in order to rescue it from the narrow rut of prejudice in which it had been confined, to valorise it, and to use it, in a way, as a weapon against the constant plotting that bedevilled the Société des Artistes Indépendants which led to attacks on foreign artists in the press. Yet what was to all appearances an act of faith in the future can also be seen as a defensive move silently aware of its being too late to be effective. However well-founded it might be, the emergence of a concept, of an artistic category, rarely changes the course of events. The existence of the School of Paris was proclaimed only a few short years before the Depression and the onset of a bellicose humour that would bring tragedy – clandestinity, exile or death – to many of the artists whose names are now associated with it. Recognition had come just as the history of the school was drawing to an end.

Immediately reprinted in *Les Berceaux de la jeune peinture. L'École de Paris* (1925) [FIG. 2], Warnod's visionary essay, apparently light in tone, succeeded perfectly not only in placing the School of Paris within the universal history of art, but in setting it in the history of a city, of a time and of a generation of restless and passionate artists whose works, over a quarter of a century, spanned a vast spectrum of styles, extending from the most rigorously ascetic Cubism, through the diversity of Expressionism, to the most poetic of Realism. In view of this, it is only right that André Warnod should be credited with coining the term, and this name of a thousand faces, be attributed to him and his "book of recollections".

ALL ABOARD FOR PARIS!

Sophie Krebs

No one would mention the foreigners had they not descended on Paris in droves at the start of the 20th century, for reasons reflecting the general political, economic and social situation, as well as personal – indeed, highly private – motivations, transforming the French capital into a "nomadic, cosmopolitan"[1] place. Paris at this time was a hub of intensive interactions between the French community and these foreigners – interactions that were often characterised by the occasional clash and even suspicion. The city was also, indisputably, the capital of the art world at this time and, simultaneously, a leading intellectual centre; this is what motivated professional and student artists alike to stay and study here, taking up residence on the city's two hills, firstly Montmartre and then Montparnasse. Unlike all the other migratory flows arriving in France during the same period, these artists, whatever their nationality, mingled, forming open and cosmopolitan networks – the very opposite of a "ghetto" – even though their national identities did not truly disappear. This phenomenon was so marked that critics in the 1920s labelled it the "École de Paris": foreigners who had come to Paris, to the "school" of Paris – that of the great masters – to learn the secrets of modernity, and to travel its paths of success and liberty. This movement, or rather this eclectic gathering with neither leader nor doctrine, encompassed all the styles of the time that opposed academism: Cubism, independent art, Primitivism, Realism, Expressionism and so on. Yet while the School of Paris dominated through to the late 1920s, it was not the only one on the artistic scene. Surrealism attracted many foreigners in the latter half of the 1920s and through the whole of the following decade, as did abstraction, which, from 1925 onwards, saw all its latest trends concentrated in Paris. These were relatively organised and international groups, centred on Paris and, as such, must be differentiated from the School of Paris, which lacked any real international reach. In the 1930s, the flow of voluntary migration came

---

1   Gladys Fabre, "Qu'est-ce que l'École de Paris ?", in Jean-Louis Andral and Sophie Krebs, eds, *L'École de Paris, 1904-1929, la part de l'Autre*, exh. cat., Paris, Musée d'Art Moderne de la Ville de Paris, 2000, pp. 25–40.

to a standstill; the tide turned as international artists returned to their countries of origin, often due to the crisis that had thrown the art market and the global economy into turmoil.[2] Another wave of migration replaced it, this time a forced one in often tragic circumstances. These migrants were, above all, exiles. Paris, for a time, became the last refuge for artists escaping totalitarian regimes and, ultimately, a bridgehead towards other emerging centres – London and New York – which did not as yet have all the advantages Paris could offer. Only the outbreak of another war would bring to an end this movement that had begun more than half a century earlier.

"MONTMARTRE LONG BEFORE MONTPARNASSE"[3]

It is difficult to quantify the number of artists[4] who arrived in Paris at the turn of the 20th century. In their recollections we can observe numerous common experiences: the same awestruck arrival, followed by a hand-to-mouth existence concealing poverty and solitude, styled by some as "bohemian living". There were those whose fame has endured – a fame that often came at the price of great sacrifices: Kees van Dongen of the Netherlands, the Czech František Kupka, Pablo Picasso from Spain, Constantin Brancusi of Romania, Jules Pascin of Bulgaria, Louis Marcoussis from Poland, the Italians Gino Severini and Amedeo Modigliani, Byelorussians Marc Chagall and Chaïm Soutine – the list is far from exhaustive. Artists of more than thirty nationalities[5] were present in the years before 1914; even more nationalities would be represented after the First World War. The call was very strong, but those who achieved a breakthrough and success were few and far between.

The stream of arrivals was constant – except during the First World War – prompting the question: why Paris? The reasons advanced by historians and by the artists themselves are often complementary. The former highlight the socio-economic and cultural factors that led the latter to choose the French capital: the low cost of living, the studios, the many and relatively inexpensive art schools, the range of teachers and their reputation, the proliferation of outlets, exhibitions and galleries – all contrasting with the impoverished cultural offerings, lack of political freedom, social constraints and disturbances of various kinds in their countries of origin. For these foreign artists, Paris was the land of liberty, in every sense of the word, and this was especially true for Jewish artists.[6] It was also a pre-eminent artistic centre, home to the great masters who had been revolutionising the art world since the mid-19th century – Claude Monet, Paul Cézanne, Auguste Renoir and so on. The liberal morals very specific to Paris in the first half of the 20th century played their part, too. This emotionally charged vision helped to create the myth of Paris.

In this context the French capital was *the* place to be, and one that had its own very distinctive character. It had escaped the effects of rampant, dehumanising urbanisation and preserved a village-like quality – a relaxed, friendly ambience alongside the buzz of the metropolis. This is very probably what made Montmartre and Montparnasse so successful. And perhaps it has not been sufficiently emphasised that the new arrivals were living and working alongside writers who were busy celebrating Paris and boosting the reputation of this new generation of artists.[7]

2   Tériade, "La fin de l'École de Paris ou le retour des enfants prodigues", *L'Intransigeant*, 15 March 1932.

3   André Warnod, *Les Berceaux de la jeune peinture. L'École de Paris*, Paris, Albin Michel, 1925, p. 15.

4   Some commentators have estimated that there were 40,000 French and international artists in Paris between the two wars. See Serge Fauchereau, "Paris, capitale artistique", in Suzanne Pagé and Aline Vidal, eds, *Les Années 30 en Europe. Le temps menaçant, 1929-1939*, exh. cat., Paris, Musée d'Art Moderne de la Ville de Paris, 1997, pp. 489–92. Looking at the figures for the Salon des Indépendants, in 1910 there were 837 exhibitors; in 1914, 1320; in 1925, 1991; in 1929, 2381. The number of members was larger – 1920: 1141 (20 per cent international); 1925: 3447 (27 per cent international). We can estimate the number of foreign artists as between 10,000 and 20,000, varying in different periods.

5   The number of nationalities represented at the Salon des Indépendants was 33 in 1920, 55 in 1925, from all corners of the globe. It should be noted, however, that the break-up of Europe following the First World War increased the number of European countries.

6   France had been seen as the homeland of liberty following the emancipation of the Jews in the Revolution – a reputation that remained intact despite the Dreyfus Affair.

7   Louis Chevalier, *Montmartre du plaisir et du crime*, Paris, Robert Laffont, 1980: "Besides, most of them [the artists], the most famous ones, once success came – largely thanks to the dedication of the writers, their friends, journalists and panegyrists when they chose to be – hastened to leave this place of poverty where nothing would remain of their fleeting presence had not these same writers, recounting their own youth, also conjured in passing their ingrate phantoms." These writers include people such as Salmon, Carco, Dorgelès, Warnod and Mac Orlan, their first reminiscences being published in the 1930s, although most came after the Second World War. In the 1920s, many writers produced novels with subject matter directly drawn from the lives of painters. For example, André Warnod, with *Lina de Montparnasse*, Paris, La Nouvelle Revue Critique, "Les Maîtres du Roman", 1928 and Michel Georges-Michel, with *Les Montparnos*, Paris, Fayard, 1923.

It was in Montmartre that the first group of cosmopolitan artists gathered, mixing with French writers and creating the model of the kind of network that would be exported to Montparnasse – one of friendship and solidarity, as much as aesthetics and commerce. The group around Picasso[8] in Montmartre was a kind of brotherhood, a "laboratory", with a studio (the Bateau-Lavoir [FIG. 1]), used as a place for meetings and discussions, and a cabaret, Au Lapin Agile, where a wider circle mixed with other artists, poets and bohemian characters, adding a picturesque touch. It was in this context – at once very close and very open – that Cubism was invented. Some artists associated with Fauvism met there, too – André Derain, Maurice de Vlaminck, Raoul Dufy and Van Dongen – which adds a more complex dimension to the concept of "network".

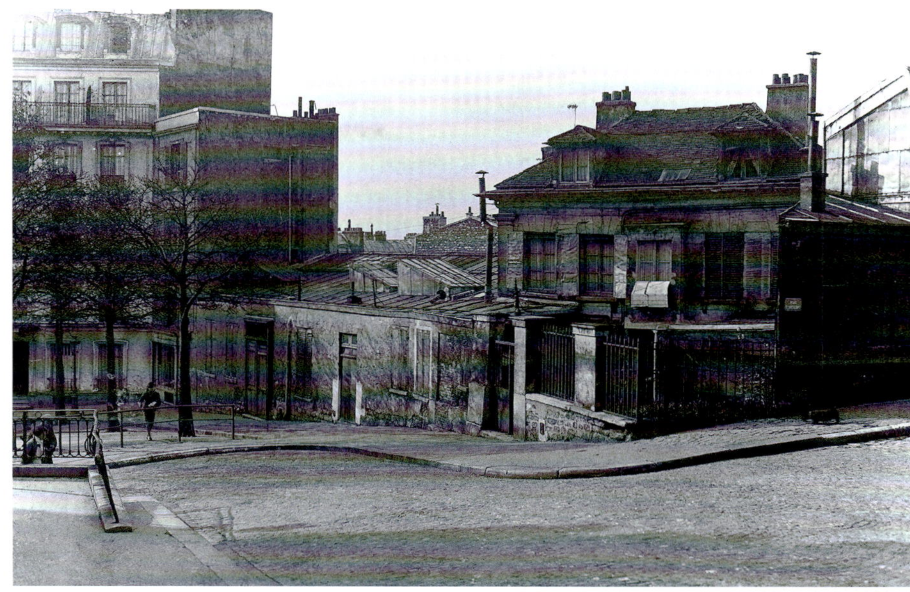

FIG. 1
The Bateau-Lavoir in Montmartre, 1950s
Unknown photographer
Roger-Viollet, RV-33822

In parallel, and partly intersecting with this first circle, there were the Spaniards of Montmartre – Paco Durrio, Ramon Sunyer, Ramon Pichot, Ignacio de Zuloaga, Manolo, Julio González and so on – forming a national community alongside several Italians who arrived in 1906, the most famous among them being Severini and Modigliani, and some Germans, such as Grete Wiegels and Otto Freundlich. This little world met, gathered together and took part – or not – in artistic events in conjunction with French artists. The same phenomenon appeared in heightened form in Montparnasse, where along with this cosmopolitan "mix", national groupings were defined, extending beyond aesthetic criteria.

These supportive communities first appeared in Montmartre at the start of the century. André Warnod locates their origins in his book *Les Berceaux de la jeune peinture*:[9] subscription associations[10] were set up (for example the monument dedicated to the local caricaturist Gavarni was funded by the Society of Painters and Lithographers), often instigated by the many cartoon artists working in the locality, or to support the families of artists in need. Dances were already being organised, such as the Bal Gavarni. Even though foreign artists are not specifically mentioned, we should remember that Van Dongen, Kupka, Marcoussis, Juan Gris and others made a living from producing humorous graphic works. The same kind of arrangements would also be seen in Montparnasse, where foreign academies, associations and cafés organised banquets, dances and exhibitions.[11]

Montmartre, the favoured *quartier* of the School of Paris, was the "birthplace of independent art", according to Warnod, who saw it as paradoxical that "in the dilapidated setting of the Butte's little streets – so old-fashioned, so steeped in stifling tradition – there could spring up, so new, so clear, so bold, so simple, the spirit that would inspire a whole generation of artists and writers".[12] It was this Paris – popular, with a village-like atmosphere, at once nostalgia-tinged and marginal – that was captured by the photographers who arrived in the 1920s (André Kertész, Brassaï, following in the footsteps of Eugène Atget). Their work created the image of an anti-monumental, emotional Paris that made the city the capital of modernist photography[13] and still underlies its success today.

8   Including Max Jacob, Guillaume Apollinaire, André Salmon and Georges Braque; described by Fernande Olivier in *Picasso et ses amis*, Paris, Stock, 1933 (available in English as *Picasso and His Friends*, trans. by Jane Miller, New York, Appleton-Century, 1965).
9   A. Warnod, *Les Berceaux de la jeune peinture* …, op. cit.
10   The French law on associations was introduced in 1901.
11   See "Abécédaire", in J.-L. Andral and S. Krebs, eds, *L'École de Paris, 1904-1929, la part de l'Autre*, op. cit., pp. 367–97.
12   A. Warnod, *Les Berceaux de la jeune peinture* …, op. cit.
13   Herbert Molderings, "Nouvelles images de Paris", in J.-L. Andral and S. Krebs, eds, *L'École de Paris, 1904-1929, la part de l'Autre*, op. cit., pp. 71–84.

"THE BABEL OF MONTPARNASSE"[14]

Long before Warnod picked up on the term "School of Paris", with its twin poles of Montmartre and Montparnasse, Guillaume Apollinaire had announced the artistic community's migration from one to the other – although the two centres, Montparnasse and Montmartre, existed simultaneously. In an article published in 1914 and then reprinted by the magazine *Montparnasse*[15] when its publication resumed, he wrote:

> Montparnasse is already replacing Montmartre. One hill replacing another – but it's still mountaineering, art on the summits. The apprentice artists aren't happy in today's Montmartre, hard to climb, full of fake artists, deluded industrialists … In Montparnasse, by contrast, you can find real artists, dressed like Americans … And what a delightful place this is, where all the skies are for outdoor use, a land of open air and terraces: at the Lilas, where the main figures are Paul Fort, Diriks, Mercereau, Giannattasio, Charles Guérin, Flandrin, Mme Marval, etc.; at La Rotonde, where you can see Kisling, Max Jacob, Rivera, Friesz and others; at Le Dôme, frequented by Basler, Goetz, Flechtheim, Pascin, Levy and all the *dômiens* [*sic*], finally at the Petit Napolitain, where Gwozdecki, Pierre Roy, De Chirico and Modigliani take refreshment; and last of all at the Versailles, where Marquet, Benoni, Auran and so on attend. The cafés in this district are oases …[16]

The reasons that drove artists to "emigrate" were certainly those mentioned by Apollinaire (pleasure tourism, the "mafia" presence), but also the constant building works (the completion of works on the Sacré-Cœur, the creation of Rue Caulaincourt and Avenue Junot – eradicating the "Maquis" shantytown, an anarchist den, the excavation of the Nord-Sud Métro line – facilitating the artists' departure to the other side of the city), combined with impoverished living conditions; because, for many artists, this was "misery Montmartre" (Roland Dorgelès) or "Montmerdre", which translates, roughly, as "shit hill" (Apollinaire) – somewhere you got out of the minute you were successful.

At the same time, several centres were emerging in Montparnasse. Le Dôme [FIG. 2], from 1905 onwards, was mainly frequented by German-speaking artists like Béla Czóbel, Wilhelm Uhde, Sonia Terk (who was married to Uhde at the time), Alfred Flechtheim, Walter Bondy, Henry Bing, the Brummer brothers, Carl Einstein, Hans Purrmann and Adolphe Basler. In the *Paris-Journal* of 2 July 1914 Apollinaire reported:

> Le Dôme is the café on the Raspail-Montparnasse intersection. The 'dômiers' are the German painters who gather here. And under this name, 'der Dome' – which to Germanic ears means a cathedral (and isn't a brasserie – a beer garden – after all, the true German cathedral?), these artists exhibit their works at Alfred Flechtheim's gallery in Düsseldorf. There are twenty-three of them living in Paris; few of them, by the way, have any personal style; several are good students, with promise; some are real artists, like Pascin, a kind of modern Chinchtel, but he's not German, he's Serbian.[17]

We know, too, that Le Dôme was famous for its aesthetic discussions, often with Henri Matisse and Pablo Picasso at the centre. Some of the 'dômiers' attended the Académie Matisse after 1908.[18]

Another meeting place was La Closerie des Lilas, which was popular with poets in particular – Paul Fort, Stuart Merill, Jean Moréas, Léon-Paul Fargue and the young generation, most having decamped from Montmartre like André Salmon, Max Jacob and Apollinaire, Francis Carco, Maurice Raynal – but was also frequented by Miceslas Goldberg, Alexandre Mercereau, Florent Fels, Filippo Tommaso Marinetti and painters, including Christian Krogh,

14   Adolphe Basler and Charles Kunstler, *La Peinture indépendante en France*, II. *De Matisse à Segonzac*, Paris, G. Crès et Cie, "Peintres et sculpteurs", 1929.
15   Magazine produced by Paul Husson and Géo Charles. Two issues were published in 1914, it was suspended during the war, then the magazine appeared again in 1920.
16   Guillaume Apollinaire, "Montparnasse", *Paris-Journal*, 23 June 1914, in *Chroniques et paroles sur l'art*, Paris, Gallimard, Bibiothèque de la Pléiade, 1991, p. 784.
17   Julius Mordecaï Pincas, known as Pascin, was not Serbian, but a Bulgarian from Romania.
18   Including Hans Purrmann, Rudolf Levy, Béla Czóbel and Isaac Grünewald. The Academy opened in 1908, in the former Couvent des Oiseaux on Rue de Sèvres, and closed in 1912.

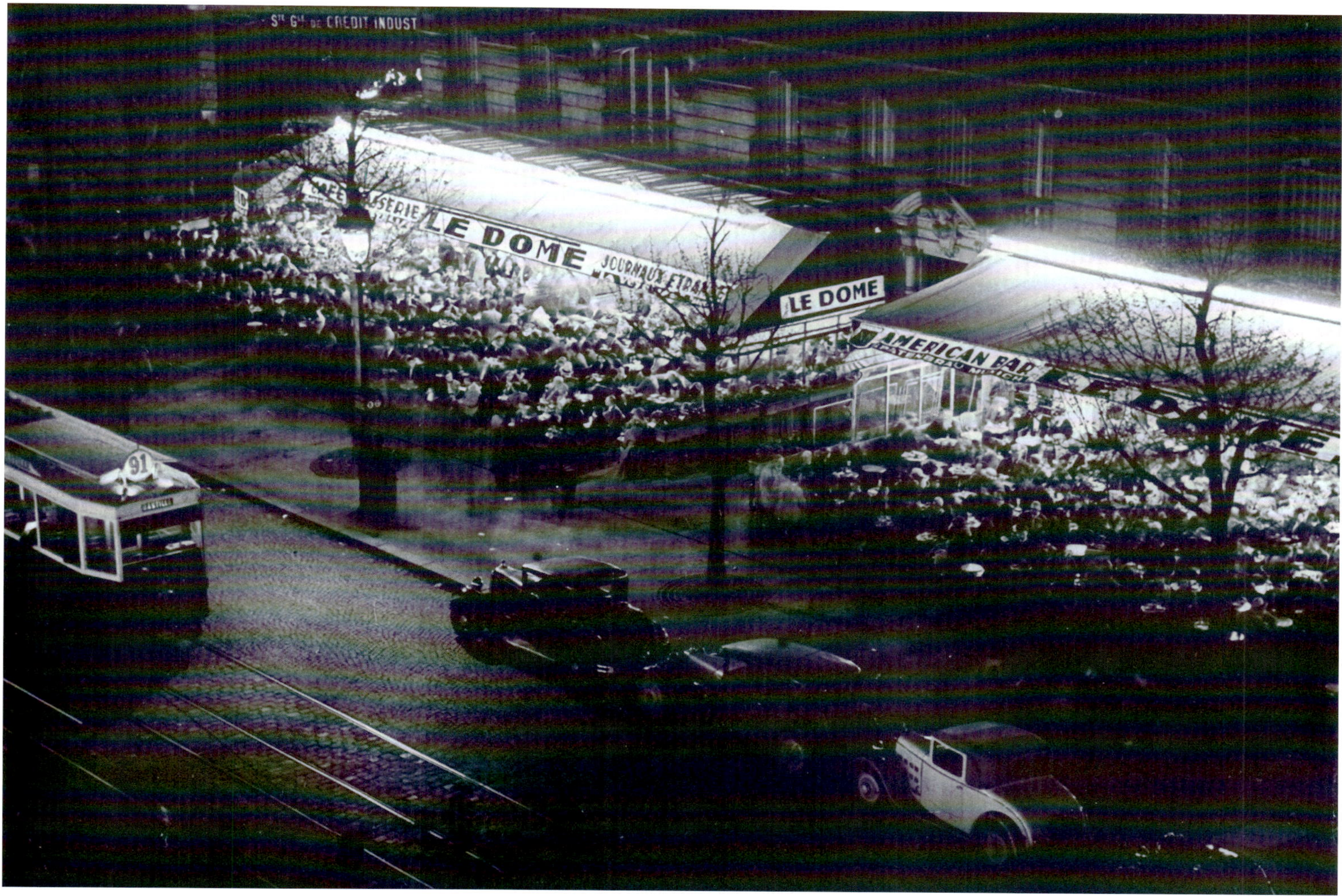

FIG. 2
Brasserie Le Dôme, 1932
Photograph by Brassaï
Private collection

Picasso and Severini. It was at La Closerie des Lilas that Symbolist poetry came to an end and Apollinaire's "new spirit" took shape. These places resonated with tradition – like a palimpsest on which new aesthetic and poetic principles were overwritten. It was surely no coincidence that the Surrealists adopted this café in their turn in the 1920s.

It would exceed the limits of the current study to list all the famous cafés (La Rotonde, La Coupole [FIG. 3], Le Parnasse, etc.), the associations with their famous balls (Union des Artistes Russes, L'Aide Amicale Aux Artistes, known as "AAAA", Maison Watteau, etc.) and the artist studios (La Ruche, Cité Falguière), quite apart from all the independent art schools that flourished in this neighbourhood (Académie Vassilieff, La Grande Chaumière, the Académie Scandinave, etc.).

Yet this vibrant activity should not overshadow the other side of the picture: the xenophobic sentiments that became increasingly apparent in the aftermath of the First World War.

THE "QUARREL OF THE FOREIGNERS"[19]

The last xenophobic attacks were not that far back: in French public opinion, the First World War had fuelled a distrust, even an outright rejection, of foreigners. Germans especially were stigmatised. Absent for around a decade, from 1914 to 1924, when some 'dômiers' returned to Paris, they remained a target for nationalist critics:

19   Expression used by Louis Vauxcelles in *L'Ère nouvelle*, 29 November 1923.

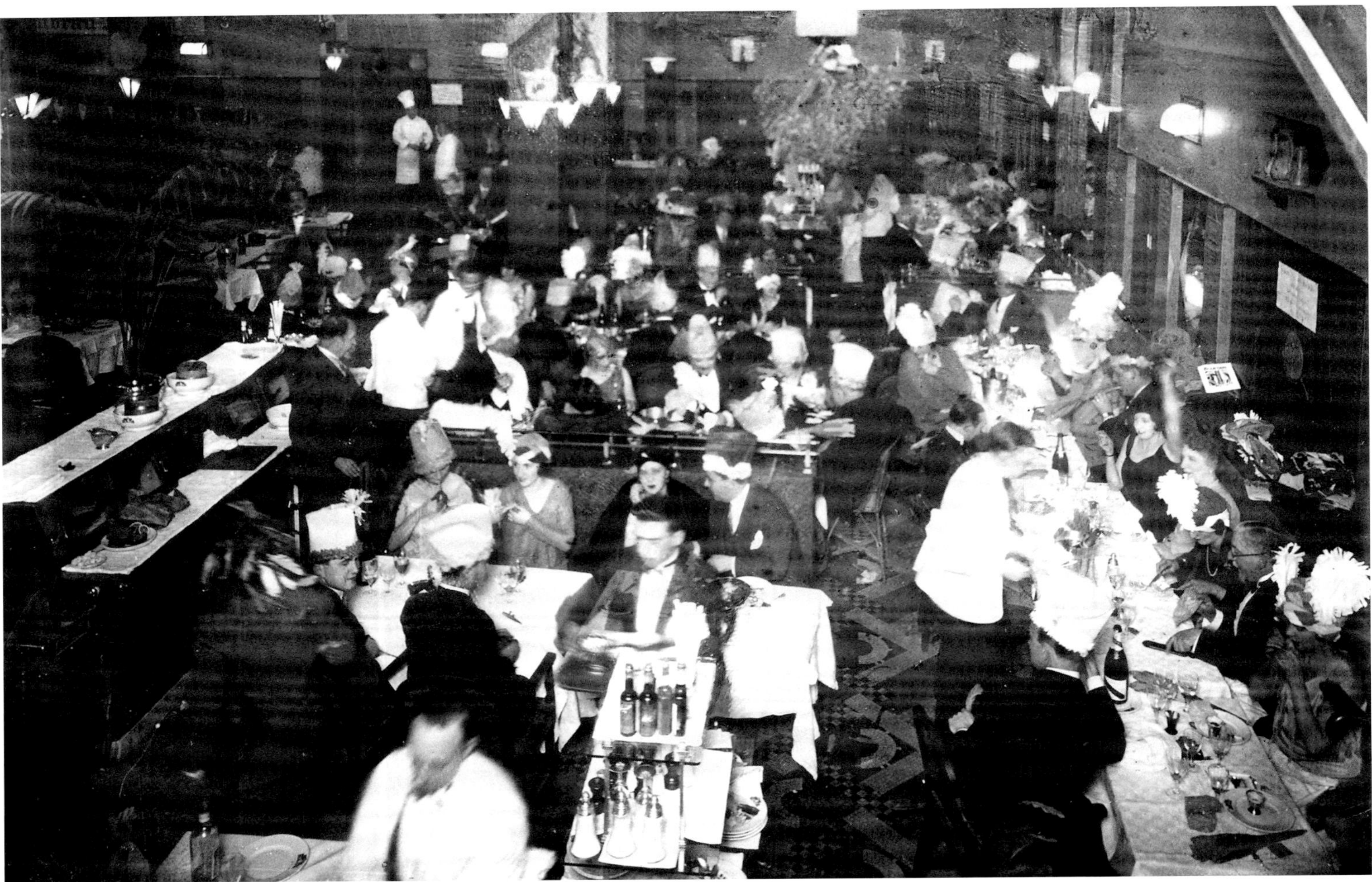

for Louis Vauxcelles, for example, who campaigned against the presence of German artists in the Exposition Internationale des Arts Décoratifs (International Exhibition of Modern Decorative and Industrial Arts) of 1925.[20] There was also the affair of the visit by American art collector Albert C. Barnes in 1922, who, accompanied by Paul Guillaume, went on a buying spree, acquiring more than fifty paintings by Soutine, a relatively unknown artist, and none at all by the painter Jean Marchand. This was just too much. Soutine was the perfect scapegoat in this dispute – foreign, Jewish, Expressionist – and therefore cast as a non-assimilated, potentially dangerous alien.

In 1923, after a stormy committee meeting, the president of the Salon des Indépendants, Paul Signac, decided to change the way works were arranged in the show. That year, artists would be placed in alphabetical order, to avoid factions and cliques (a measure targeting the Cubists), and the following year, they would be arranged by nationality and alphabetical order. The news spread through Montparnasse like wildfire. The response was swift: a joint delegation of French and foreign artists[21] asked the president to reverse the measure. Following extensive debate and further votes, the decision was upheld, causing the resignations of Léger, Zadkine, Kisling, Survage, Van Dongen and others.

This affair highlights the mobilisation of the foreigners, who joined forces against an exhibition that was purportedly democratic – its slogan was "without jury or reward" – and also that of the press, which devoted more than a hundred articles to the issue. It was on this occasion that the critic Roger Allard[22] used for the first time the term "School of Paris", which was picked up by Warnod in the following year.

20   Louis Vauxcelles, "L'art allemand peut attendre", *Le Figaro*, 1919, Fonds Vauxcelles, Bibliothèque Doucet.
21   Led by Jean-Émile Laboureur and the Dutch artist Conrad Kickert.
22   Roger Allard, "Le Salon des indépendants", *La Revue française*, 17 February 1924.

There were many reasons for this ostracism of foreigners. The Salon des Indépendants was a victim of its own success, and having to deal with a growing number of participants. It also needed to secure the funding necessary to hire the Grand Palais[23] and compete with its great rival, the Salon d'Automne, which was already staging group exhibitions by invited foreign artists. Yet the reasons advanced by Signac should not overshadow the barely disguised jealousy felt by some French painters, weakened by the First World War, and looking askance on these meteoric careers "engineered" by dealers and critics.[24] Among the latter, Vauxcelles is a good indicator of the prevailing mindset at the time: "Without wishing to slight the undeniable talents of such as Kisling, Marcoussis, Pascin, Sabbagh, Gimmi, Zadkine, Lipchitz, Hernandez and Ekegarth, it is necessary to observe proportions carefully when a group is formed. There are, after all, some people in Montparnasse who have not yet become assimilated."[25]

Allard, meanwhile, criticised the foreign artists for forgetting what they owed to French art and for coming in order to "profit" from French generosity:

> We should say, too, that the foreign artists, some of them at least, have a tendency to forget what they owe to our modern French schools. Trained, mostly in our classes, they seek to promulgate, outside France, the concept of a certain School of Paris, in which distinctions between masters and imitators, on the one hand, disciples and copyists, on the other, are blurred, to the advantage of the latter. The most mediocre having most interest in this confusion, which they energetically encourage, it goes without saying.[26]

Warnod, in 1925, expressed roughly the same idea: "They create, in default of anything else, a very profitable disturbance. French artists should not rest on their laurels; moreover, there are among the foreign artists some great original artists who, for their part, give more than they take. They pay for the others, the followers, the imitators, the counterfeiters."[27] He viewed this assorted crowd as an opportunity for French art, providing it with access to new markets.[28]

For others, the arrival of foreigners "wishing to assimilate the virtues of the French school"[29] was a danger to French art which risked being "contaminated":

> It seemed to me that the innermost spirit of France was endangered by the influx of internationals who, whatever might be said of them with strange impudence and wide-eyed optimism, do not become in any way French while among us – on the contrary, injecting harmful viruses into the minds of our young people … A methodical, hateful assault is being attempted, across the whole of post-war Europe, against the spirit, the discipline, the culture, the grace of Rome, of the Renaissance, by Germano-Slavism.[30]

These far-right conspiracy theories, of contamination defiling the purity of the French race, of the cause of France's decadence, were applied to foreign artists, just as they were to Italian or Russian workers. Which led Salmon to observe that "critics so very eager to absolve themselves of any overly garish, heavy-handed nationalism, would none the less trouble themselves to disencumber French painting by sending back across the border a good number of foreigners accustomed to the climate of our Salons".[31] In short, no one was spared from the wave of xenophobia.

Among the foreign artists themselves, the affair elicited a certain amount of bitterness. Kisling, for example, wrote to Lipchitz: "It makes me laugh to think that we're foreigners everywhere, even in Paris. It makes me laugh

23 From 1920 onwards, the Salon des Indépendants was held in the Grand Palais in the month of February.
24 In *Le Ruy Blas* of 15 February 1923, we can read (in an unsigned article): "Perusing the catalogue … all we see is names with *off*, with *ski*, with *bers*, with *sonn*, with *agh*. So these 'independents' are therefore mostly foreigners. What are they doing in our country, these foreigners? How do they make a living? … Not from art, which is just as well, because it would be regrettable to see French art lovers' money lining the pockets of foreigners when our own painters find it so difficult to survive."
25 Louis Vauxcelles, *Le Carnet de la semaine*, 8 February 1923. It is worth recalling that the Ministry of the Interior had set a quota for foreign members of the Salon des Indépendants; this quota, of 33 per cent, was never reached.
26 R. Allard, "Le Salon des indépendants", op. cit. In this piece he was the first to use the term "School of Paris" for the "parisianised" foreign artists resident in city.
27 André Warnod, "L'École de Paris", *Comœdia*, 27 January 1925.
28 The *dômiers* were especially effective as intermediaries for German collectors of French art.
29 Louis Vauxcelles, *Excelsior*, 18 February 1924.
30 Camille Mauclair, *L'Ami du peuple*, 1 August 1929.
31 André Salmon, "Chroniques", *L'Art vivant*, 15 October 1925.

a little to see Basler, Meyer and others, Rosenberg, Kahnweiler, etc., against foreigners, Jews or converts … but in another way, it's sad to see this ridiculous confusion."[32] And shortly after this, to the same correspondent:

> Tell me if, with all this fuss about foreigners, you're exhibiting at the Independents – I think not, and yet maybe it would be interesting to exhibit none the less. Really, the way people think these days is all wrong – who are they going to put Pissarro, Van Gogh, Sisley or Picasso with – and that most Parisian of all Parisians, Van Dongen?[33]

While Zadkine exploded with anger: "Why more compartments and concentration camps?"[34]

THE END OF THE SCHOOL OF PARIS

At the close of the 1920s, at the height of success for all these artists, the economic crisis spelled the end of what some people called the "Années folles", the roaring twenties – an expression that was widely used in the literature of the interwar years. Many US-based collectors stopped buying art, causing difficulties for numerous Parisian galleries and therefore for their artists, too. In the early 1930s, the tide turned. Some artists left Paris: Foujita, ruined, returned to Japan in 1930, Kisling moved to the Côte d'Azur, Chagall went travelling, Soutine lived partly outside Paris, Pascin committed suicide in 1930 and so on.

In 1932, Tériade noted that the School of Paris was effectively non-existent, its "scholars" having returned to their homelands: "The fact is that the many exhibitions bringing together artists of all latitudes, all races and especially all colours – like a delicous *macedoine* washed down with copious wine – seem to be forgotten events in 1932."[35] Now artists preferred to exhibit by nationality, a trend that started in the late 1920s. The School of Paris no longer had a place in 1930s Paris, which saw the return of nationalism. Exhibitions were staged with the aim of bringing artists together under their national banners – shows like "Italian painters of Paris" (1928, Salon de l'Escalier), "A group of Italians in Paris" (1929, Galerie Zak), "Modern Polish art" (1929, Éditions Bonaparte) and "American artists of Paris" (1932, Galerie de la Renaissance). From 1932 onwards, these shows were joined by exhibitions at the Musée National des Écoles Étrangères Contemporaines (National Museum of Contemporary Foreign Schools), based in the Jeu de Paume in the Tuileries Garden.

This museum was exceptional in that it reserved a room for the School of Paris among those devoted to German, Belgian, Italian and other international schools. Yet the status of the School of Paris remained ambiguous, its isolation seemingly arranged to ensure "that no contamination might impair the glory of artists whose nationality has been perfectly defined and recognised by embassies".[36] It is moreover among the School's initial defenders that we find its most virulent critics in the 1930s – Waldemar-George among them. He analysed all the elements underlying its creation: its amalgamation with French painting, its independence of sources or precursors, its status as a fashion fad, its aesthetic diversity – and concluded that this was not French art.[37] The critic thus ended any hope of universalism, of an art without borders, created by the generation he had himself supported. The concept of national tradition, in his view the source of artistic renewal, was as irreducible as the national character supposedly retained by the foreign artist living in France, confounding any "naturalisation" and therefore refusing assimilation.

Other movements also attracted foreigners to Paris. Since 1925 and the exhibition "L'Art d'aujourd'hui" ("Today's Art"), for example, the French capital had been one of the centres of abstract art. Piet Mondrian was

32   Letter from Kisling to Jacques Lipchitz, 8 March 1923, Reuben Lipchitz archives.
33   Letter from Kisling to Jacques Lipchitz, 22 November 1923, Reuben Lipchitz archives.
34   Ossip Zadkine, *Le Bulletin de la vie artistique*, 15 January 1924.
35   Tériade, "La fin de l'École de Paris ou le retour des enfants prodigues", op. cit.
36   Ibid.
37   Waldemar-George, "École française ou École de Paris", *Formes*, July 1931.

back in Paris from 1920 onwards, and was joined by his compatriot Theo van Doesburg in 1927; Wassily Kandinsky, another leading figure of abstraction, left Berlin for Paris when the Nazis came to power;[38] the Belgian Michel Seuphor, founder of the group Cercle et Carré (1929), was also in Paris, as were Robert and Sonia Delaunay and František Kupka. The movement's diversity was confirmed with the formation of the Abstraction-Création group (1931), spanning the full range of trends in abstraction and including many international artists both in Paris and beyond. This clearly shows the difference between the School of Paris and an international group. Yet abstract art, shunned by the critics, did not attract a network of journalists and writers capable of influencing critical attitudes and the public taste. This, it seems, is what led its events to remain largely private in nature for a long period.

Surrealism, meanwhile, supplanted the School of Paris in the late 1920s and adopted quite similar methods: networks of cafés, galleries, very strong links with writers and so on. And just as Parisian abstract movements connected outwards to other international centres (in Berlin, Moscow and Switzerland, for example), so did the Surrealists, organising international exhibitions in the 1930s (in Prague, London, Tenerife, etc.), supporting national movements while preserving the pre-eminence of the French capital.

The School of Paris, though, was incapable of generating an international network or movement, due both to its absence of theory and the fanatical individualism of the artists involved. For most of them, the fact of merely being in Paris was enough to establish their modernist credentials.

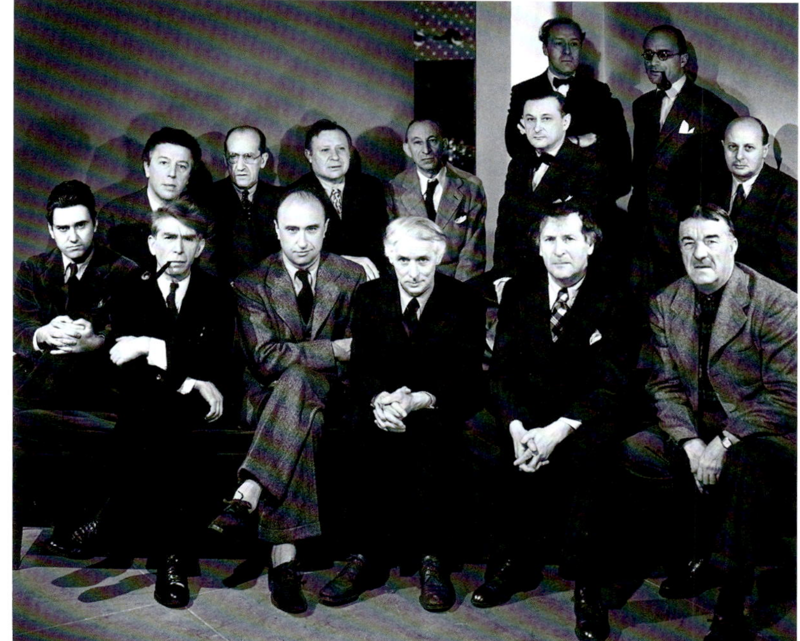

FIG. 4
Artists taking part in the exhibition "Artists in Exile" at the Pierre Matisse Gallery, New York, March 1942
Photograph by George Platt Lynes
New York, The Museum of Modern Art Archives, IN620.12

A GROUP PHOTOGRAPH

It all happened, then, in the cosmopolitan ambience of Montparnasse. It was here that movements took shape and dispersed, that discussions were held, often in the same cafés, in the footsteps of Apollinaire. The protagonists were joined by all kinds of interconnections and personal relationships. The model Kiki is a case in point, linking artists like Kisling, Foujita, Man Ray and Léger – and other women, too, moved between different groups (Youki was the companion first of Foujita, then Robert Desnos), clearly showing the close proximity in which these various individuals were operating. Remarkably, when both French and international artists fled into exile during the Second World War this entire community – representing the School of Paris, abstraction and Surrealism – came together in New York for the 1942 "Artists in Exile" exhibition at the Pierre Matisse Gallery. The group photograph taken at the time has become famous [FIG. 4], showing Roberto Matta, Ossip Zadkine, Yves Tanguy, Max Ernst, Marc Chagall, Fernand Léger, André Breton, Piet Mondrian, André Masson, Amédée Ozenfant, Jacques Lipchitz, Pavel Tchelitchev, Kurt Seligmann and Eugène Berman: five French artists and nine foreign. And it's highly likely that the members of this little group all knew each other already from way back – having met, no doubt, on the terrace of Le Dôme, or La Rotonde, in Montparnasse.

---

38   Already in contact with Christian Zervos and having had an exhibition in Paris in 1929, Kandinsky chose the French capital for its cosmopolitanism. In a letter to Josef Albers of 9 January 1934, he describes this aspect of the city as highly restorative following recent experiences, expressing his belief that the French, secure in their sense of national identity, did not see this diversity as in any way threatening. See *Josef Albers and Wassily Kandinsky: Friends in Exile – A Decade of Correspondence, 1929–1939*, ed. Nicholas Fox-Weber, New York, Hudson Hills, 2010.

MONTMARTRE

① Rue Caulaincourt Studios
73, Rue Caulaincourt, Paris XVIII

② Bateau-Lavoir
13, Place Émile-Goudeau, Paris XVIII

MONTPARNASSE

③ Académie de la Grande-Chaumière
14, Rue de la Grande-Chaumière, Paris VI

④ Constantin Brancusi's studio
8, Impasse Ronsin, Paris XV

⑤ Chana Orloff's studio
7 bis, Villa Seurat, Paris XIV

⑥ Pablo Picasso's studio
11, Rue Victor-Schœlcher, Paris XIV

⑦ Vavin intersection:
Cafés La Coupole, Le Dôme, La Rotonde
102–8, Boulevard du Montparnasse, Paris VI & XIV

⑧ Cité Falguière
Quartier Necker, Paris XV

⑨ La Closerie des Lilas
171, Boulevard du Montparnasse, Paris VI

⑩ La Ruche
2, Passage de Dantzig, Paris XV

OTHER PLACES

⑪ École des Beaux-Arts
14, Rue Bonaparte, Paris VI

⑫ Gare de l'Est
Place du 11 novembre 1918, Paris X

⑬ Gare du Nord
18, Rue de Dunkerque, Paris X

⑭ Gare Montparnasse
17, Boulevard de Vaugirard, Paris XV

⑮ Grand Palais
3, Avenue du Général-Eisenhower, Paris VIII

Petit Palais
Avenue Wilson-Churchill, Paris VIII

⑯ Musée du Louvre
Rue de Rivoli, Paris I

The locations given are the present-day addresses.

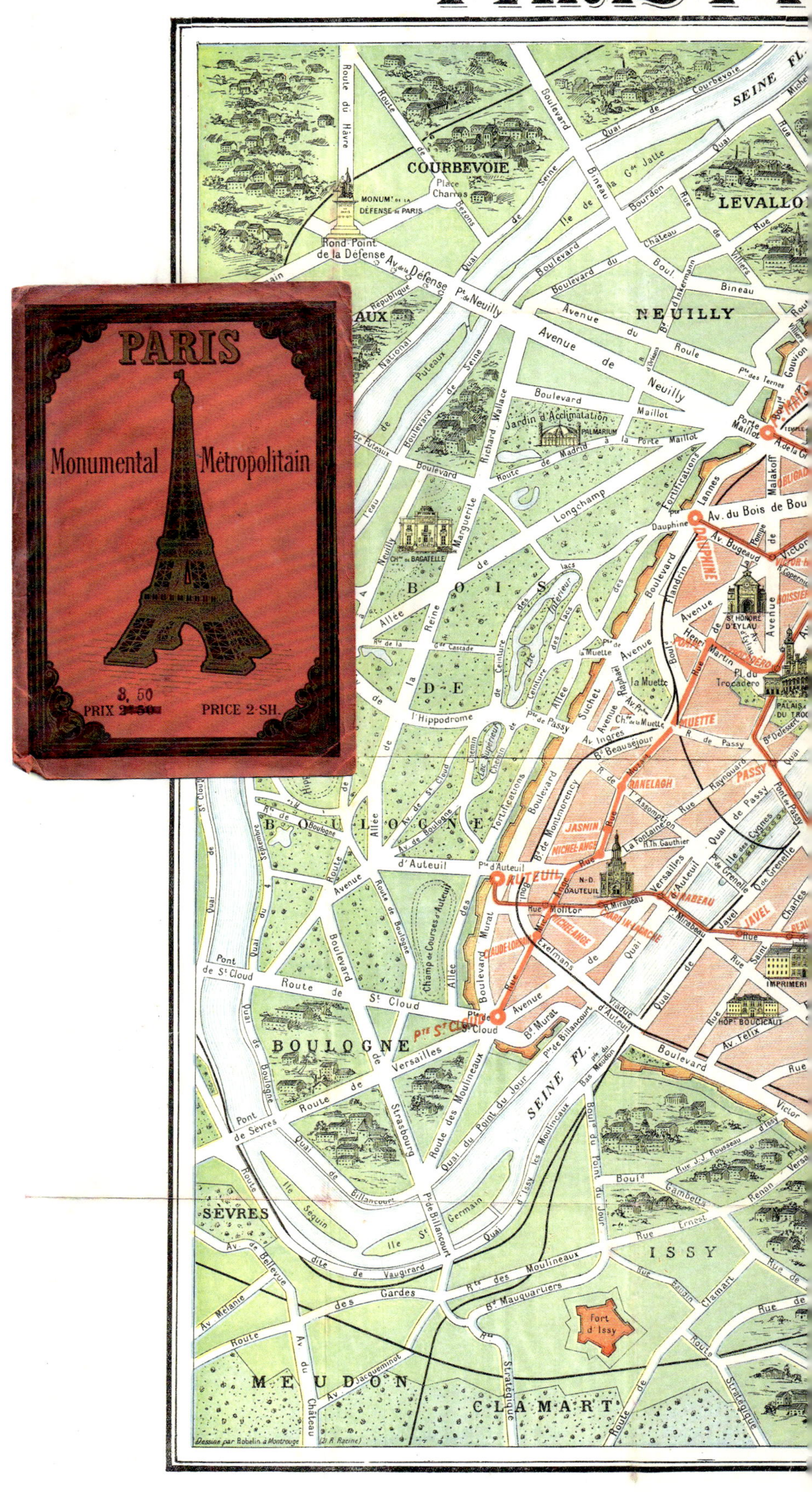

Paris Monumental et Métropolitain,
Paris, Robelin, *c.* 1920

EXHIBITED WORKS

**MASTERS OF COLOUR –
FROM FAUVISM TO ABSTRACTION**

FOREIGN CUBISTS

MARC CHAGALL AND LA RUCHE

**AMEDEO MODIGLIANI AND THE
ARTISTS OF MONTPARNASSE**

PARIS SEEN BY ...

**AROUND SOUTINE –
PARISIAN PORTRAITS**

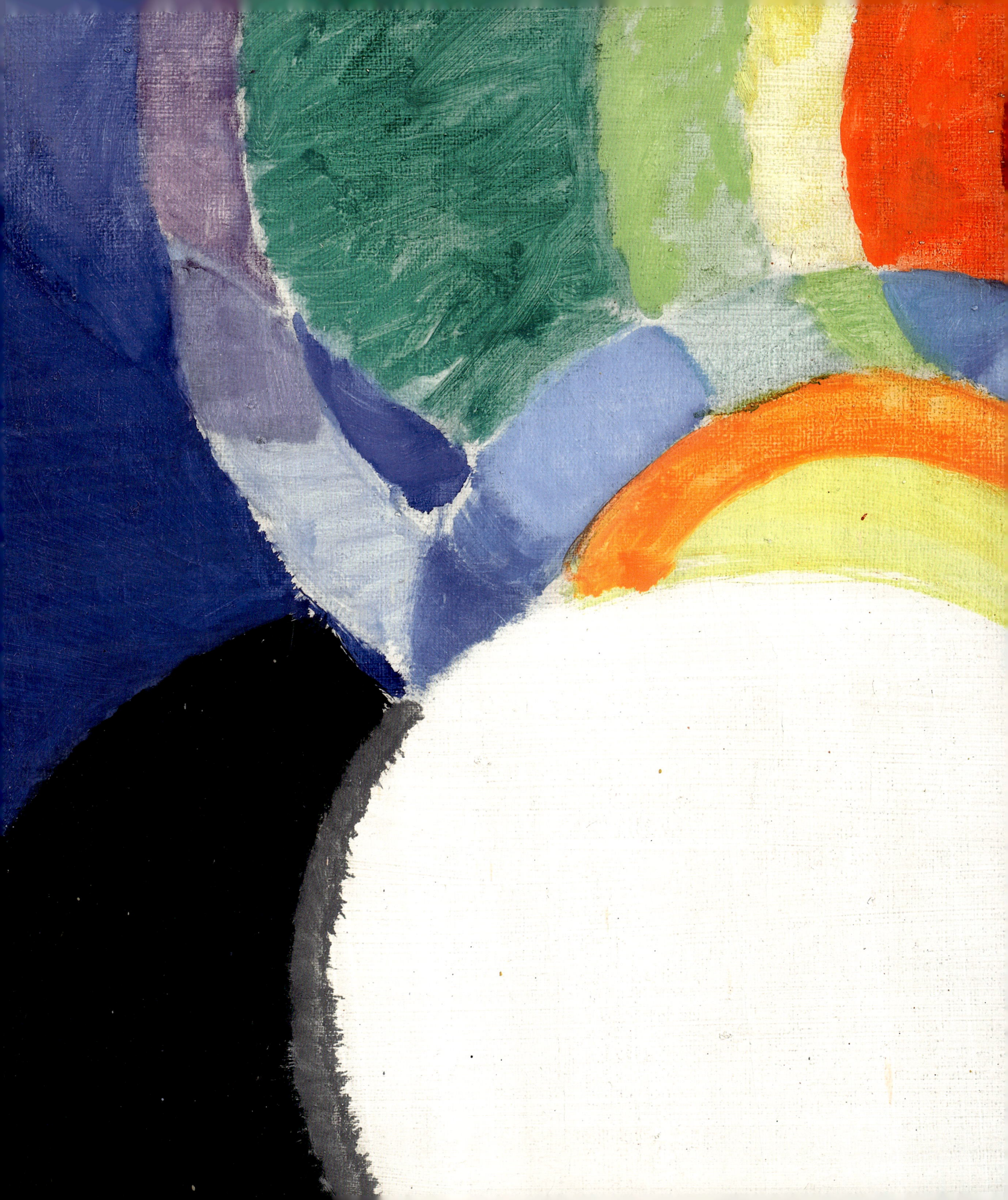

MASTERS OF COLOUR – FROM FAUVISM TO ABSTRACTION

Anna Hiddleston-Galloni

For artists arriving in Paris at the beginning of the 20th century, the city abounded with new creative energies, experimenting with radical expressions of colour and form. Pablo Picasso, who came to Paris for the first time in October 1900, was a vital and stimulating presence. The bright palette of his portrait of the writer and fashionable chronicler of Parisian society Gustave Coquiot [CAT. 1], which served as a frontispiece to the catalogue of Picasso's first show in Paris at Galerie Ambroise Vollard in 1901, owes much to Toulouse-Lautrec in its use of stark contrast. This later gave way to the monochromatic paintings of the Blue and Rose periods between 1904 and 1906.

Picasso's innovative contributions to the avant-garde were echoed in the work of other young artists based in Paris who took similar creative risks, resulting in Fauvism, one of the first avant-garde modernist movements of the 20th century. Spearheaded by Henri Matisse, André Derain, Maurice de Vlaminck and Albert Marquet, Fauvism was inspired by the examples of Van Gogh and Gauguin in its use of intense colour, not only as a vehicle for describing light and space, but also as a means of communicating the artist's emotional state. The Fauves ("wild beasts") – a term coined by Louis Vauxcelles after the scandal caused by the display of their paintings at the Salon d'Automne in 1905 – were a group of French painters and one Dutch, Kees van Dongen, who arrived in Paris in 1897. Van Dongen set up his studio in the Montmartre neighbourhood, even living for a short time at the Bateau-Lavoir artist residence in 1906, where he was pulled into the avant-garde circle of artists gravitating around Picasso, settled there since 1904. Van Dongen immersed himself deeply in the life of Montmartre and built his reputation through his use of incandescent colour. Although his palette grew slightly darker in 1909, his paintings of the dancers at the Folies-Bergère, a music hall next to his studio, analyse the crude effect of the modern white electric lamps that Van Dongen was one of the first to use in his studio [CAT. 2].

Other foreign artists, such as František Kupka from Prague and Sonia Terk-Delaunay of Russian origin, followed a similar path, drawing on Fauvism's radical innovations as a stepping-stone for the development of an abstract style. Kupka's pioneering use of overall yellow in *The Yellow Scale* from 1907 not only reveals the artist's understanding of colour as a quantity and quality of light, but also as an expression of inner feeling [CAT. 5]. Like Van Dongen's, Kupka's compositions were inspired by scenes of Parisian nightlife, depicted in vibrant colours. The glowing green of the courtesan's scarf and shoes in *The Archaic* painted in 1910 [CAT. 6] creates areas of light that structure the work in anticipation of the abstract paintings to come. Indeed, the following year, directly inspired by Isaac Newton's chromatic circle, Kupka produced one of the first abstract compositions in the history of art [CAT. 10]. The undulating arabesque lines of *Study for Amorpha, Fugue in Two Colours* subsequently evoked the musical form of a fugue, playing on the interaction of warm and cold tones to create a lyrical sensation [CAT. 9].

In the autumn of 1912, at a conference held on the occasion of the Salon de la Section d'Or, the poet Guillaume Apollinaire used the word "Orphism" for the first time to describe not only Kupka's work but also that of Robert and Sonia Delaunay, foreseeing an art of pure colour. Sonia Delaunay arrived in Paris in December 1906, and her friendship with Wilhelm Uhde rapidly brought her into contact with the avant-garde. Her first works painted in Paris, such as her portrait of *Philomena* [CAT. 4], combine Russian embroidery techniques and textiles inspired by popular Russian culture with French stylistic motifs. Reacting against the monochrome of Analytic Cubism, from 1912 she concentrated on depicting light through simultaneous colour contrasts, creating abstract paintings based on squares of colour inspired by patchwork [CAT. 8]. Her impact on the artists of the time is evident in the work of the Portuguese painter Amadeo Souza Cardoso also in Paris since 1906. A close friend of Amedeo Modigliani and Constantin Brancusi, his unique imagery draws upon Sonia Delaunay's subtle use of coloured rhythms, which he integrated into compositions oscillating between abstraction and figuration [CAT. 7].

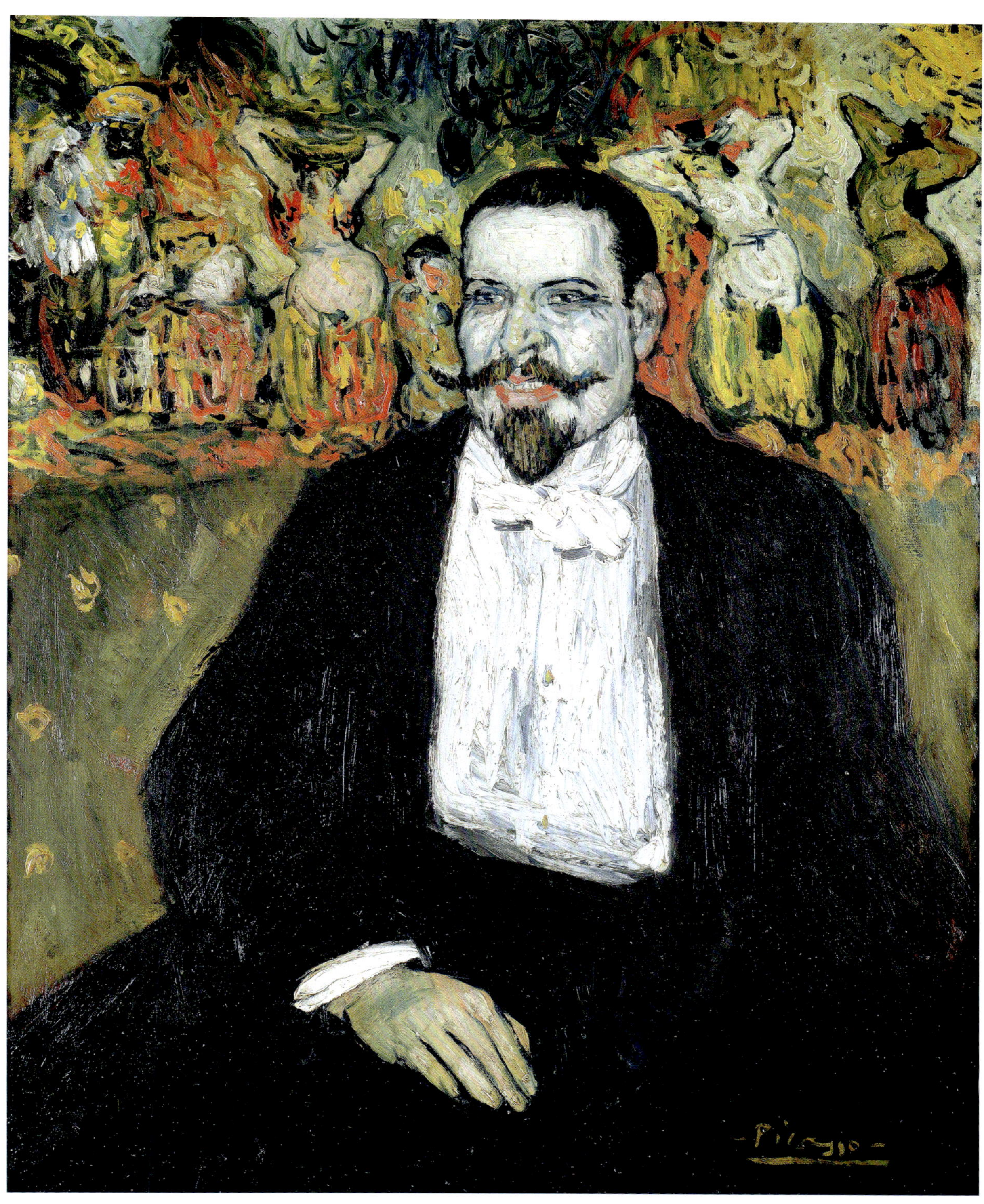

CAT. 1
Pablo Picasso (1881–1973)
Gustave Coquiot, 1901

Oil on canvas, 100 × 81 cm

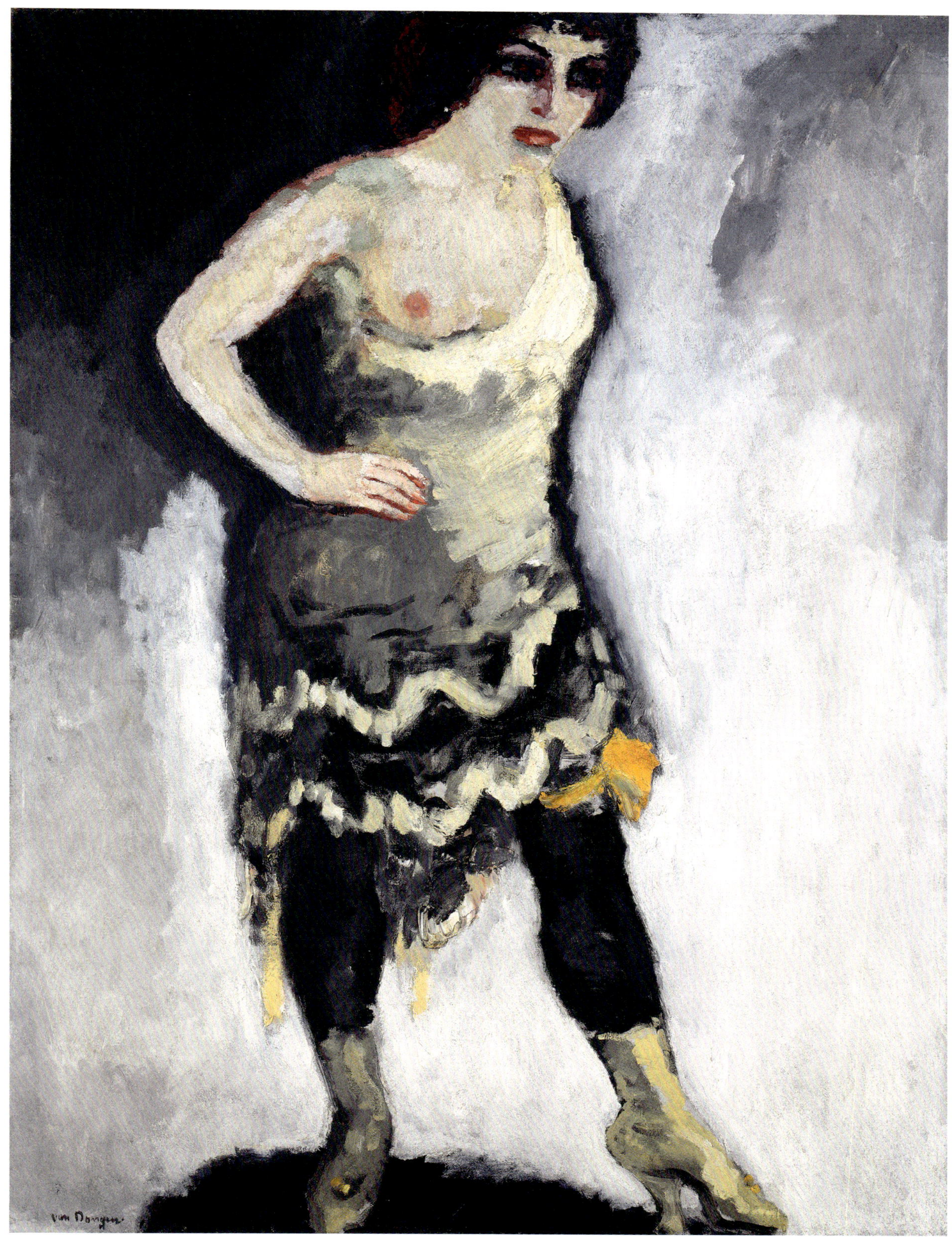

CAT. 2

Kees van Dongen (1877–1968)
Nini, Dancer at the Folies-Bergère, c. 1909

Oil on canvas, 130 × 97 cm

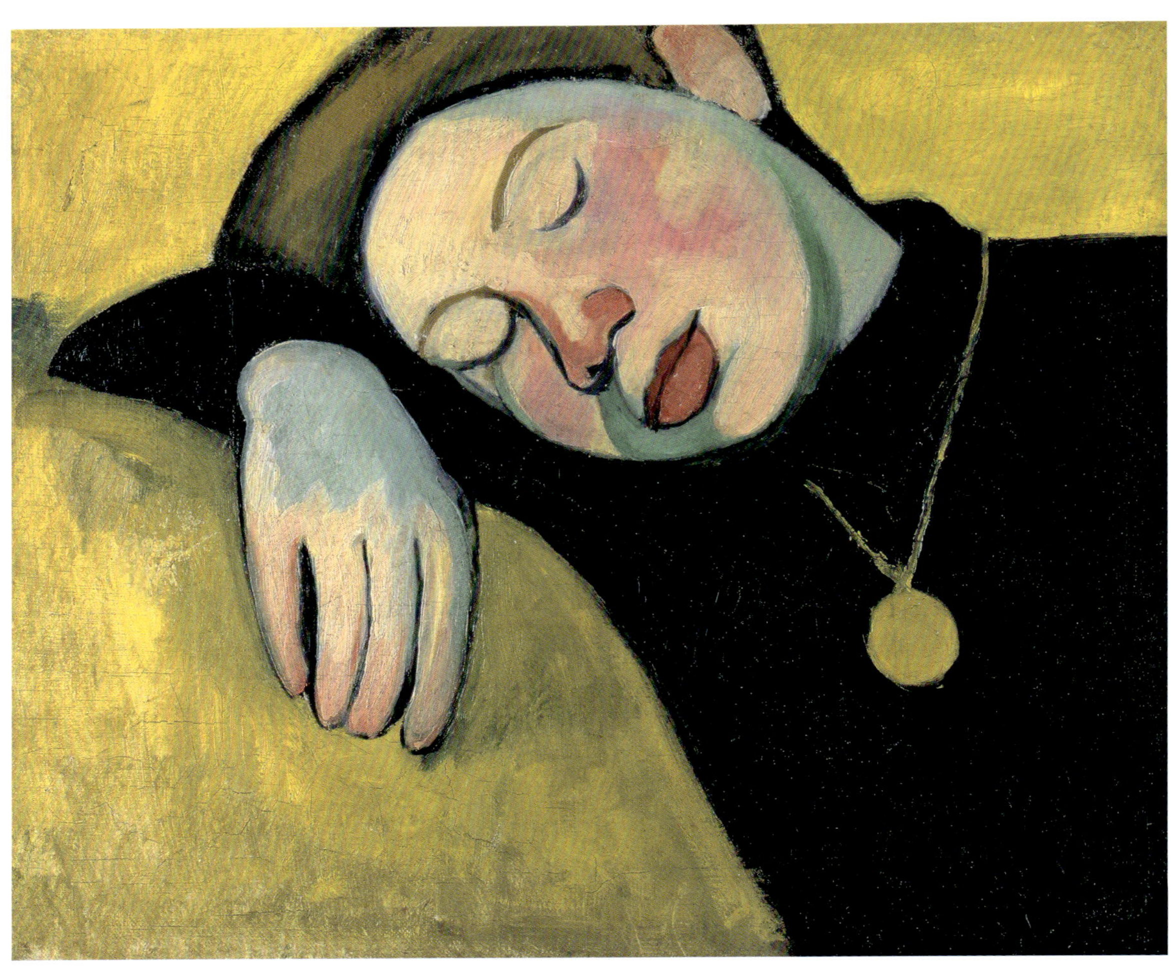

Sonia Delaunay (1885–1979)
Young Girl Sleeping, 1907

Oil on canvas mounted on wood panel, 46 × 55 cm

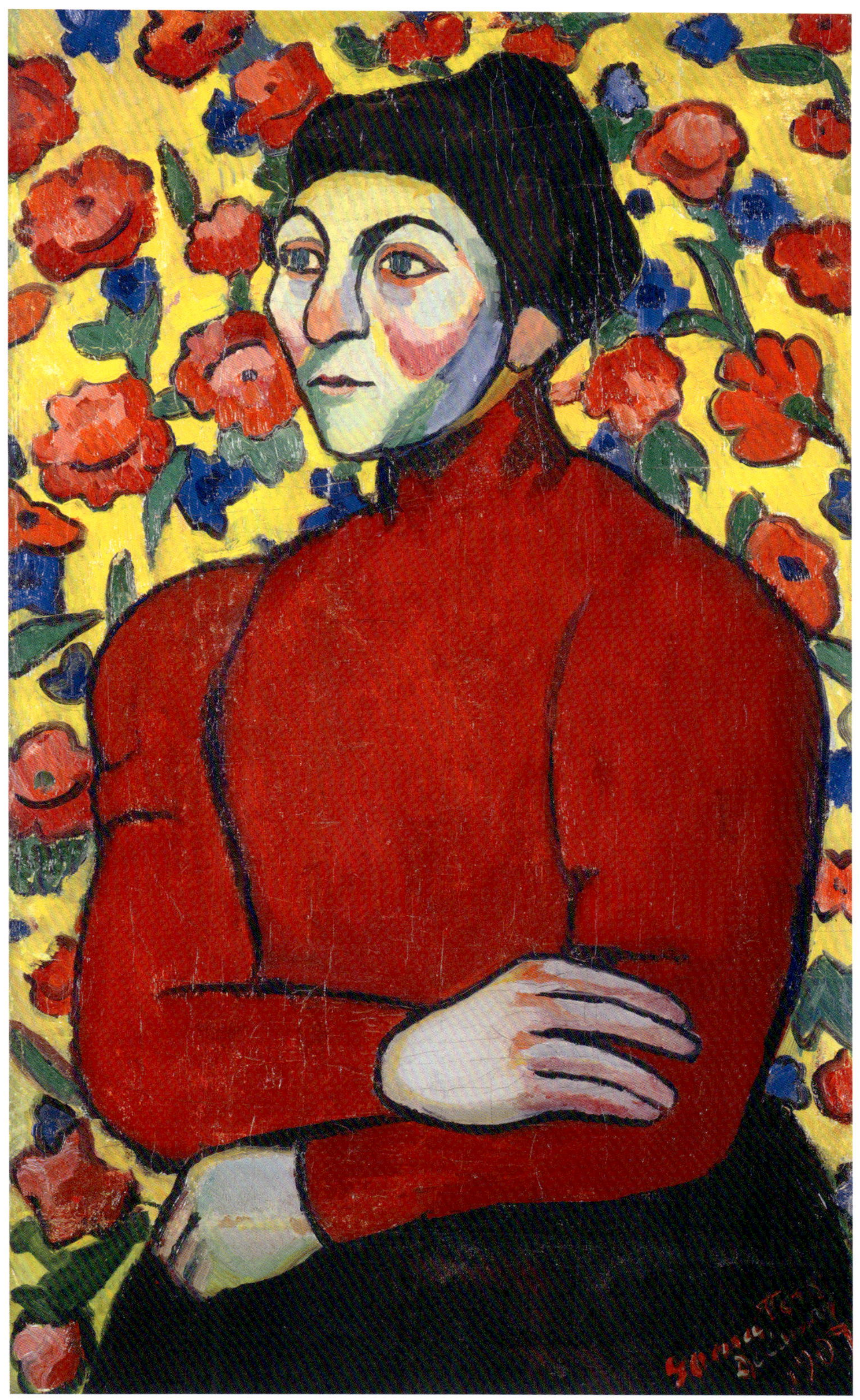

CAT. 4

Sonia Delaunay (1885–1979)
Philomena, 1907

Oil on canvas, 92 × 54.5 cm

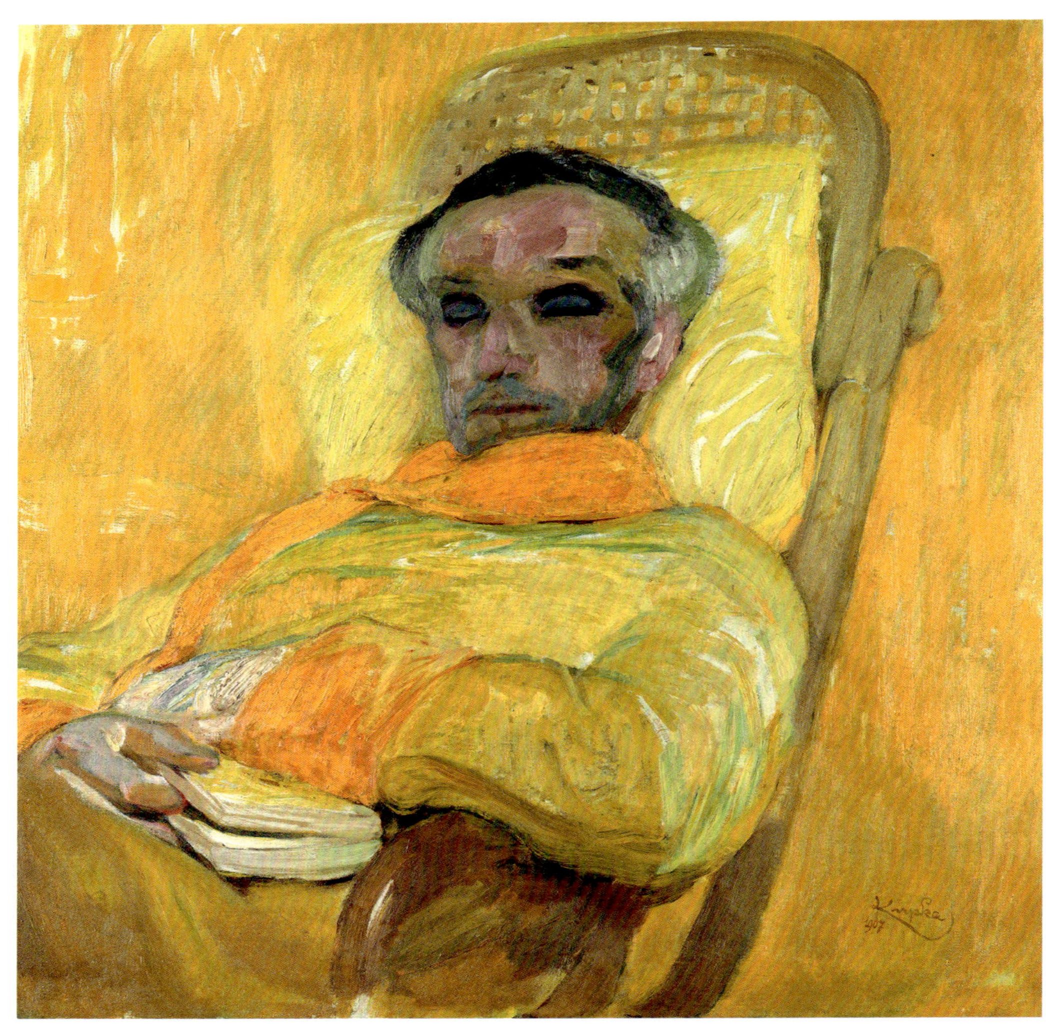

CAT. 5
František Kupka (1871–1957)
The Yellow Scale, 1907

Oil on canvas, 79 × 79 cm

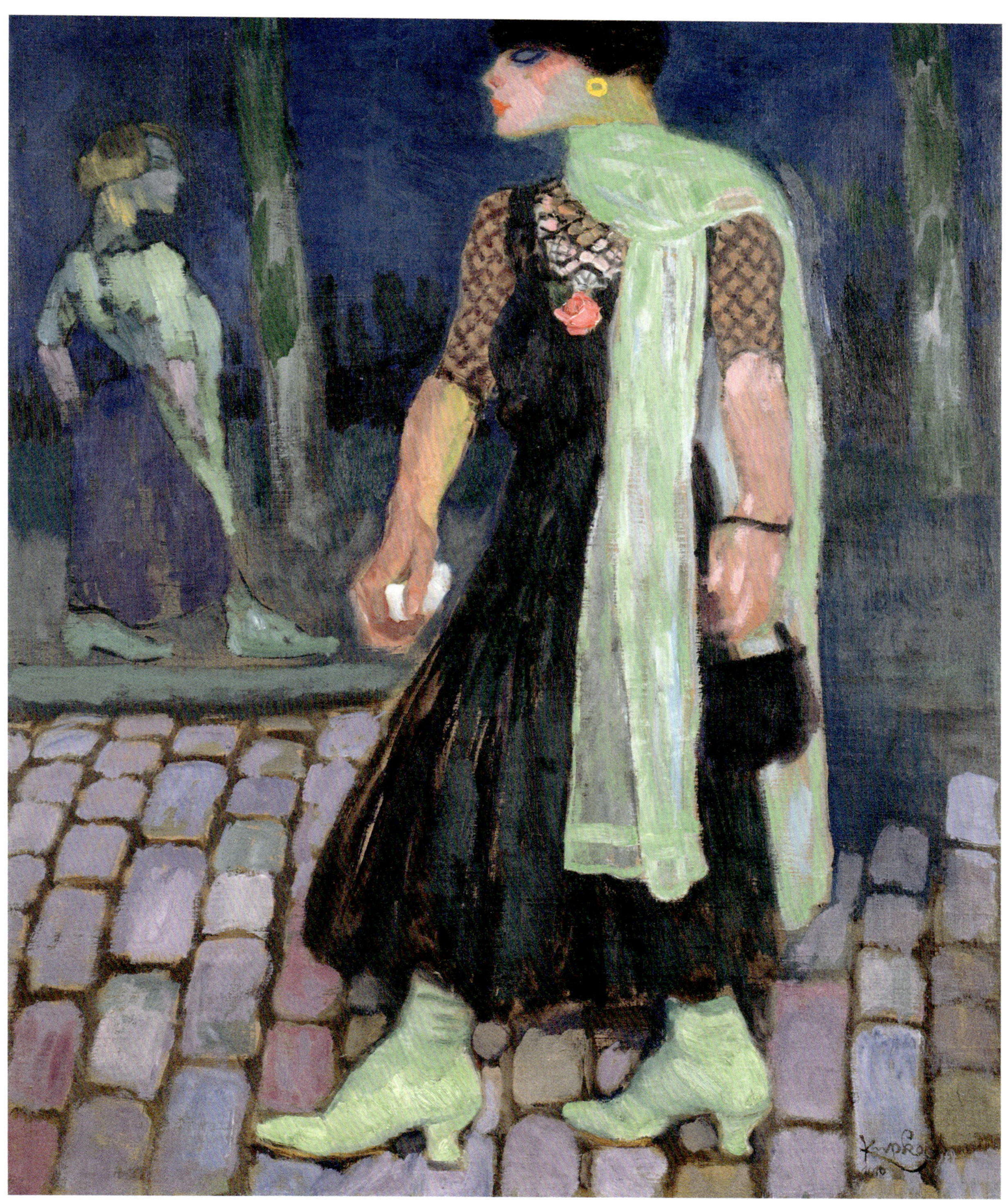

CAT. 6

František Kupka (1871–1957)
The Archaic, 1910

Oil on canvas, 110 × 90 cm

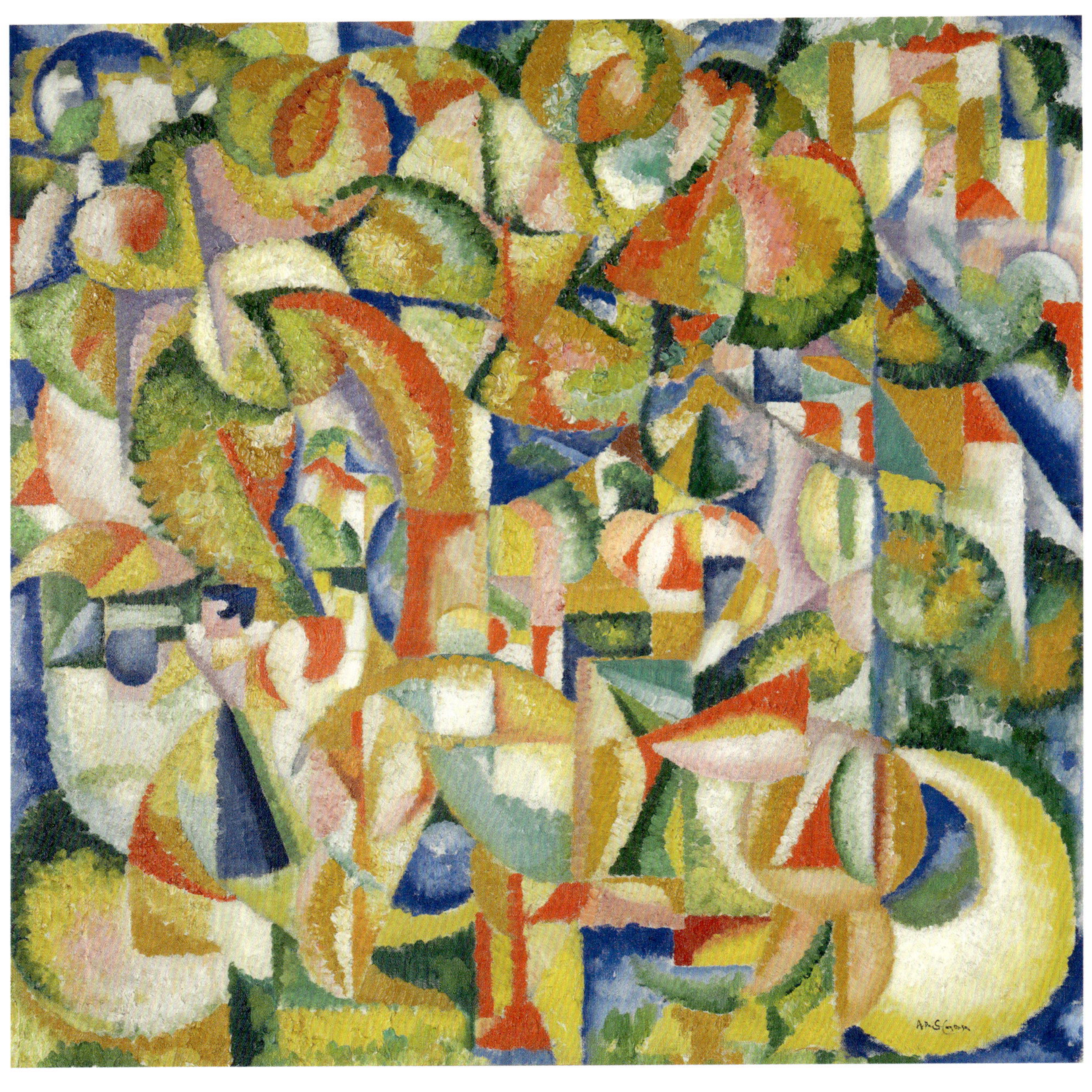

CAT. 7
Amadeo de Souza-Cardoso (1887–1918)
Riders, 1913

Oil on canvas, 100 × 100 cm

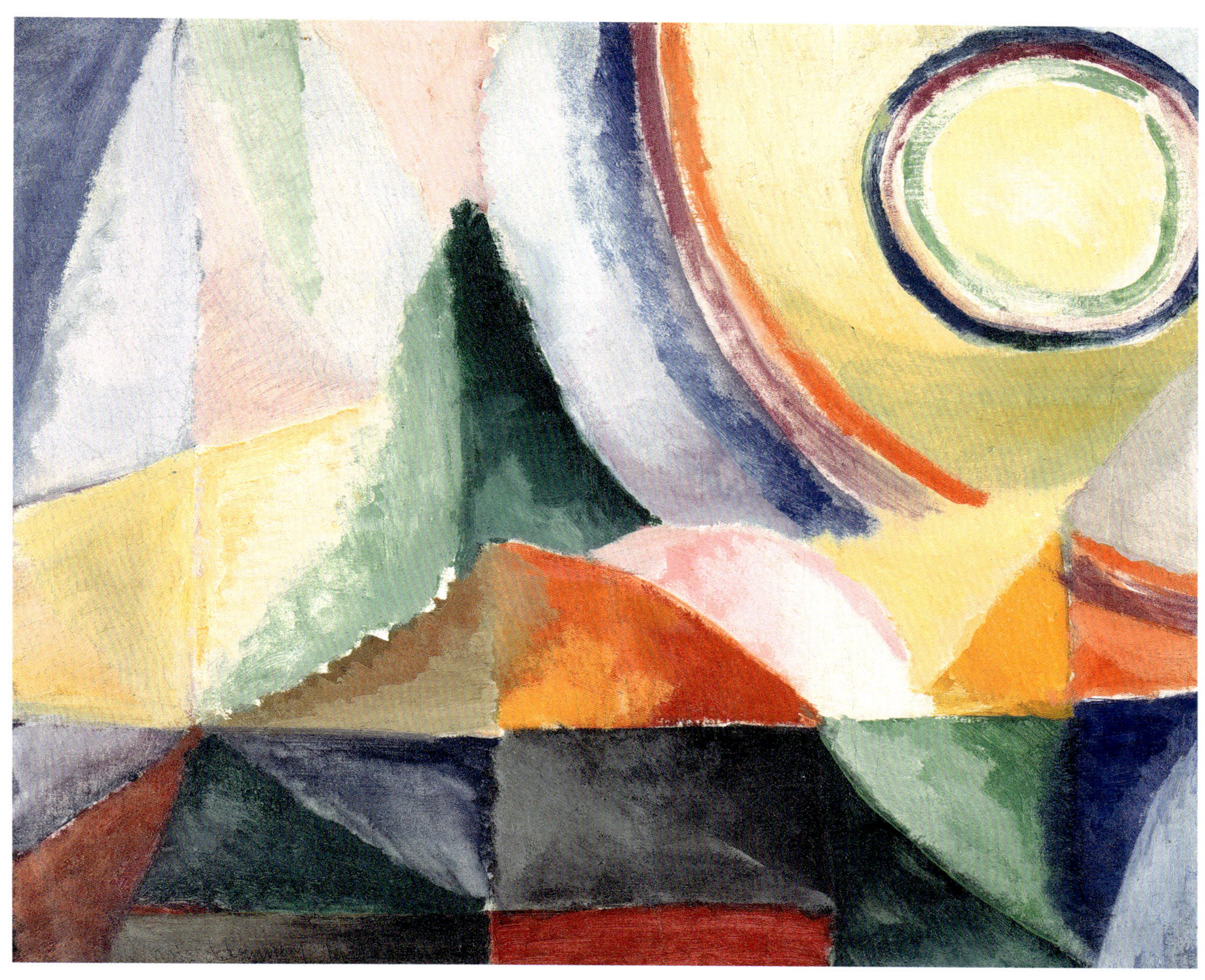

Sonia Delaunay (1885–1979)
Simultaneous Contrasts, 1912

Oil on canvas, 46 × 55 cm

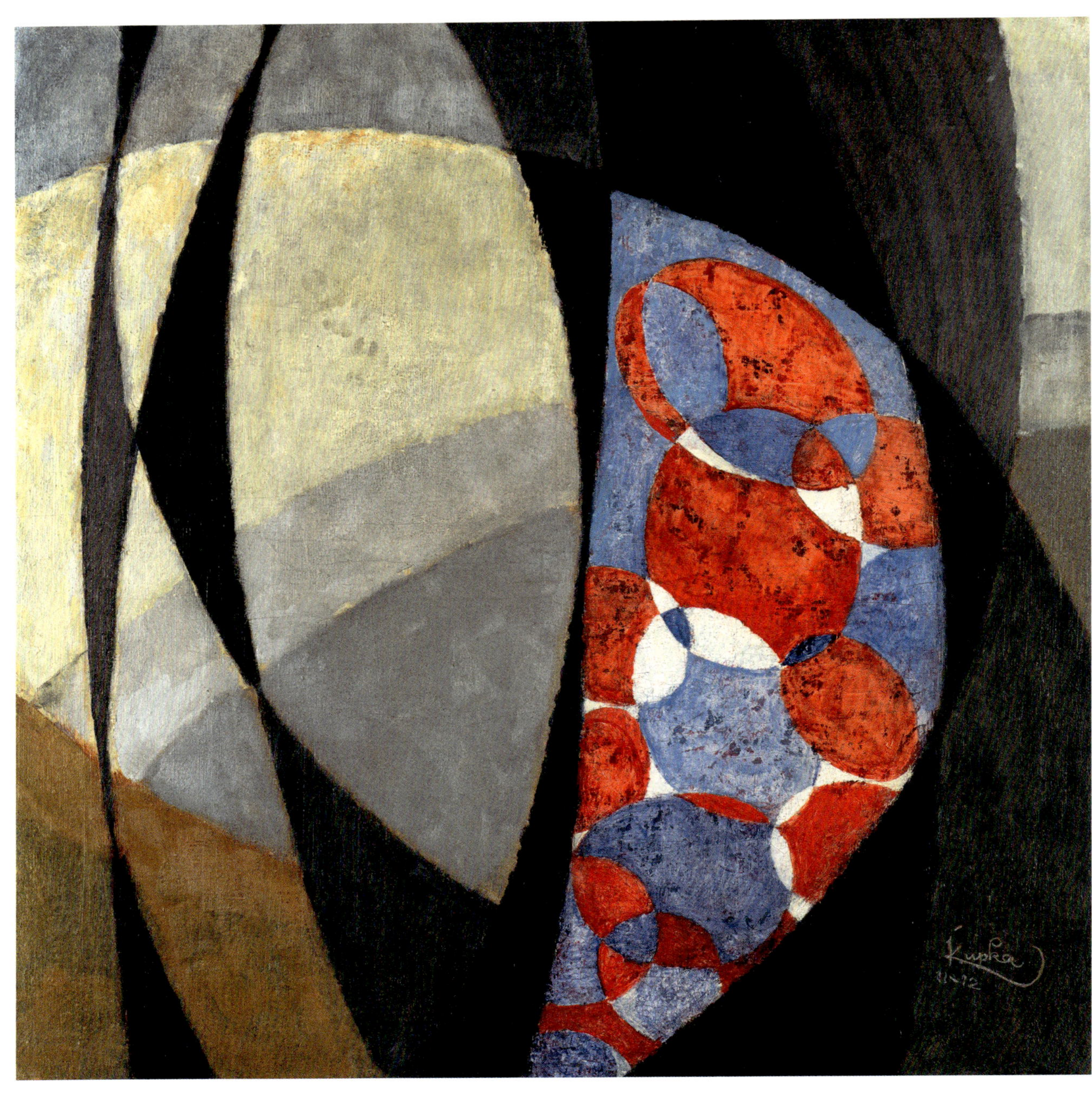

CAT. 9
František Kupka (1871–1957)
Study for Amorpha,
Fugue in Two Colours, 1911–12

Oil on canvas, 66 × 66.5 cm

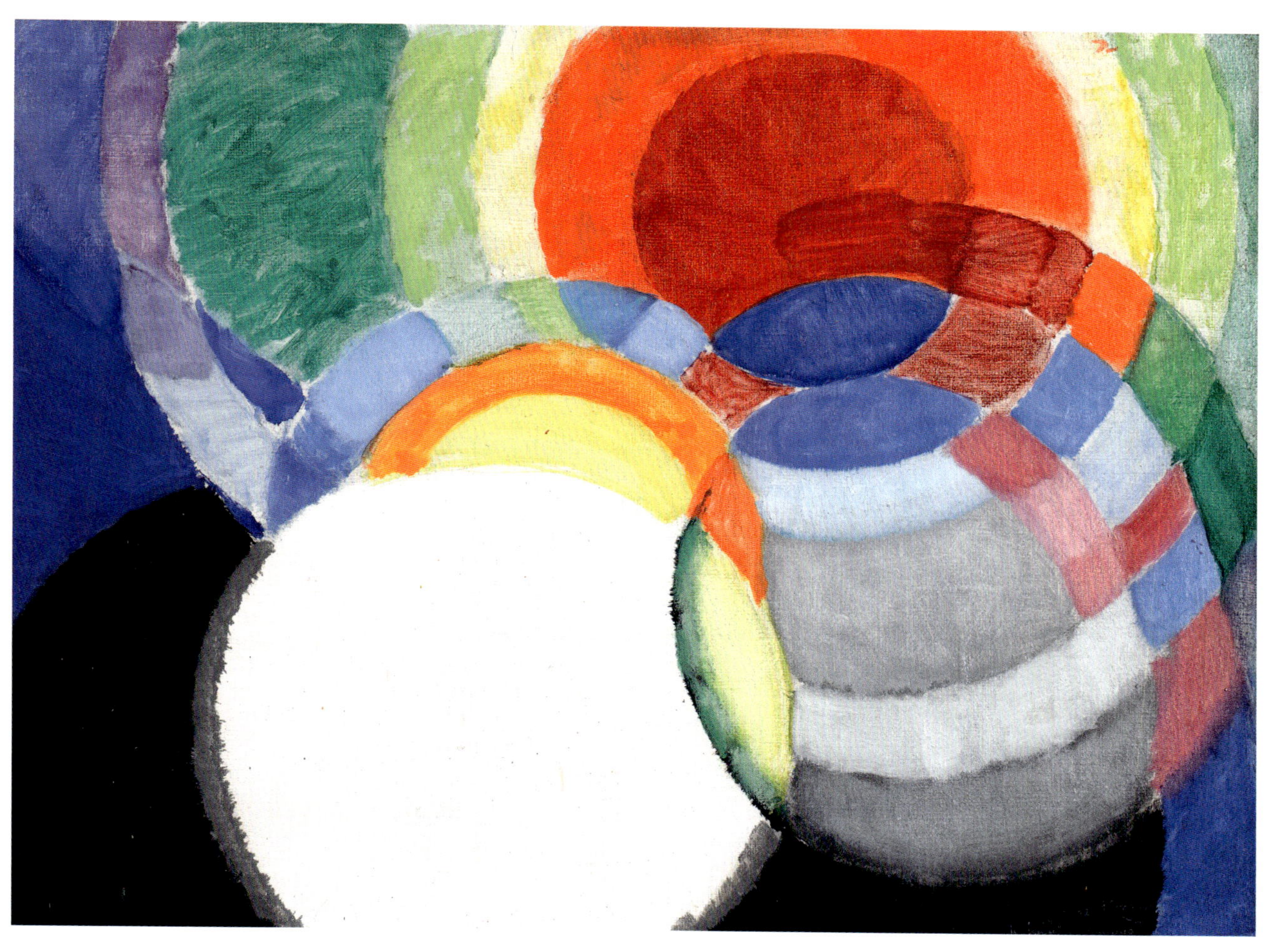

František Kupka (1871–1957)
Disks of Newton: Study for
Fugue in Two Colours, 1911–12

Oil on canvas, 49.5 × 65 cm

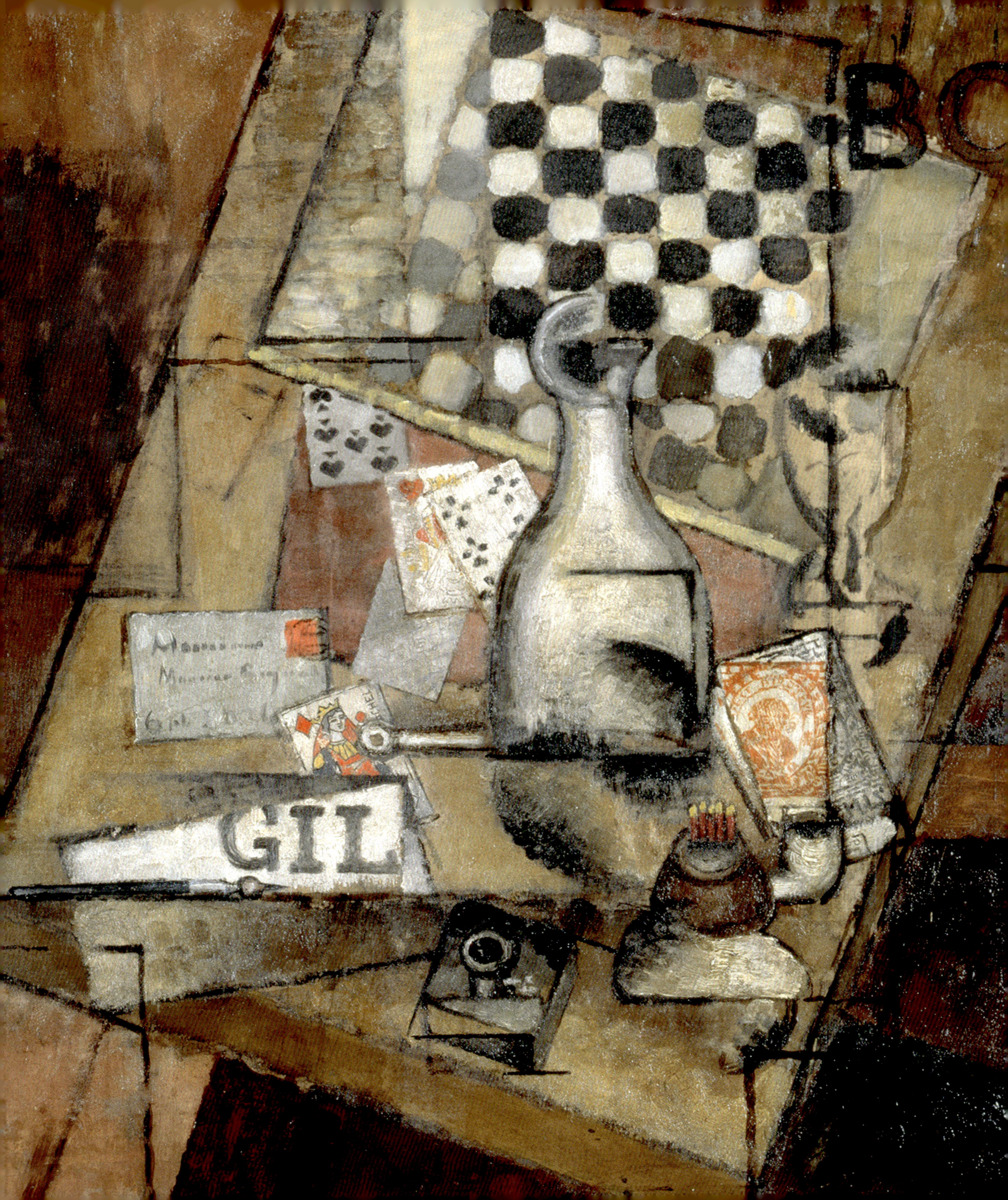
BC
GIL

FOREIGN CUBISTS

CHRISTIAN BRIEND

More than Fauvism and the movements that preceded it, the Cubism that evolved from 1907 was closely linked to the presence in Paris of painters and sculptors from elsewhere. The new visual language that radically challenged the canons of traditional representation was due to both a Frenchman, Georges Braque, and a Spaniard, Pablo Picasso, who were supported by Daniel-Henry Kahnweiler, a German art dealer recently settled in Paris and Guillaume Apollinaire, a poet and critic of Polish descent. Making use of formal devices derived from his knowledge of the work of Paul Cézanne and his encounter with African sculpture, Picasso developed with Braque the formula for the Analytical Cubism exemplified by the *Woman Seated in an Armchair* of 1910, one of a series of paintings of seated women [CAT. 11]. Soon joined by fellow Spaniard Juan Gris, who would cultivate a more colourful version of Cubism marked by a distinctive jumbling of planes, Picasso and his French "climbing partner" would exert on their immediate contemporaries an influence no less decisive for its being underground, the two men at that point having hardly ever shown in Paris. Among them were the foreign artists who crowded more particularly the Salon des Indépendants, which, from 1911, dispensed with the filter of a jury. It was through this annual fair of new art that Cubism became a truly international formal language that rapidly spread throughout Europe. Many of the "foreign Cubists" in the French capital hailed from Eastern Europe, like the Poles Henri Hayden and Louis Marcoussis, both from Warsaw, and the Hungarian Alfred Reth. In their café and restaurant interiors [CAT. 12, 14] they adopted, to varying degrees, the Cubist innovations, with more or less complex fragmented forms arranged upon a grid, an insistence on the frontality of the support, and allusions to the "pasted papers" of Braque and Picasso, the whole rendered in muted colours. Present in force at the Salon of 1914, the Russians did not lag behind. Among them were two Muscovites close to Apollinaire – Serge Férat (born Sergei Nikolaevich Yastrebsov) and, more notably, Léopold Survage. During the First World War, Survage painted a portrait of Férat's cousin, Baroness Hélène d'Oettingen, poet, painter and patron of the arts [CAT. 18]. In this monumental composition with its colourful urban background, Hélène d'Oettingen reigns at the centre, as she presides over the salon in the Boulevard Raspail where she entertained Apollinaire's friends.

A central figure in the movement and the author of *Cubist Painters* (1913), in which he already foresaw the "dismemberment of Cubism", the poet Apollinaire was, for his part, the subject of a rather more enigmatic portrait by the Italian artist Giorgio de Chirico – this just before the outbreak of the First World War in which the poet would be seriously wounded in the head [CAT. 16]. More greatly indebted to Cubism, the Futurist Gino Severini's portrait of his father-in-law, Paul Fort, "prince of poets" and leading light of the literary circle associated with La Closerie des Lilas in Montparnasse, integrated collage of printed pages (not without humour) in Cubist fashion, accompanied by a variety of personal belongings [CAT. 17].

It was Picasso himself, with his stage curtain for the ballet *Parade*, who in 1917 gave the signal for a return to a more traditional style of representation imbued with the spirit of Italy. As evidenced by the *Young Girl with a Hoop* [CAT. 22], however, his later work does not by any means represent a disavowal of an aesthetic that continued to attract French and foreign disciples long after his own "Cubist period" had come to an end with the Great War.

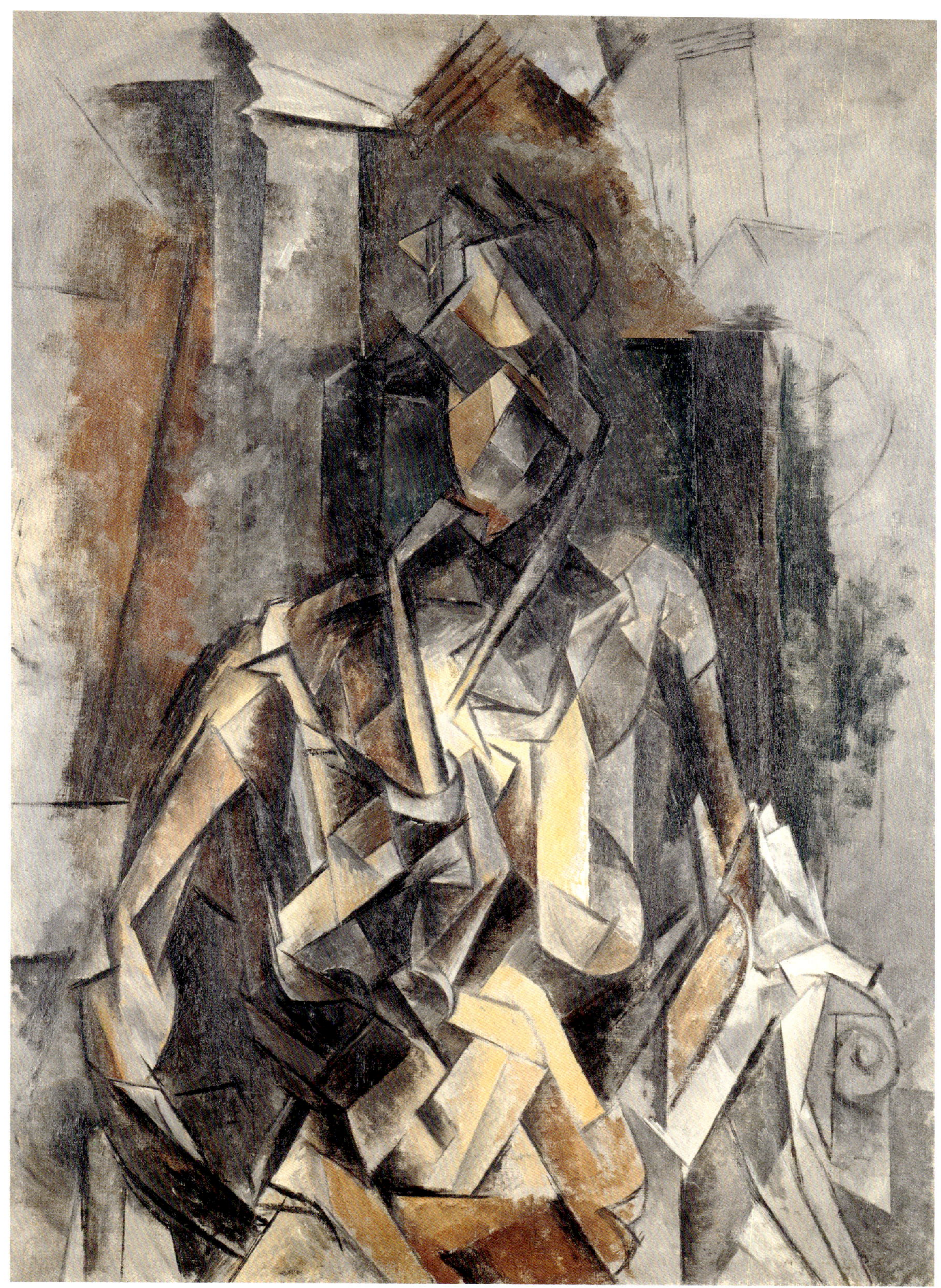

Pablo Picasso (1881–1973)
Woman Seated in an Armchair,
spring 1910

Oil on canvas, 100 × 73 cm

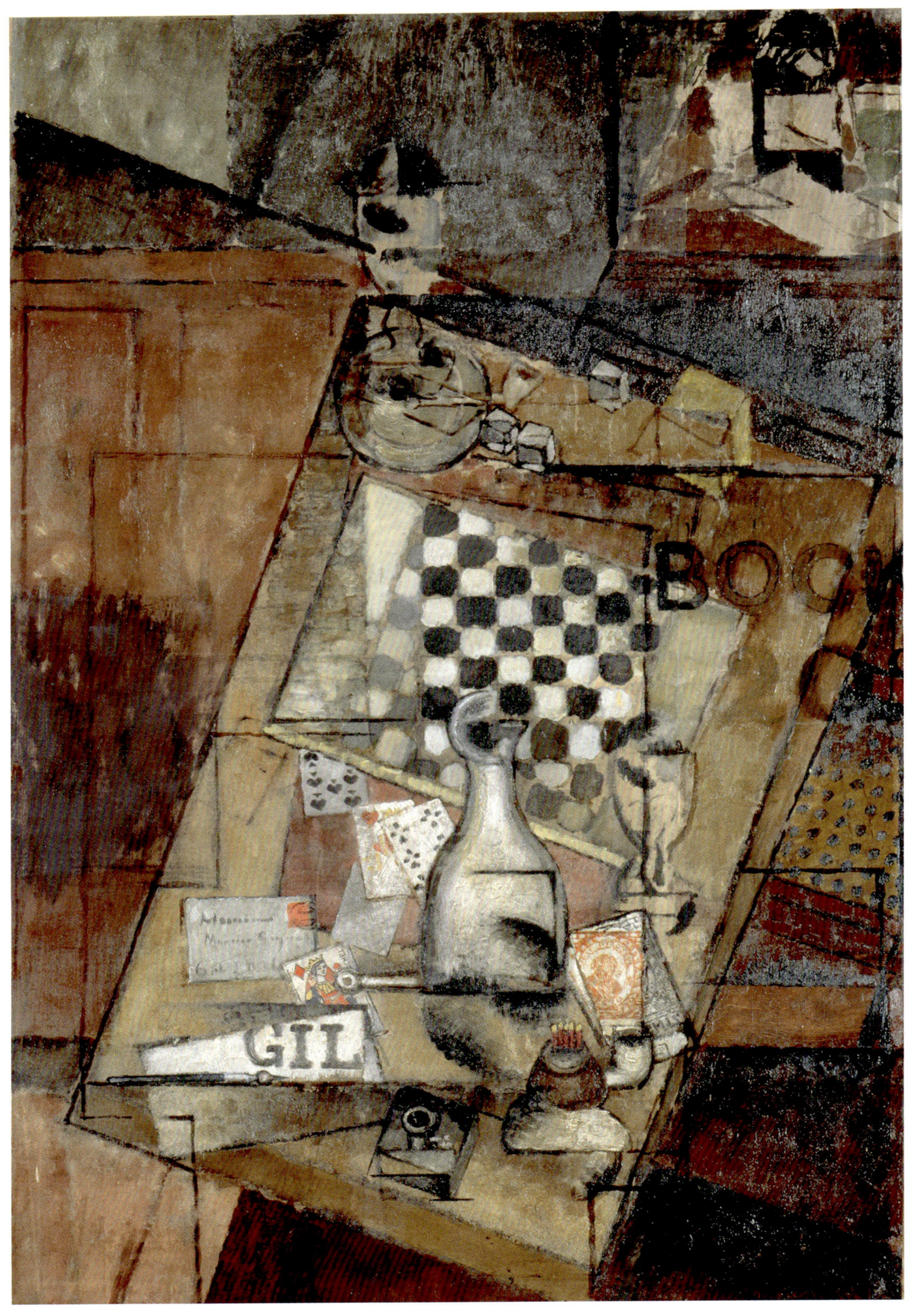

CAT. 12

Louis Marcoussis (1878–1941)
Still Life with Chessboard, 1912

Oil on canvas, 143 × 97 cm

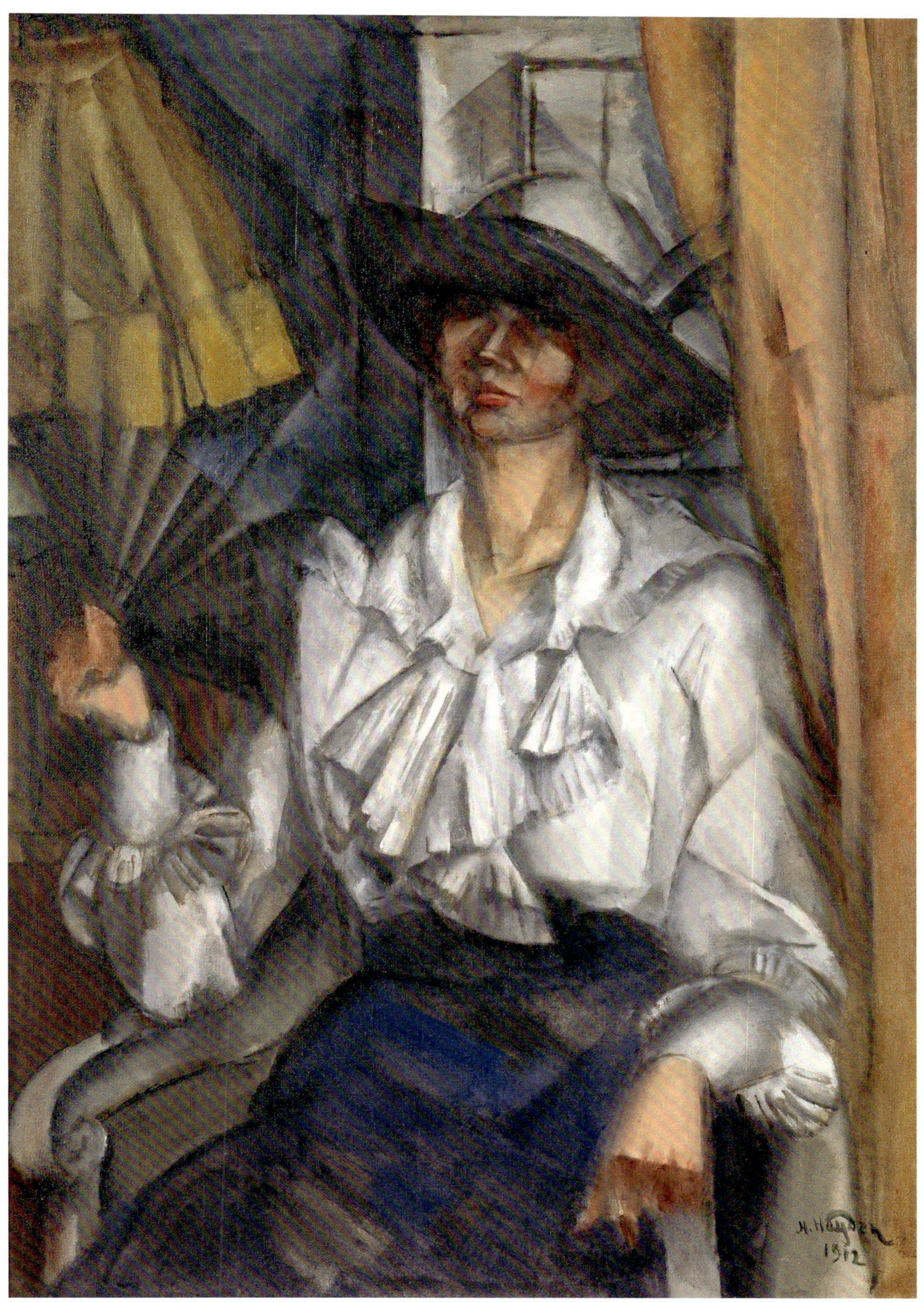

CAT. 13

Henri Hayden (1883–1970)
Parisian Woman with a Fan, 1912

Oil on canvas, 92 × 65 cm

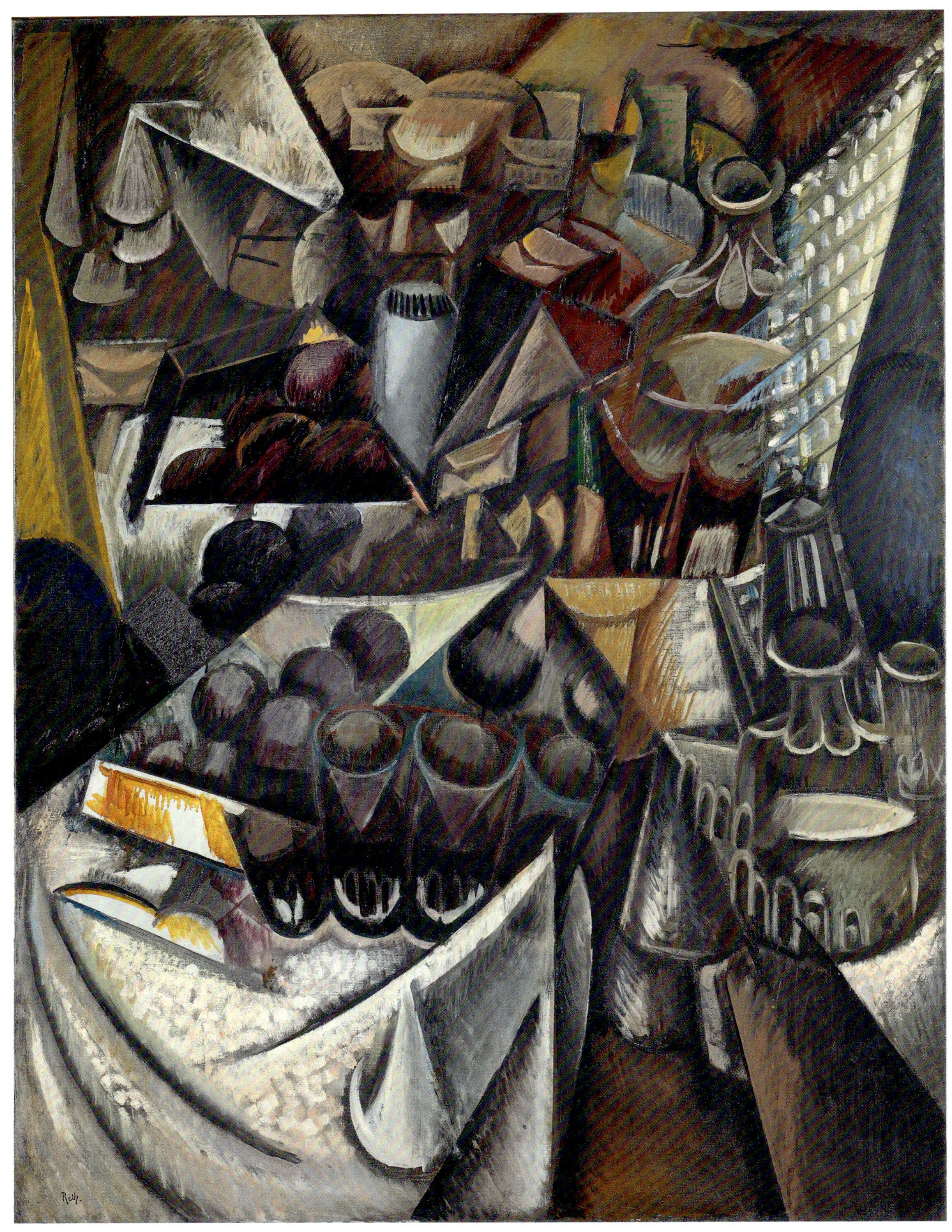

CAT. 14

Alfred Reth (1884–1966)
The Hubin Restaurant, 1913

Oil on canvas, 130 × 97 cm

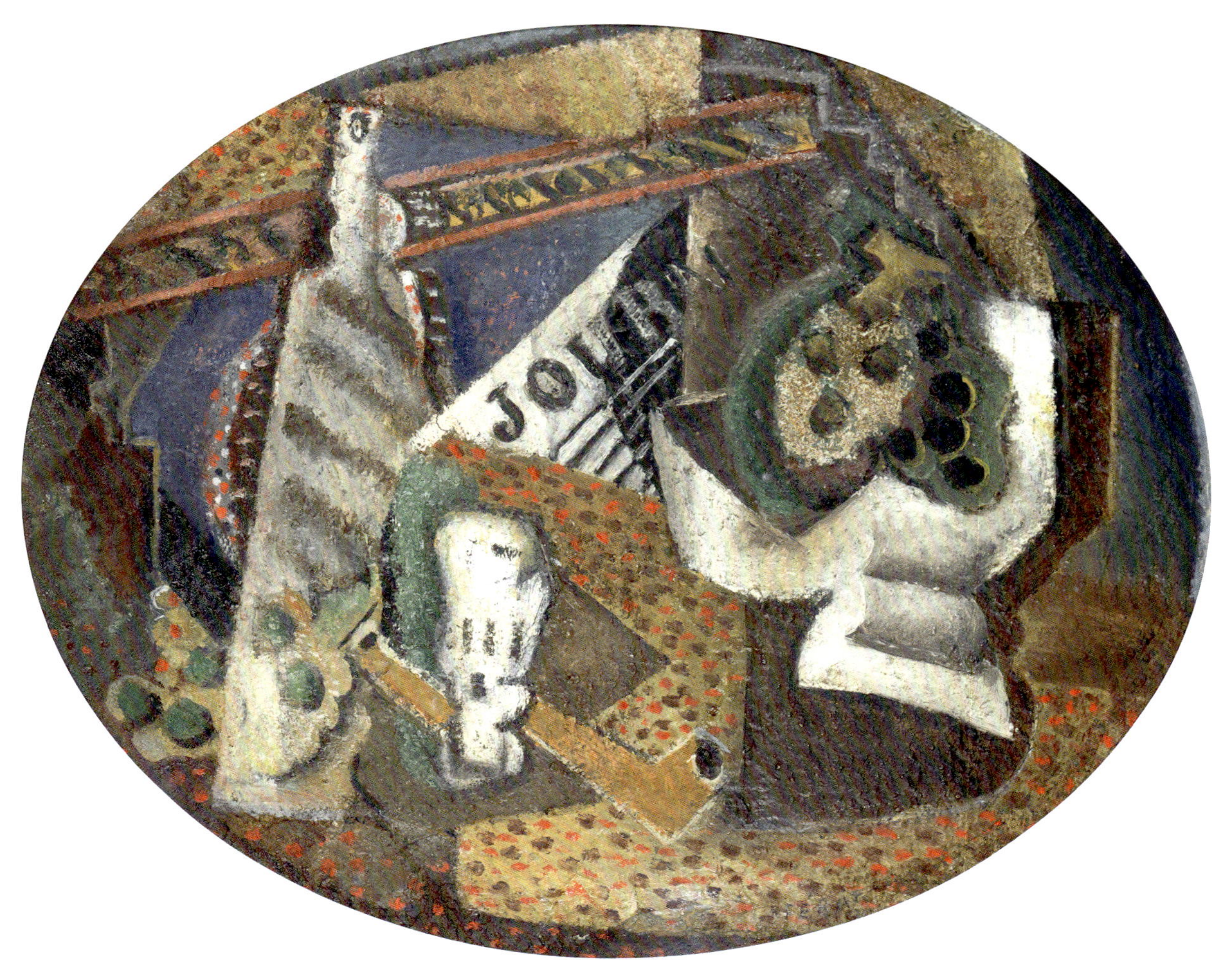

CAT. 15
Serge Férat (1881–1958)
Glass, Pipe and Bottle, 1914–15

Oil and sand on card, 45 × 55 cm

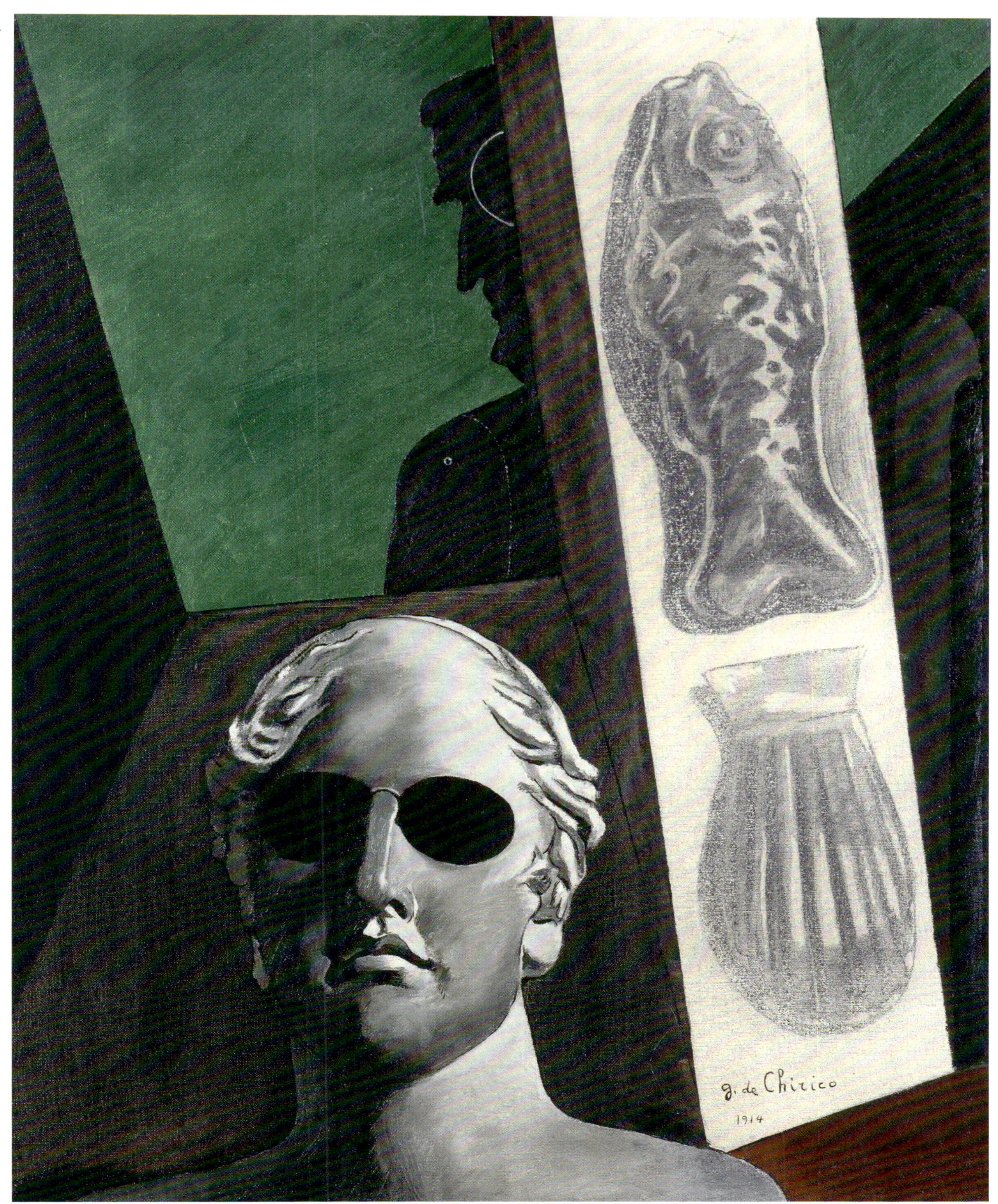

Giorgio de Chirico (1888–1978)
Premonitory Portrait of Guillaume Apollinaire,
spring 1914

Oil and charcoal, 81.5 × 65 cm

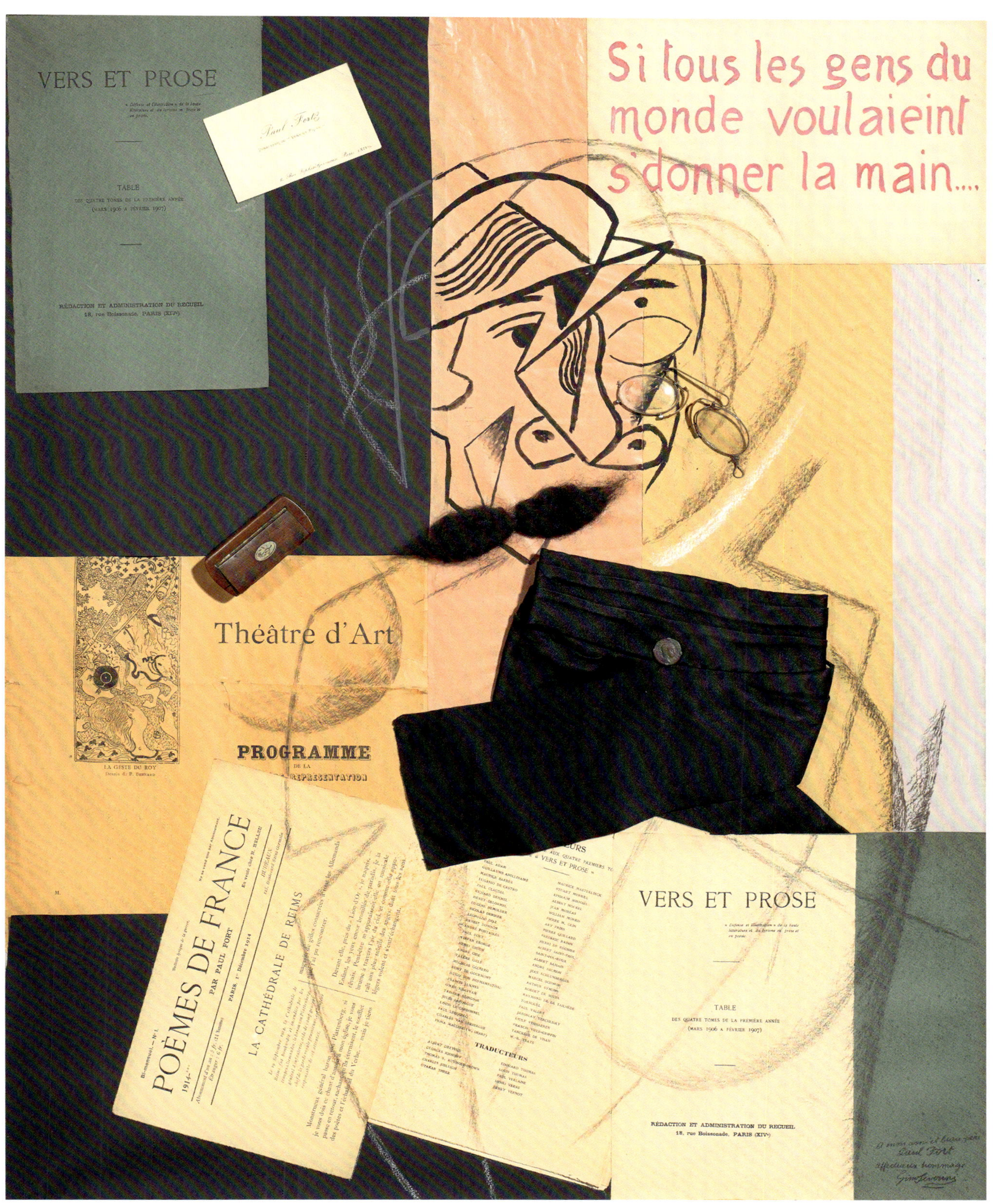

Gino Severini (1883–1966)
Portrait of Paul Fort, 1915

Oil, chalk, charcoal, Indian ink and objects on paper
glued on canvas, 81 × 65 cm

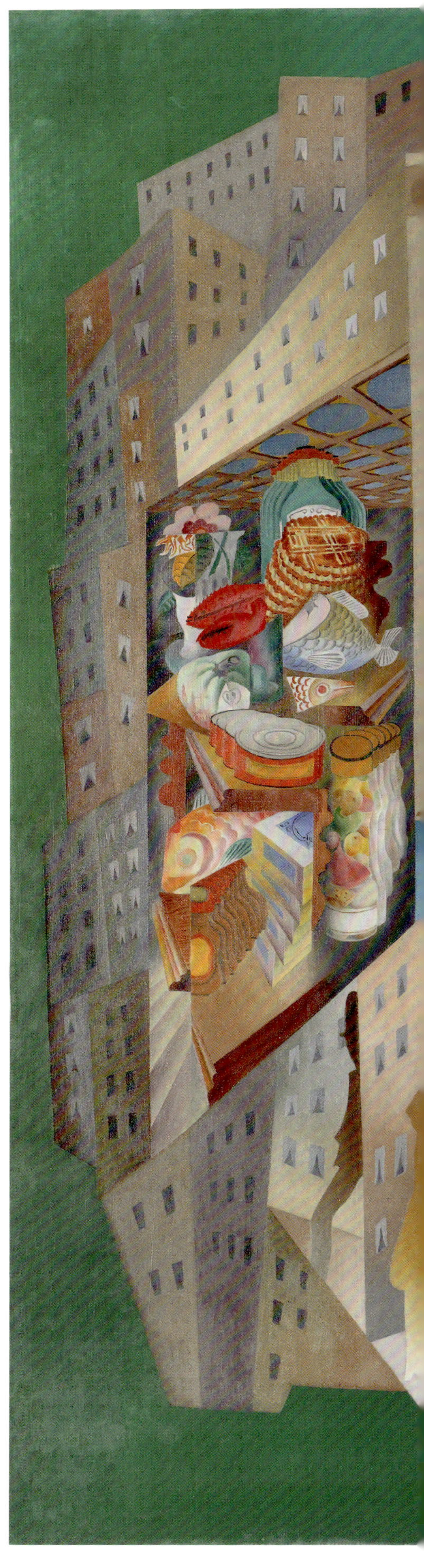

Léopold Survage (1879–1968)
The Baroness Hélène d'Oettingen, 1917

Oil on canvas, 200 × 235 cm

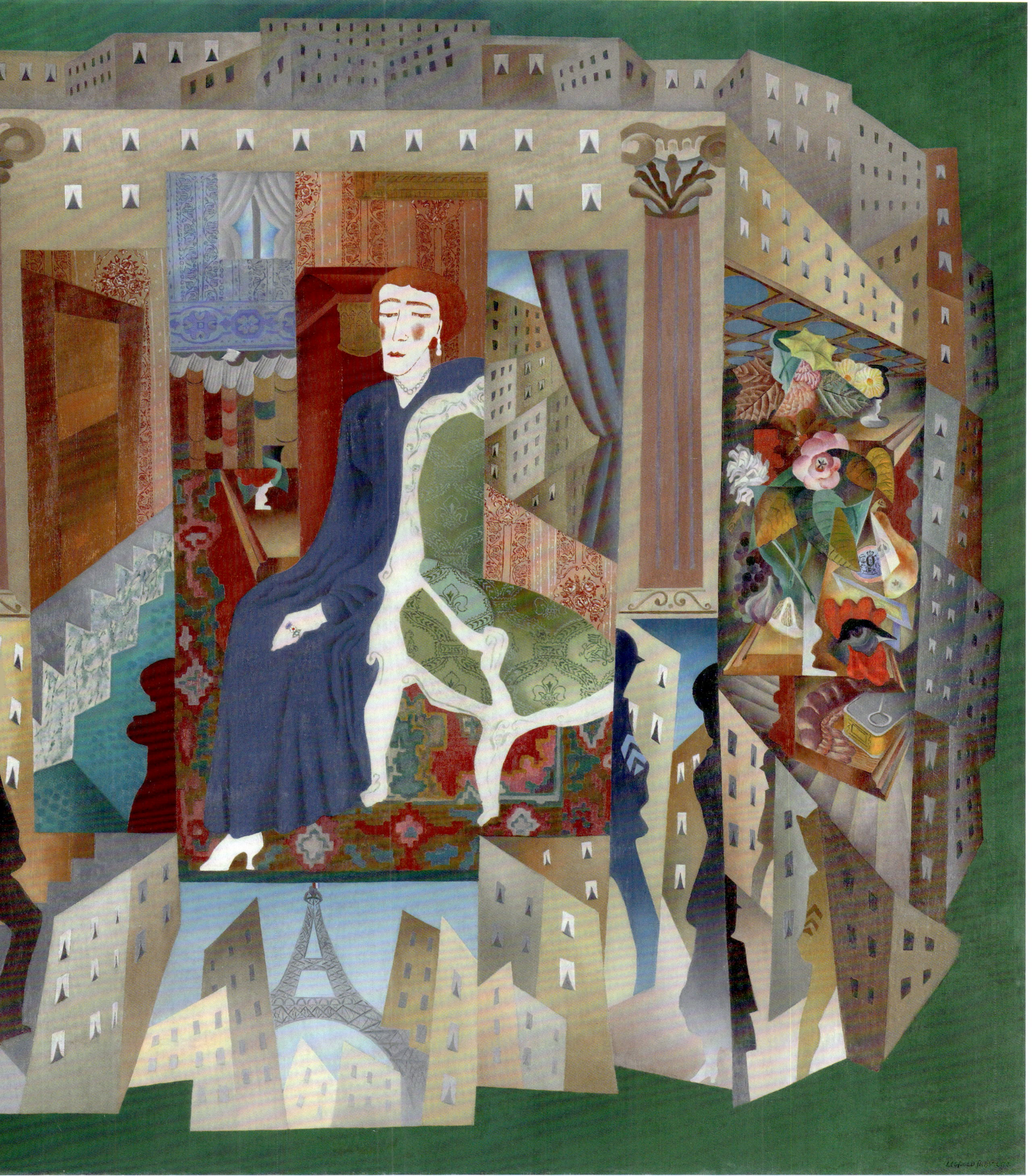

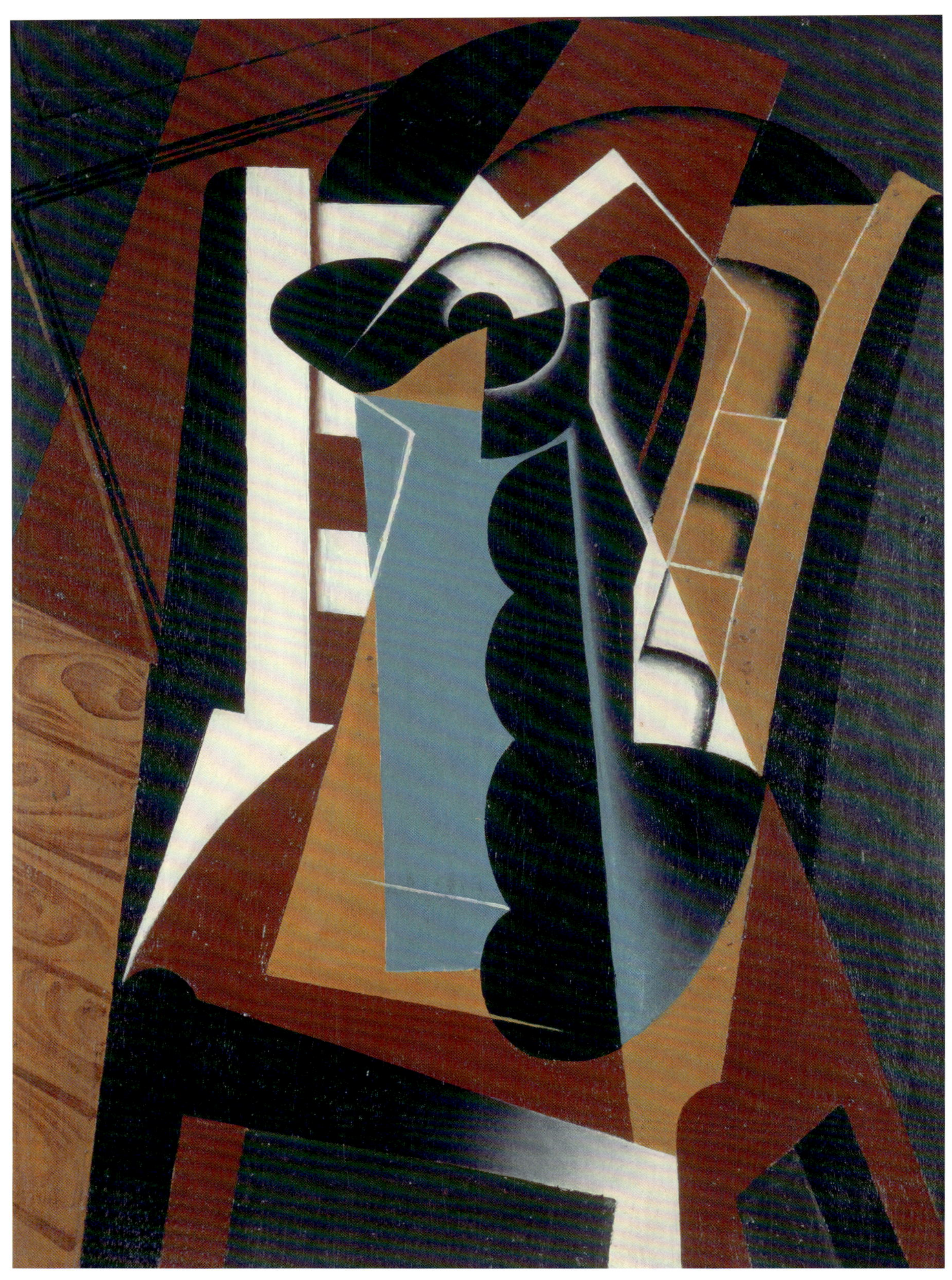

Juan Gris (1887–1927)
Still Life on a Chair, April 1917

Oil on wood panel, 100 × 73 cm

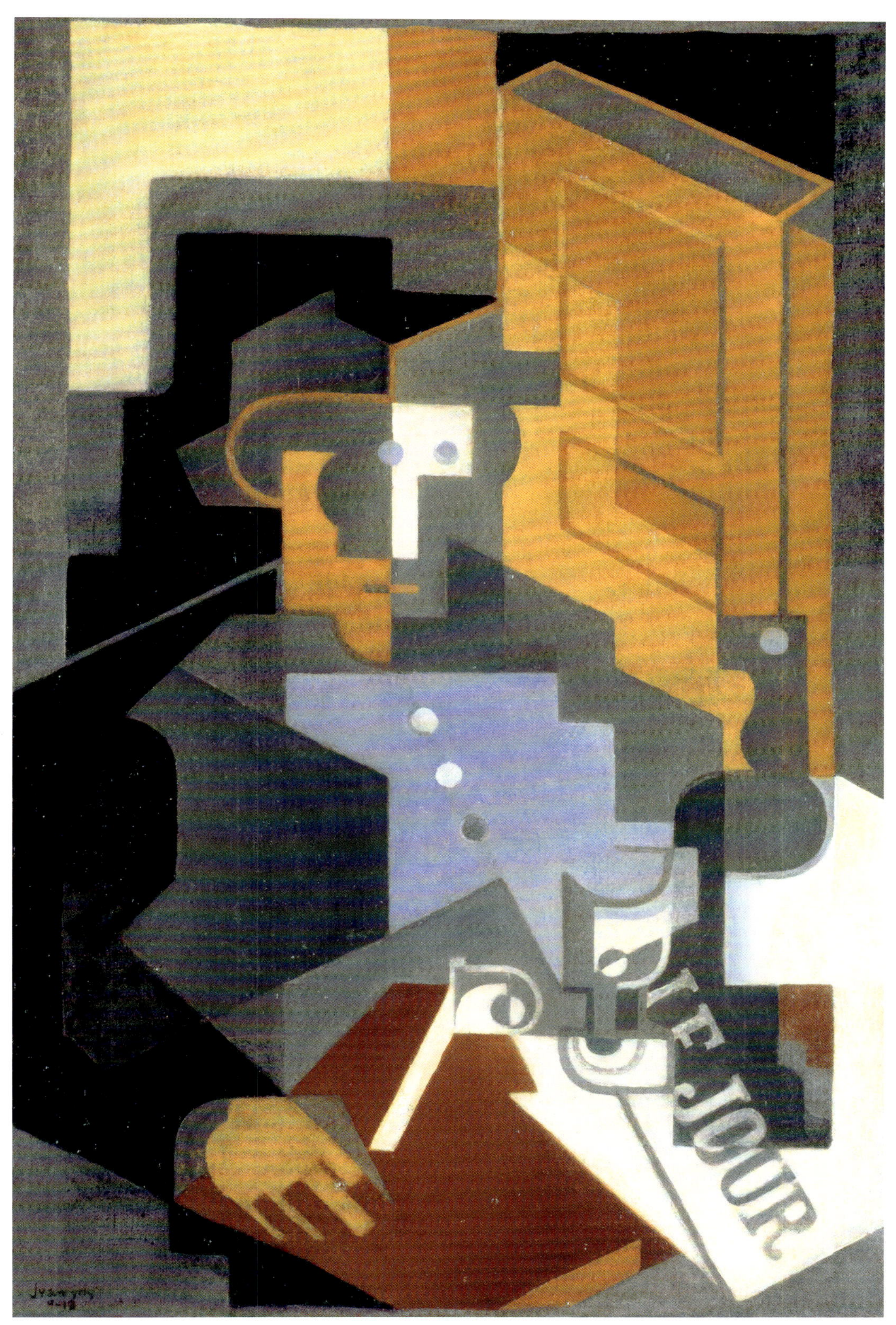

Juan Gris (1887–1927)
Man from Touraine, September 1918

Oil on canvas, 100 × 65 cm

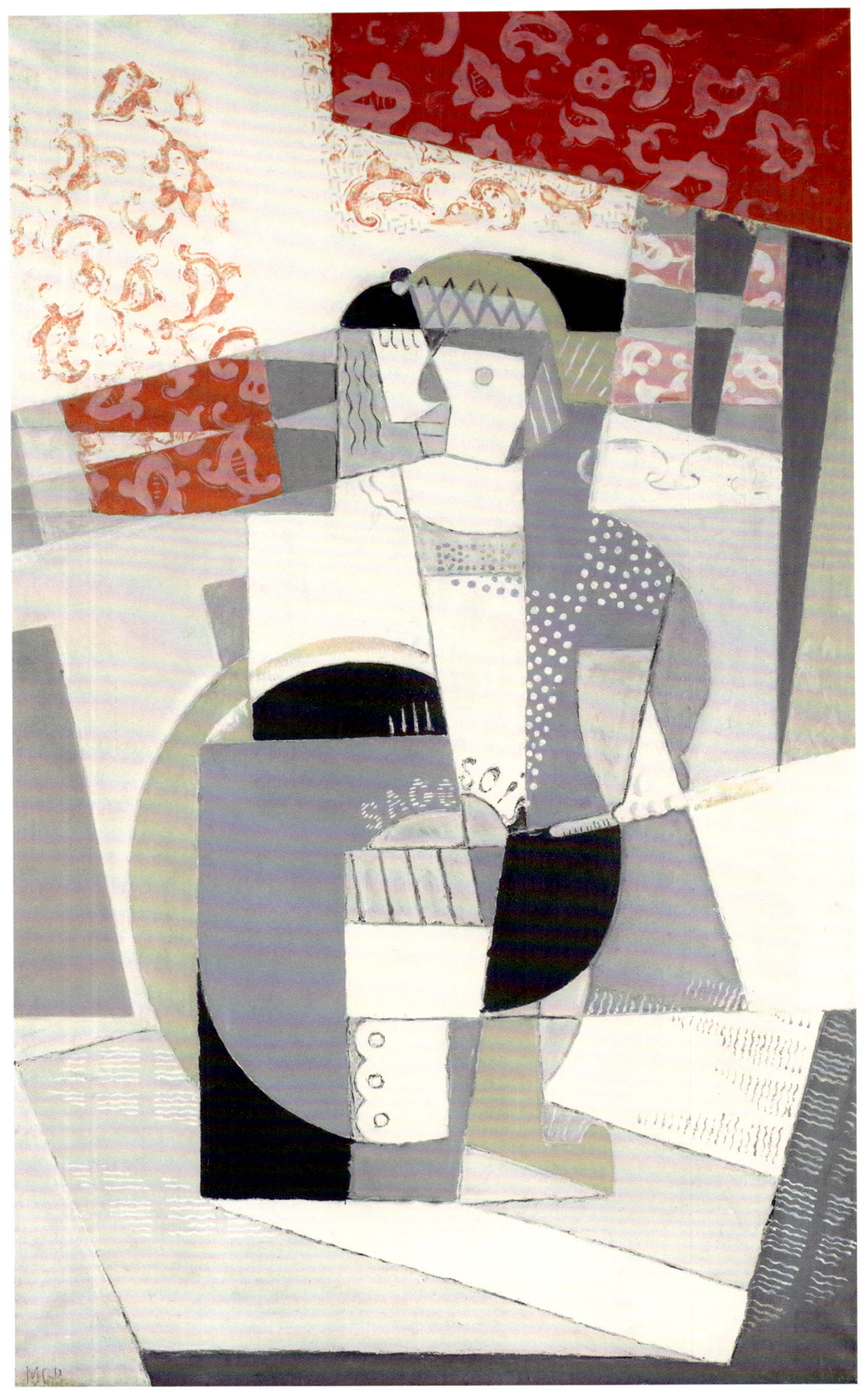

Maria Blanchard (1881–1932)
Child with a Hoop, 1917

Oil on canvas, 140 × 85 cm

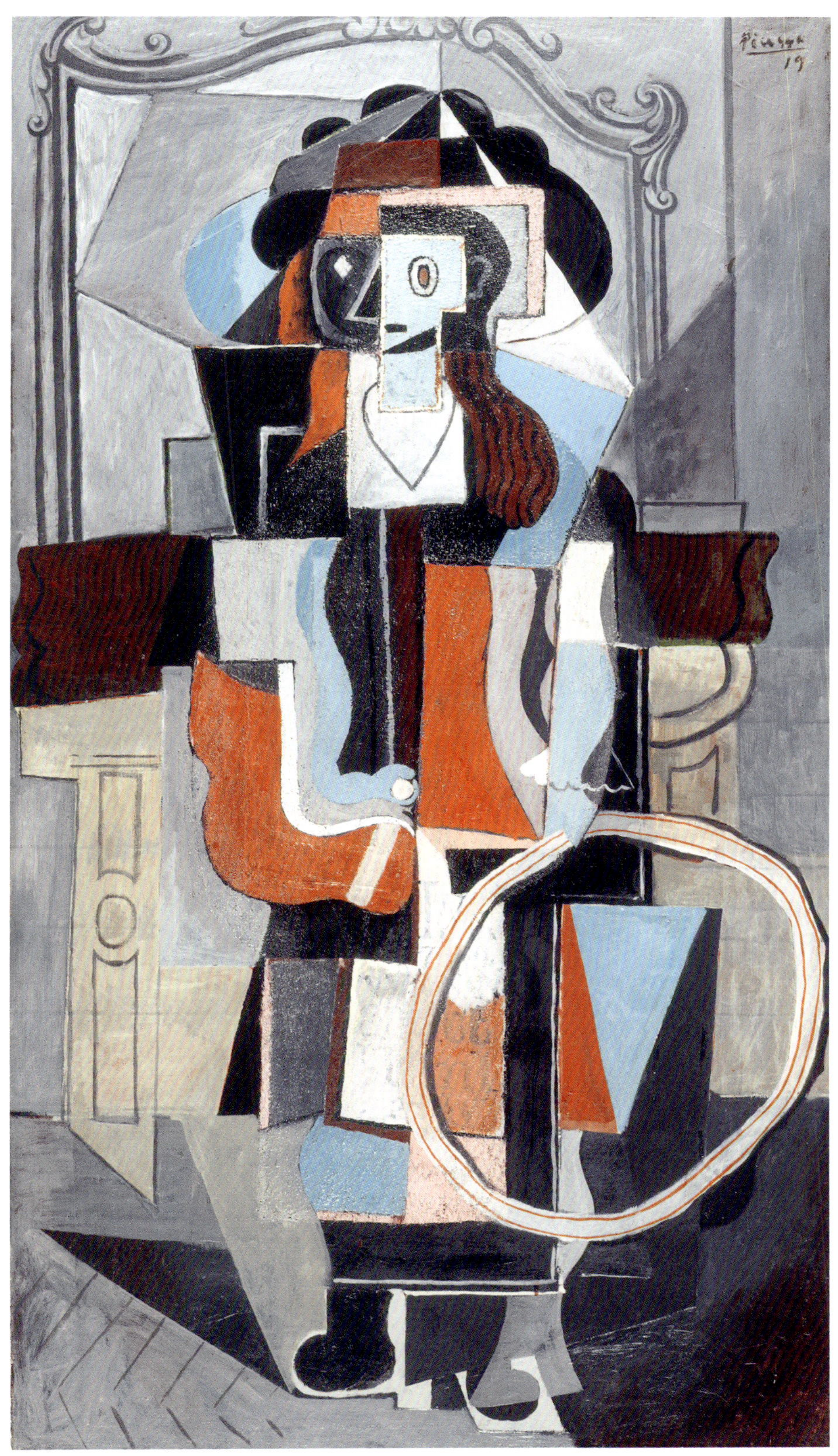

CAT. 22

Pablo Picasso (1881–1973)
Young Girl with a Hoop, spring 1919

Oil and sand on canvas, 142.5 × 79 cm

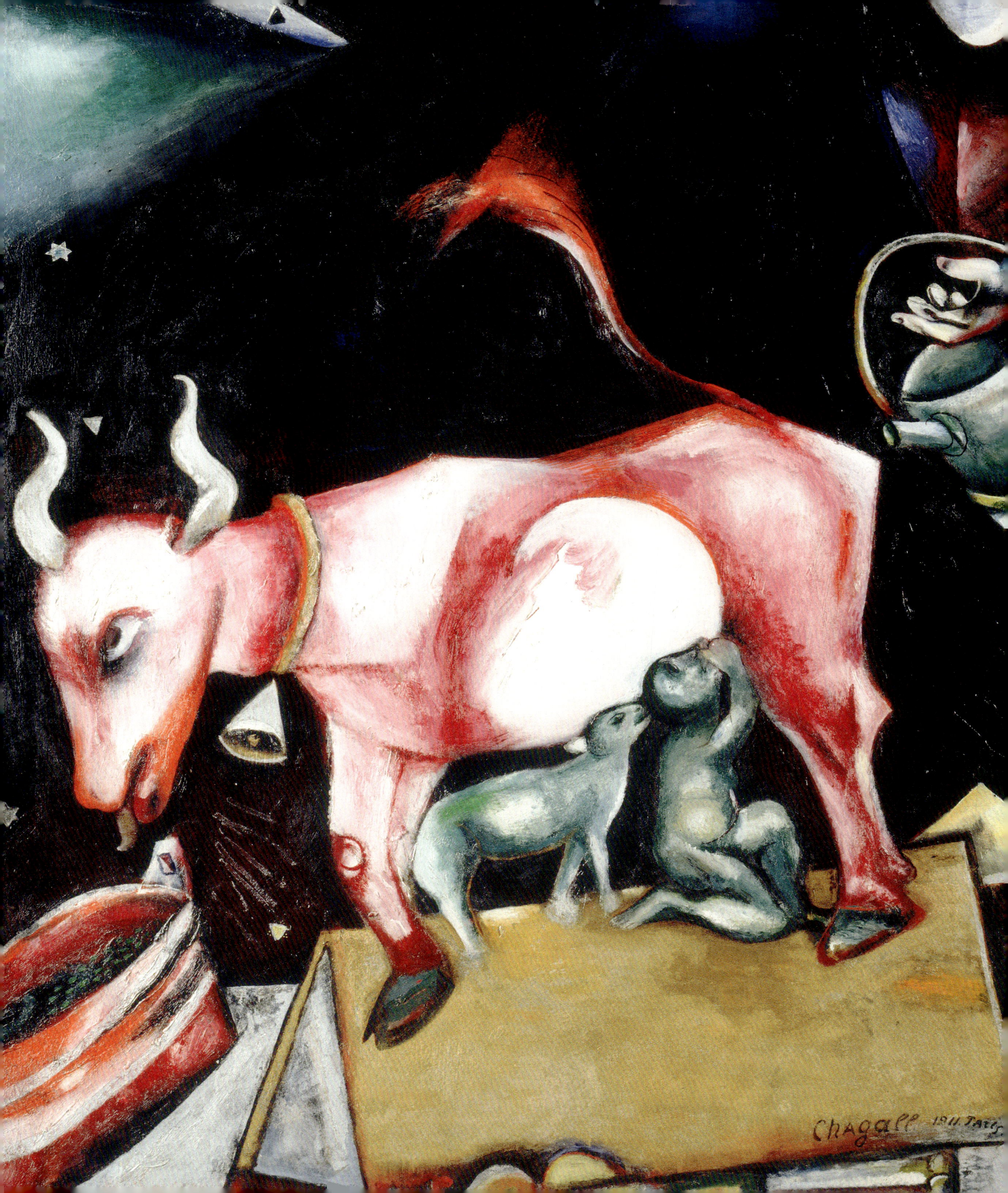

MARC CHAGALL AND LA RUCHE

ANNE LEMONNIER

La Ruche artist residence owes its existence to the academic sculptor Alfred Boucher. Having acquired an empty plot on Passage de Dantzig, in the neighbourhood of the Vaugirard slaughterhouses, he had a studio complex built on the site, repurposing the temporary structures of several pavilions from the Paris World's Fair (Exposition Universelle) of 1900, including an impressive octagonal rotunda. The site, which opened in 1902, hosted artists from diverse backgrounds, in particular those who had fled the pogroms in Eastern Europe and sought refuge in Paris. The lifestyle there was modest, even impoverished, but the bohemian atmosphere fostered vibrant creative exchanges. Thoroughly traditional artistic practices were pursued alongside more avant-garde explorations. The Italian artist-designer and poet Ardengo Soffici took up residence at La Ruche in 1903, for example, as did the Romanian sculptor Constantin Brancusi the following year. Fernand Léger, who arrived there in 1905, developed a painting style focused on the representation of three-dimensional forms; his work found resonance in that of Ukrainian sculptor Alexander Archipenko, who moved into La Ruche in 1908. Over several years these two artists were then joined by other sculptors who would also be strongly influenced by Cubism: Joseph Csáky from Hungary, Jacques Lipchitz from Lithuania and Ossip Zadkine from Byelorussia. Marc Chagall, who arrived in Paris from Byelorussia in 1911, also lived there; painting at night on sheets or on old, scraped canvases, he developed a dreamlike image world, peopled with elements derived from Jewish iconography. Remembering his time at La Ruche, he later wrote:

> While in the Russian studios a slighted model can be heard sobbing, from the ateliers of the Italians comes the sound of guitars and singing, and from the Jews heated discussions. Meanwhile, I am quite alone in my studio, working by my petrol lamp … Somewhere they are slaughtering cattle, the cows are lowing and I paint them. I used to stay up all night long."[1]

In 1912 and 1913, Pinchus Krémègne, Michel Kikoïne and Chaïm Soutine, who had remained friends since their student days at the Minsk School of Drawing and Painting, along with Mané-Katz from Ukraine, also moved into La Ruche.

Some of these artists became friends with the poets Guillaume Apollinaire, Blaise Cendrars and Max Jacob, who were regulars at the café Le Dantzig, near La Ruche. Chagall became especially close friends with Cendrars, who dedicated two of his *Dix-neuf poèmes élastiques* (*Nineteen Elastic Poems*) to the artist. Apollinaire, meanwhile, composed the poem *Rotsoge* the day after visiting Chagall's studio in La Ruche:

> Your round house where a sour herring swims
> I lack the key of eyelids …
> But your hair is the trolley
> Across Europe clad in tiny multicolored lights.[2]

It was thanks to this poet that Herwarth Walden organised an exhibition of Chagall's work in Berlin in June–July 1914, marking the artist's breakthrough in terms of public recognition.

---

1   Marc Chagall, *Ma vie,* Paris, Stock, 2003, p. 145. English translation from http://www.sothebys.com/en/auctions/ecatalogue/2016/impressionist-modern-art-evening-sale-n09567/lot.33.html where reference is given as "quoted in J. Baal-Teshuva, *Marc Chagall 1887–1985*, Cologne, 1998, p. 41".

2   Translated by Anne Hyde Greet, Calligrammes, University of California Press, 1980, pp. 97–99.
    Rotsoge, Apollinaire's name for Chagall.

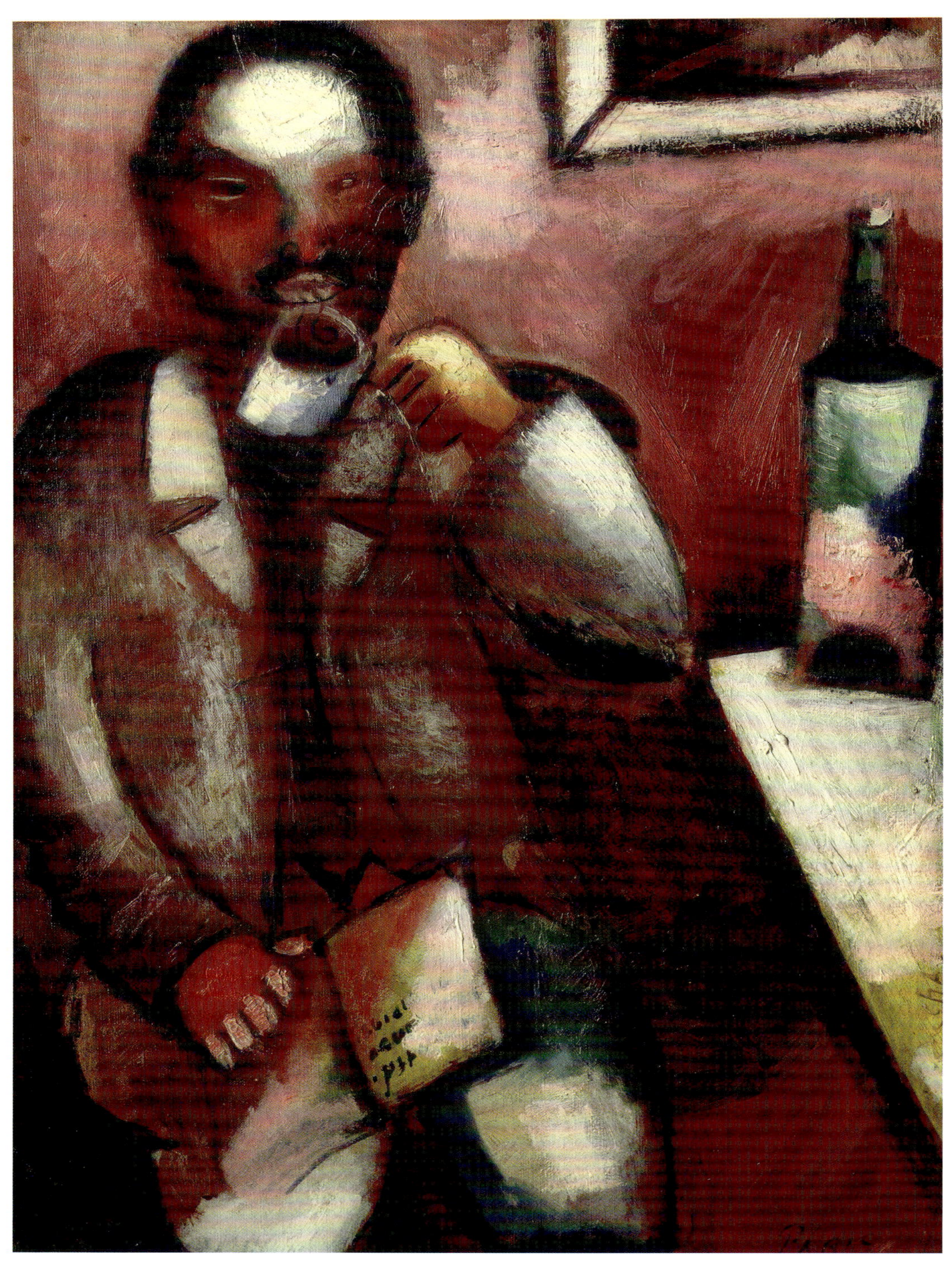

Marc Chagall (1887–1985)
Mazin, the Poet, 1911–12

Oil on canvas, 73 × 54 cm

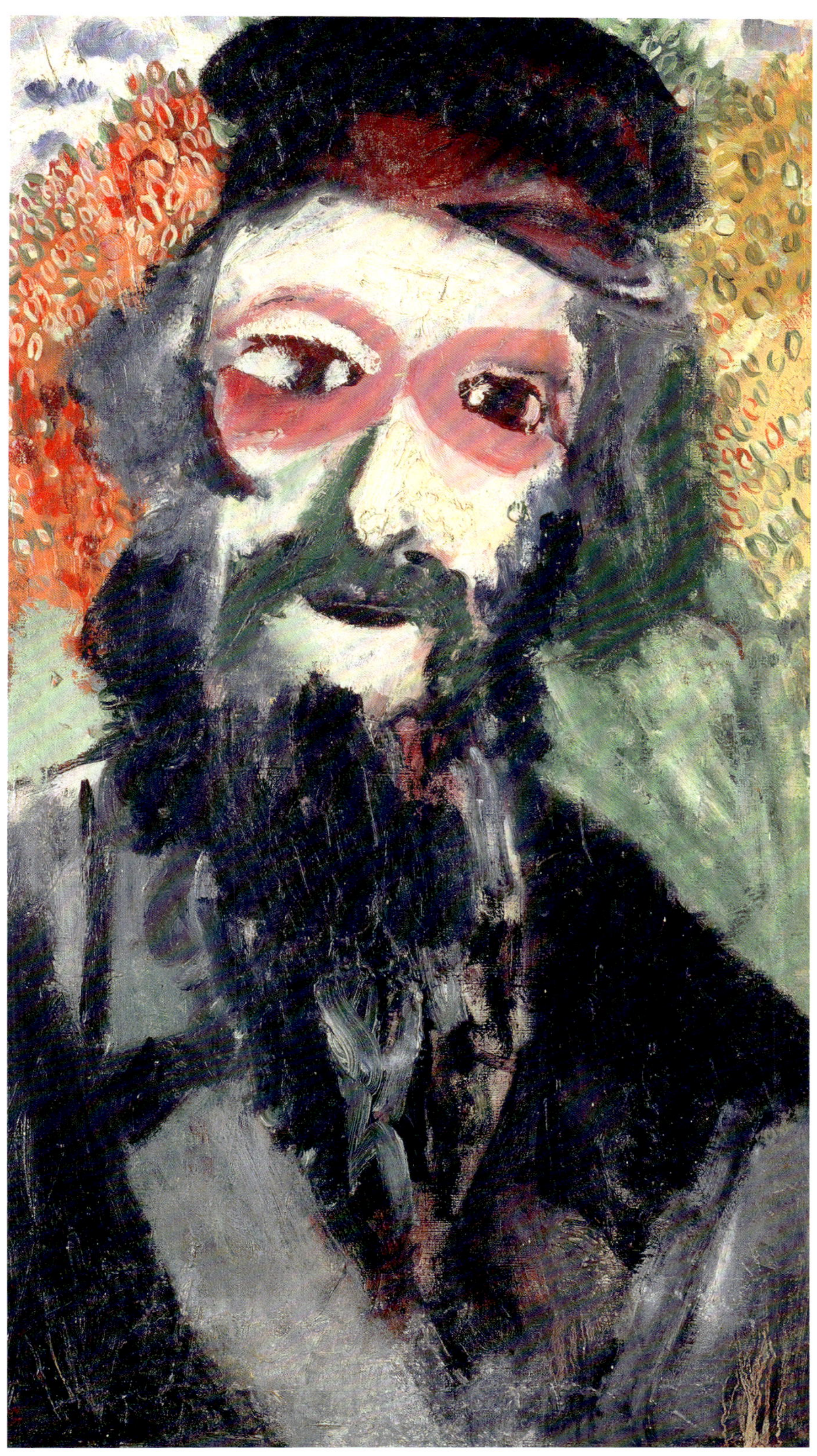

Marc Chagall (1887–1985)
The Father, 1911

Oil on canvas, 80 × 44.2 cm

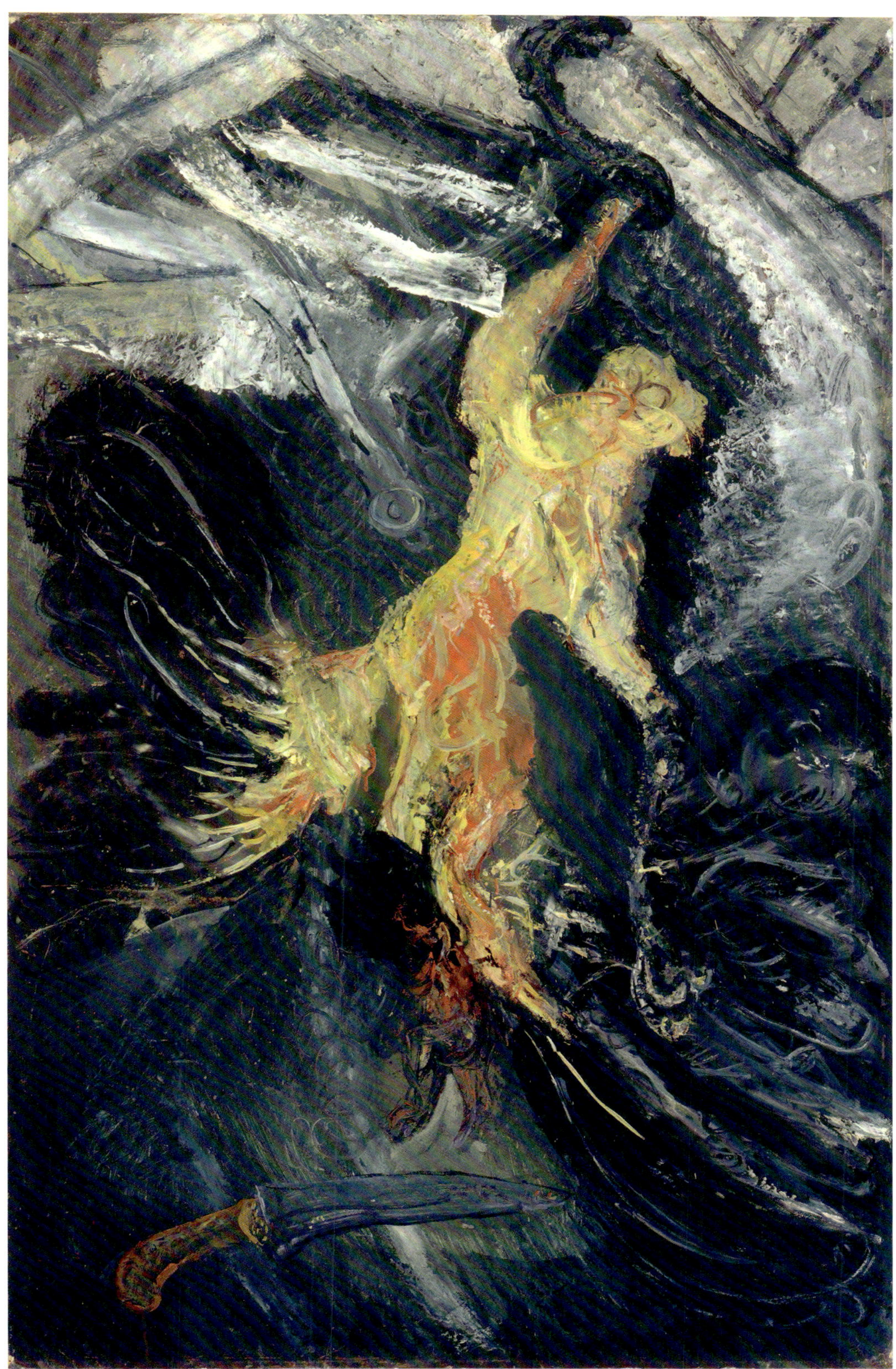

CAT. 31
Chaïm Soutine (1893–1943)
The Hanging Chicken, 1925

Oil on wood panel, 125 × 80 cm

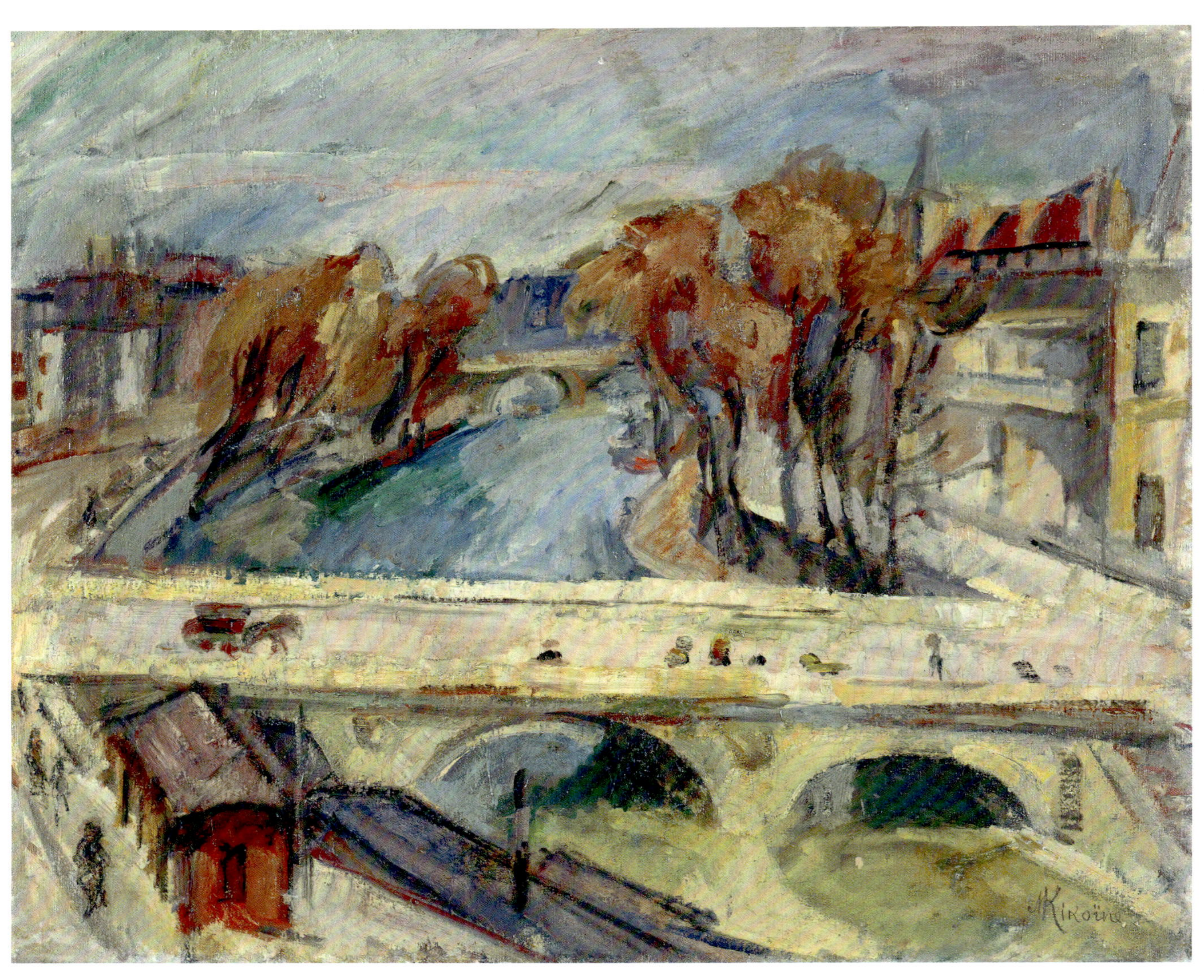

CAT. 32

Michel Kikoïne (1892–1968)
The Pont-Neuf, 1918

Oil on canvas, 60 × 73 cm

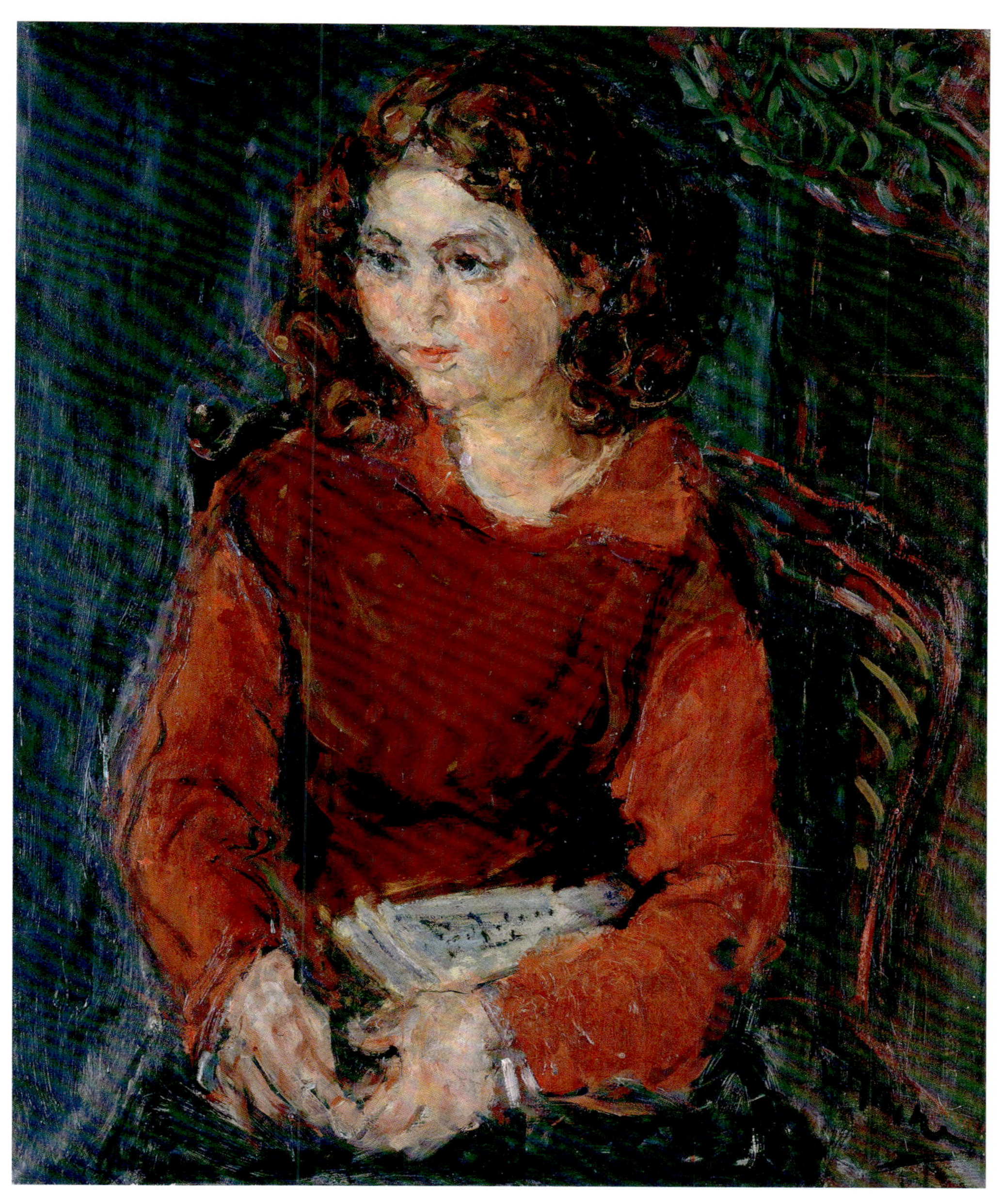

CAT. 33
Michel Kikoïne (1892–1968)
Portrait of Claire, 1927

Oil on canvas, 73 × 60 cm

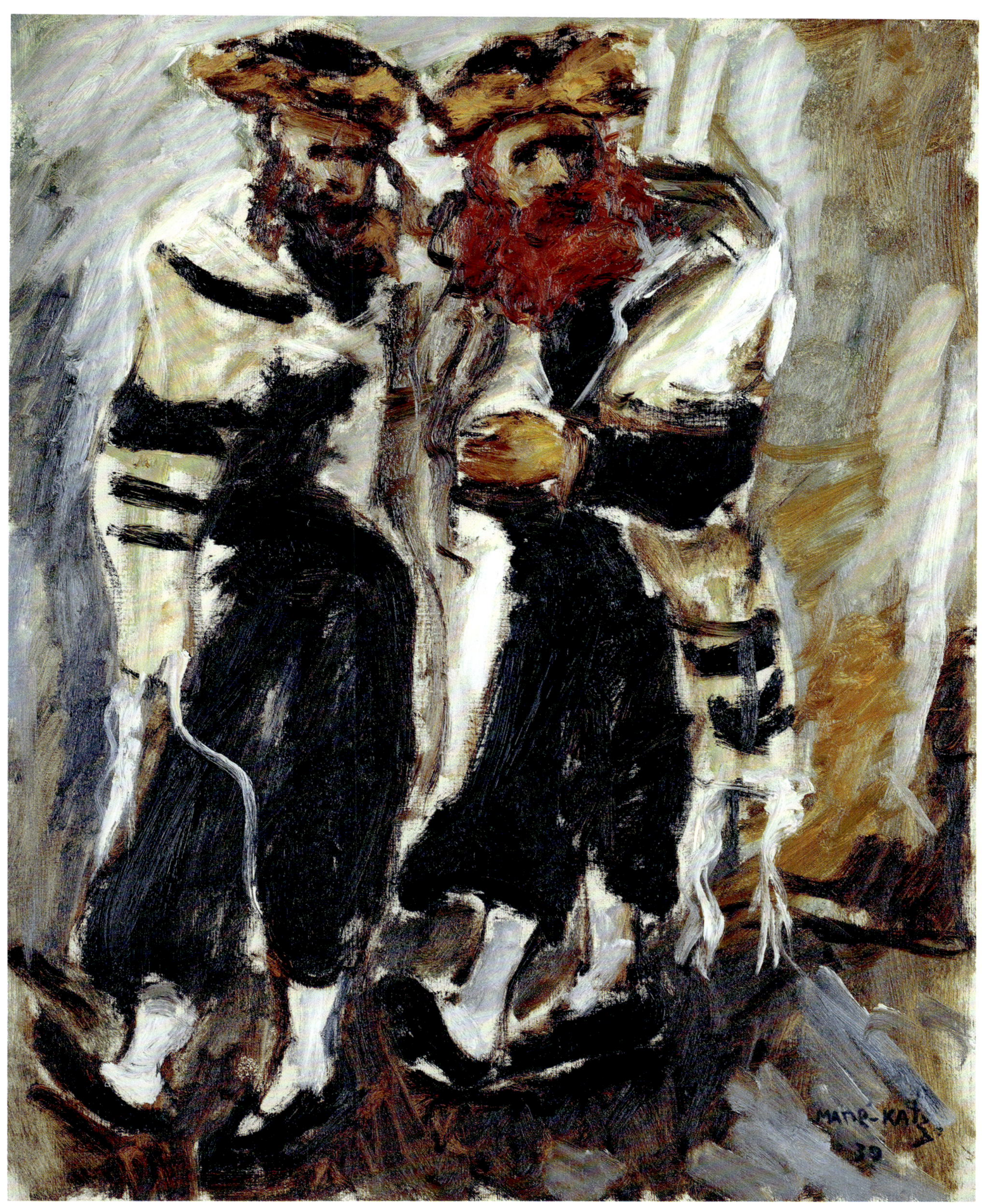

CAT. 34
Mané-Katz (1894–1962)
Two Rabbis, 1930

Oil on canvas, 92 × 72 cm

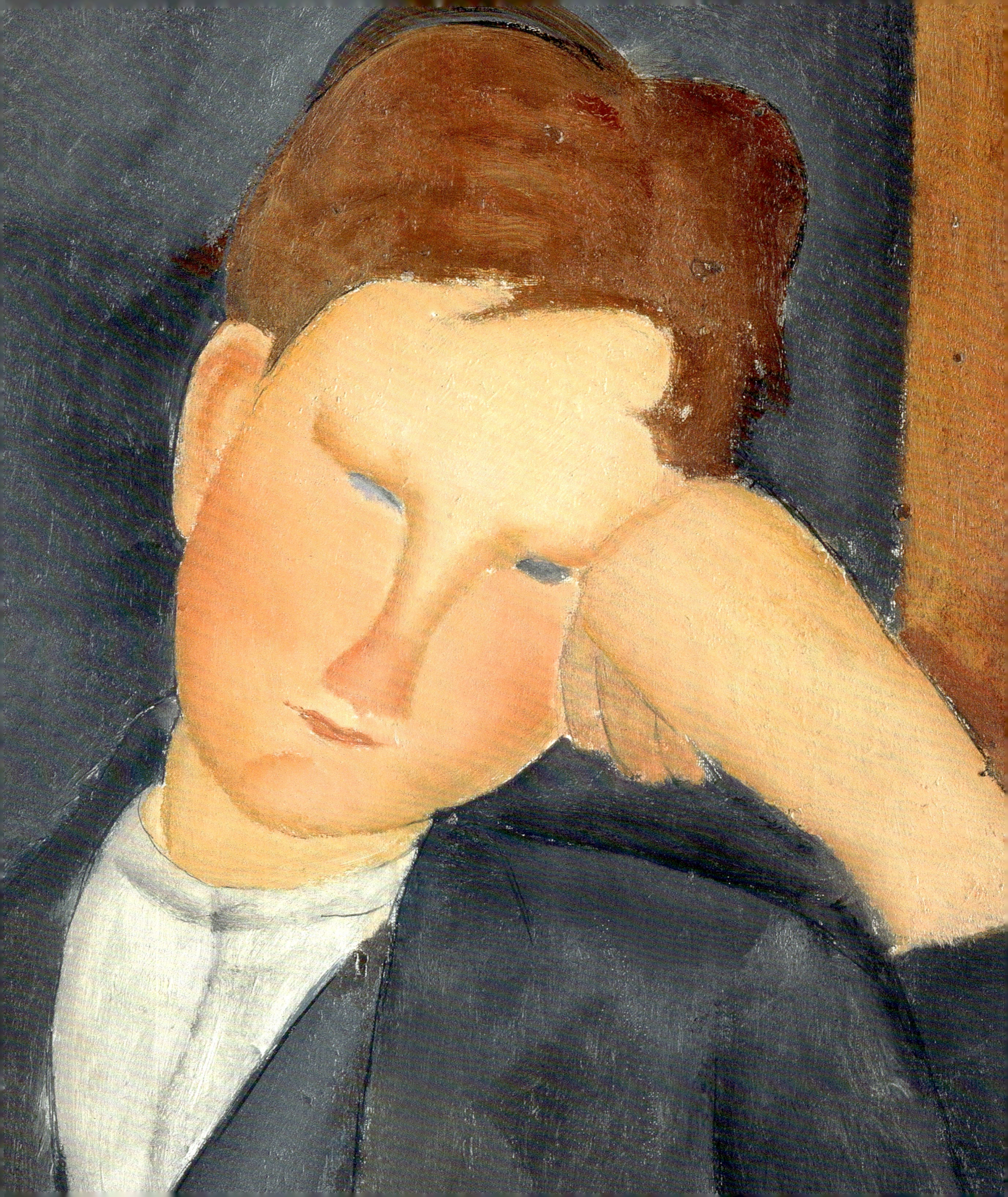

AMEDEO MODIGLIANI AND THE ARTISTS OF MONTPARNASSE

ANNE LEMONNIER

As the Montmartre cabarets gradually closed down and the poets and singers dispersed from what had been the heart of creative life in Paris in the early 20th century, Montparnasse became the new gathering place for artists from all over the world. A literary circle formed in the café La Closerie des Lilas, where the poet Paul Fort hosted lively debates whose participants included Guillaume Apollinaire, Max Jacob and André Salmon.

Meanwhile, two other cafés around Carrefour Vavin quickly became bohemian hubs in Montparnasse. The first was Le Dôme, which was a meeting place for all those seeking refuge in Paris. The Bulgarian painter Jules Pascin went there in 1905, having just arrived from Munich, where he had become known for his satirical drawings. In Paris he developed a style of soft colours and brushwork in tune with the sensuality of his subjects, including portraits of his wife, Hermine David [CAT. 41] and many female nudes.

La Rotonde, not far from Le Dôme, was the haunt of Pablo Picasso, Amedeo Modigliani, Kisling and Léonard Foujita. Foujita arrived in Paris in 1913, where he became renowned for his minutely detailed interiors in the Japanese tradition [CAT. 45] and the self-portraits through which his distinctive appearance became familiar [CAT. 46]. Like Kisling, whose portraits of women are characterised by their delicate forms and subtle colour harmonies [CAT. 44], Foujita was a fashionable figure in Paris during the Roaring Twenties. Artists also met at the wine merchant Baty's establishment and at Chez Rosalie in Rue Campagne-Première, where the owner would feed the most penniless among them, notably her compatriot Modigliani.

Like Picasso, who left the Bateau-Lavoir for Boulevard Raspail and then Rue Victor-Schœlcher, Modigliani left Montmartre for Montparnasse. Having formerly trained as a painter in Florence and Venice, in his studio located in the Cité Falguière, he devoted himself to sculpture in stone, carving hieratic figures with elongated faces whose primitivism reflected his quest for purity of form [CAT. 35, 36]. His explorations were sustained by discussions with Romanian sculptor Constantin Brancusi (whose studio was in the nearby Impasse Ronsin [CAT. 47–49]), who created, by directly carving, sculptures with purified forms and soft features. Modigliani went on to pursue his experimentation in painting, first in Rue Joseph-Bara, at the home of the Polish dealer Leopold Zborowski, who supported him financially from 1916, and then in Rue de la Grande-Chaumière, where he painted portraits in muted tones, with elongated faces and heads slightly inclined in melancholic poses. In April 1918, Modigliani left for the South of France, where he met up with some of his friends from Montparnasse, including Alexandre Archipenko, Foujita, Kisling and Chaïm Soutine. It was there that he painted the portrait of Gaston Modot [CAT. 38], a painter friend who was also a film actor. The almond eyes and stylised features of this portrait are reminiscent of Modigliani's sculptures, while the figure's frontality, immutable pose and verticality give it an august air of distinction.

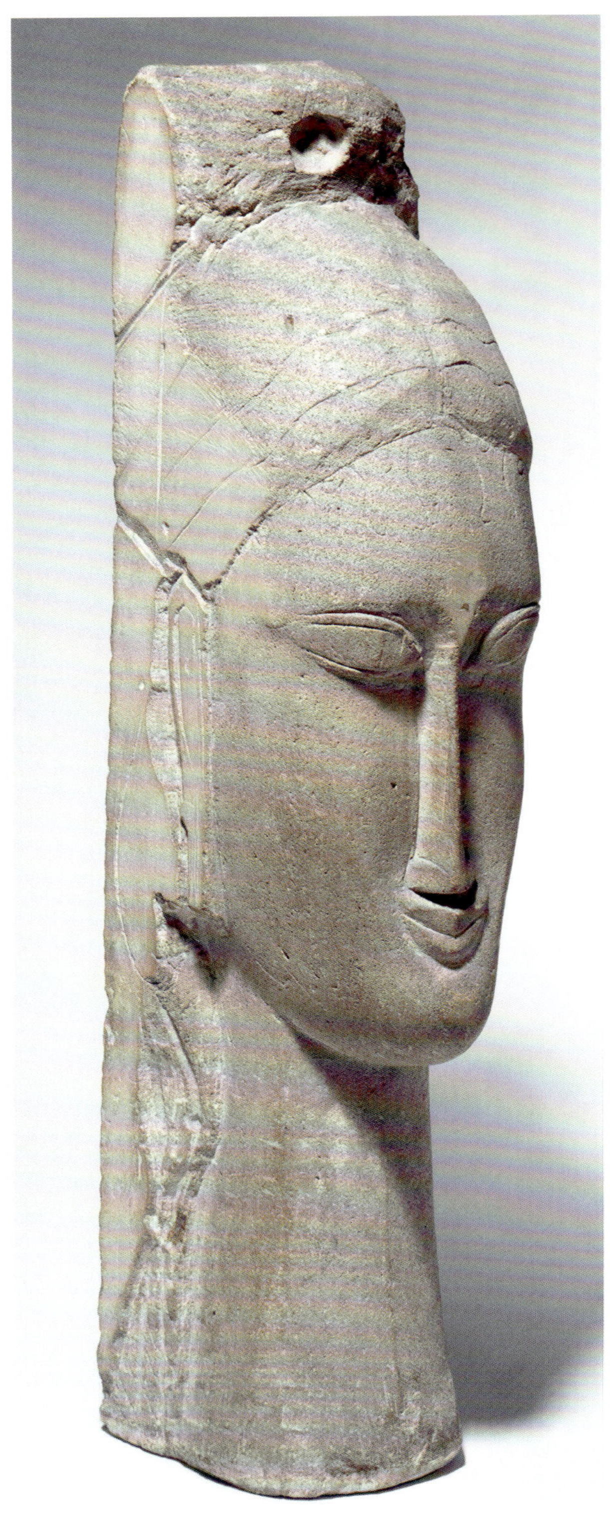

Amedeo Modigliani (1884–1920)
Woman's Head, 1912

Stone, 58 × 12 × 16 cm

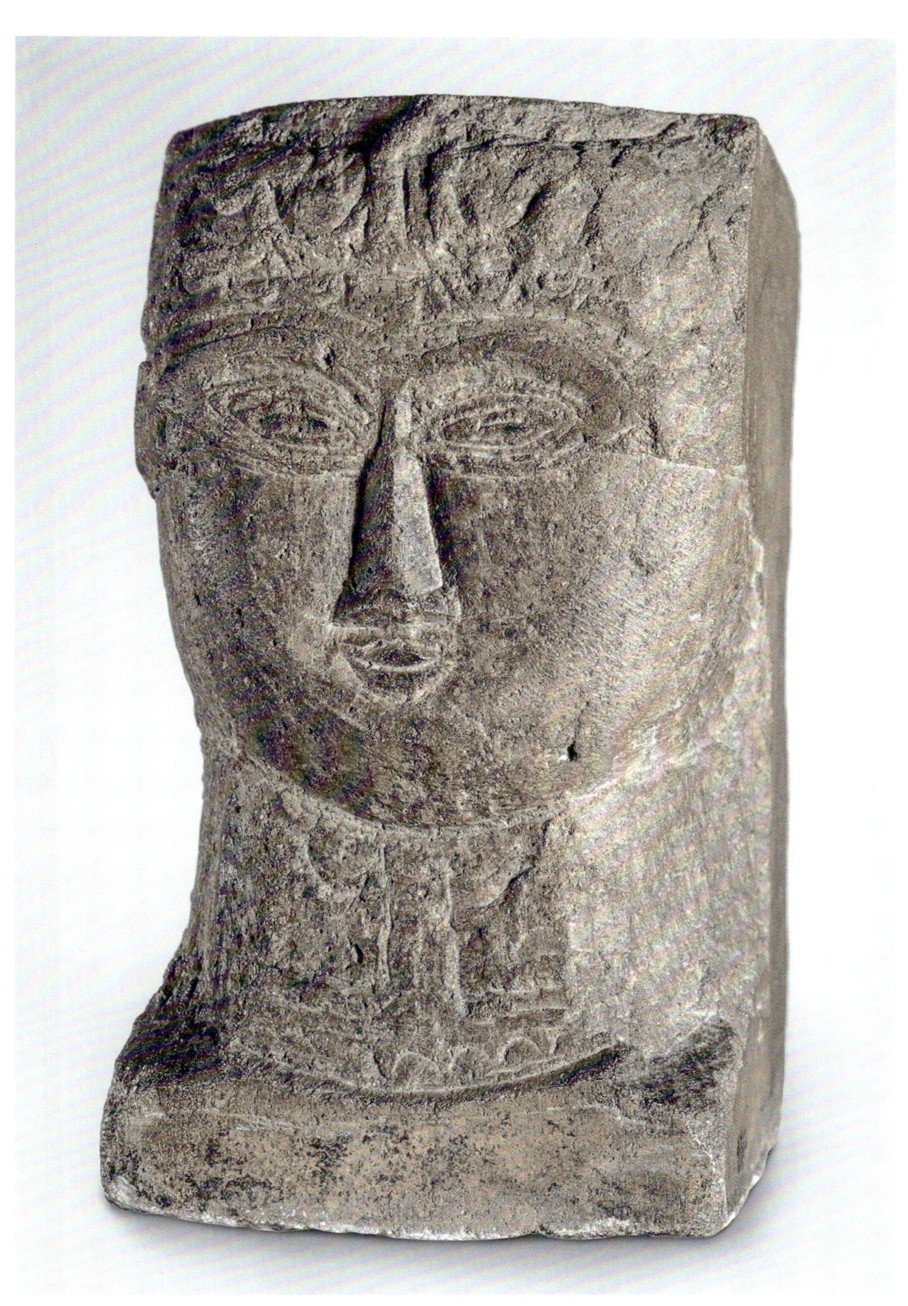

CAT. 36
Amedeo Modigliani (1884–1920)
Woman's Head, 1911–13

Stone, 47 × 27 × 31 cm

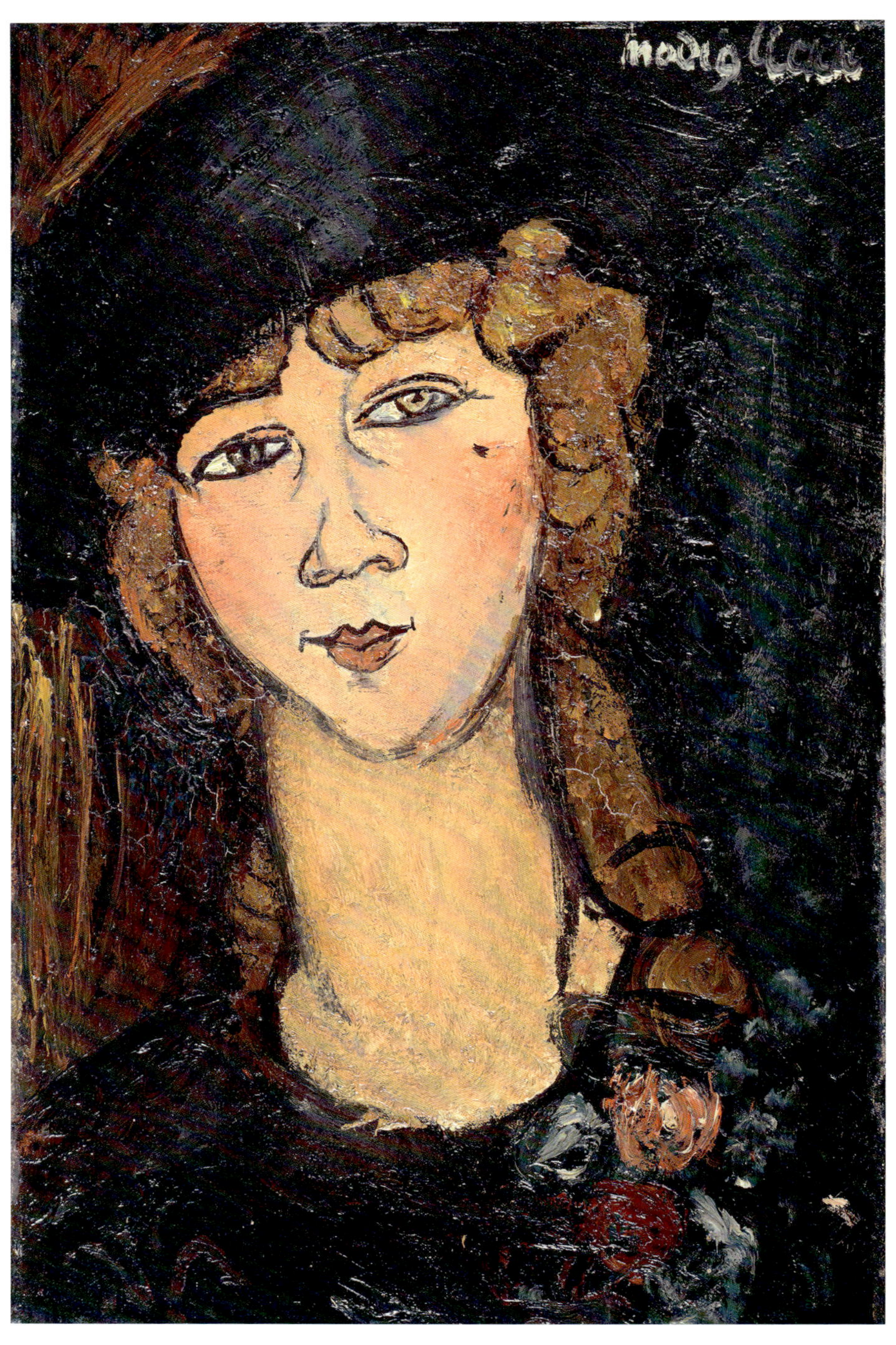

Amedeo Modigliani (1884–1920)
Lolotte, June 1917

Oil on canvas, 55 × 35.5 cm

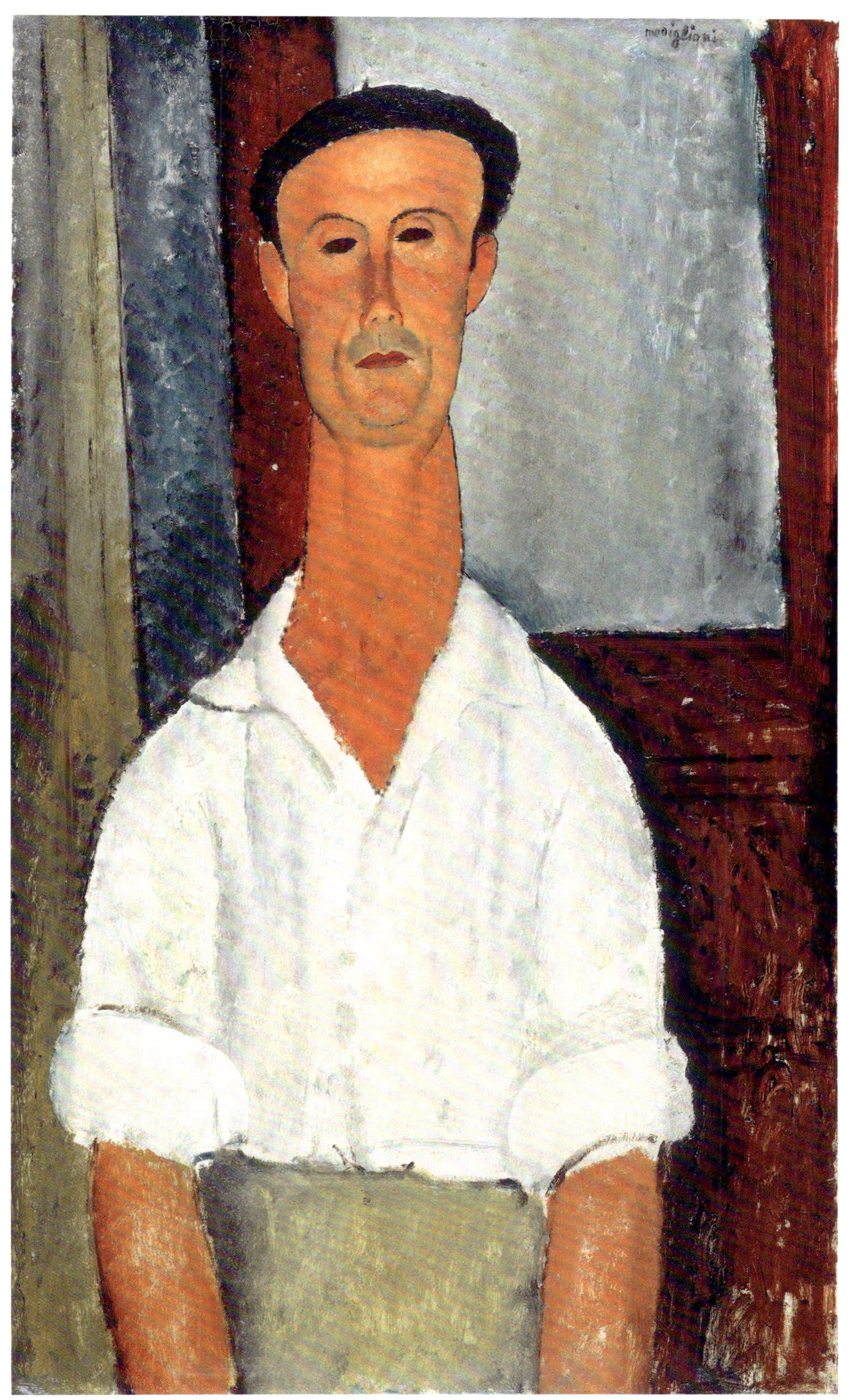

CAT. 38

Amedeo Modigliani (1884–1920)
Gaston Modot, 1918

Oil on canvas, 92.7 × 53.6 cm

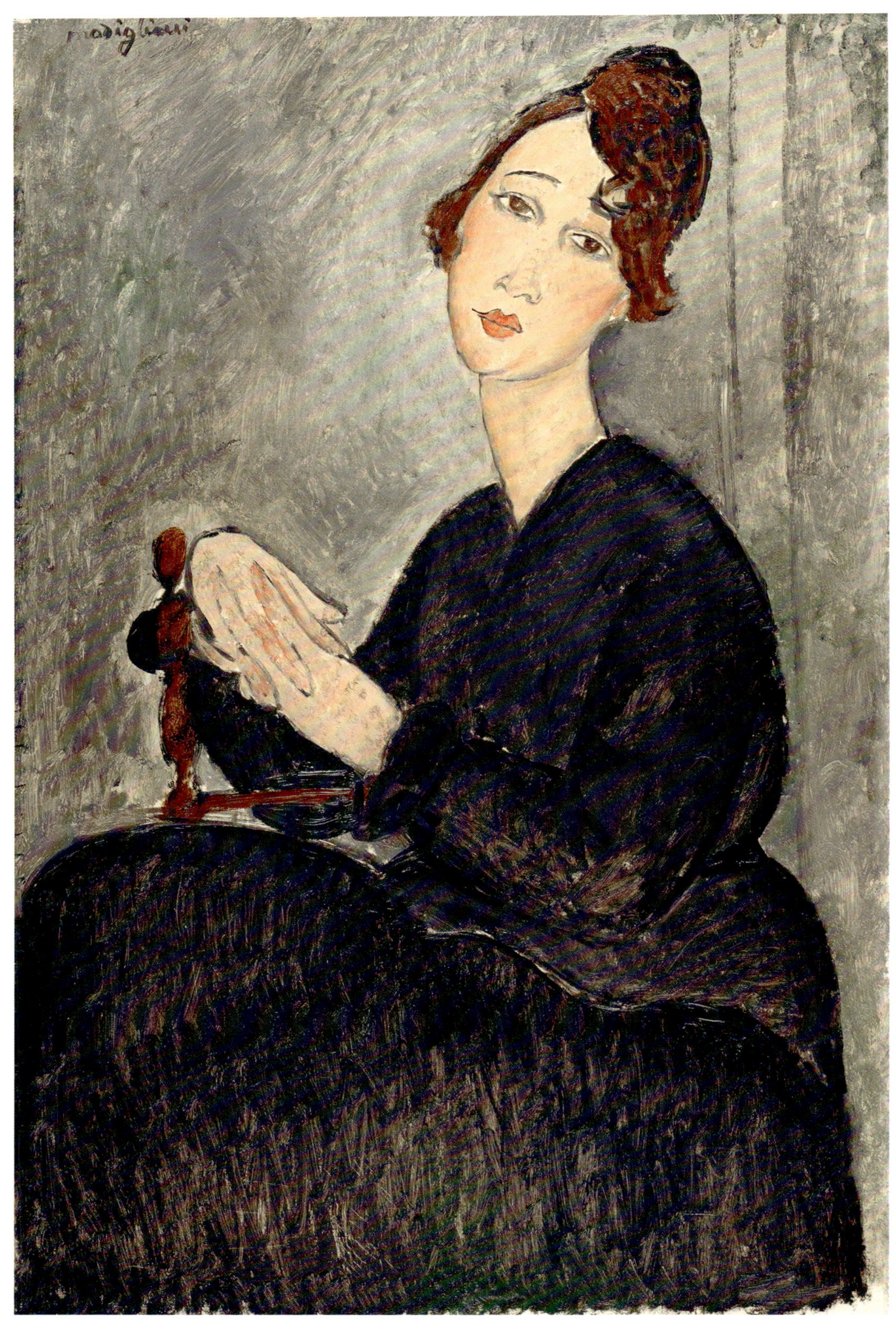

CAT. 39

Amedeo Modigliani (1884–1920)
Portrait of Dédie (Odette Hayden), 1918

Oil on canvas, 92 × 60 cm

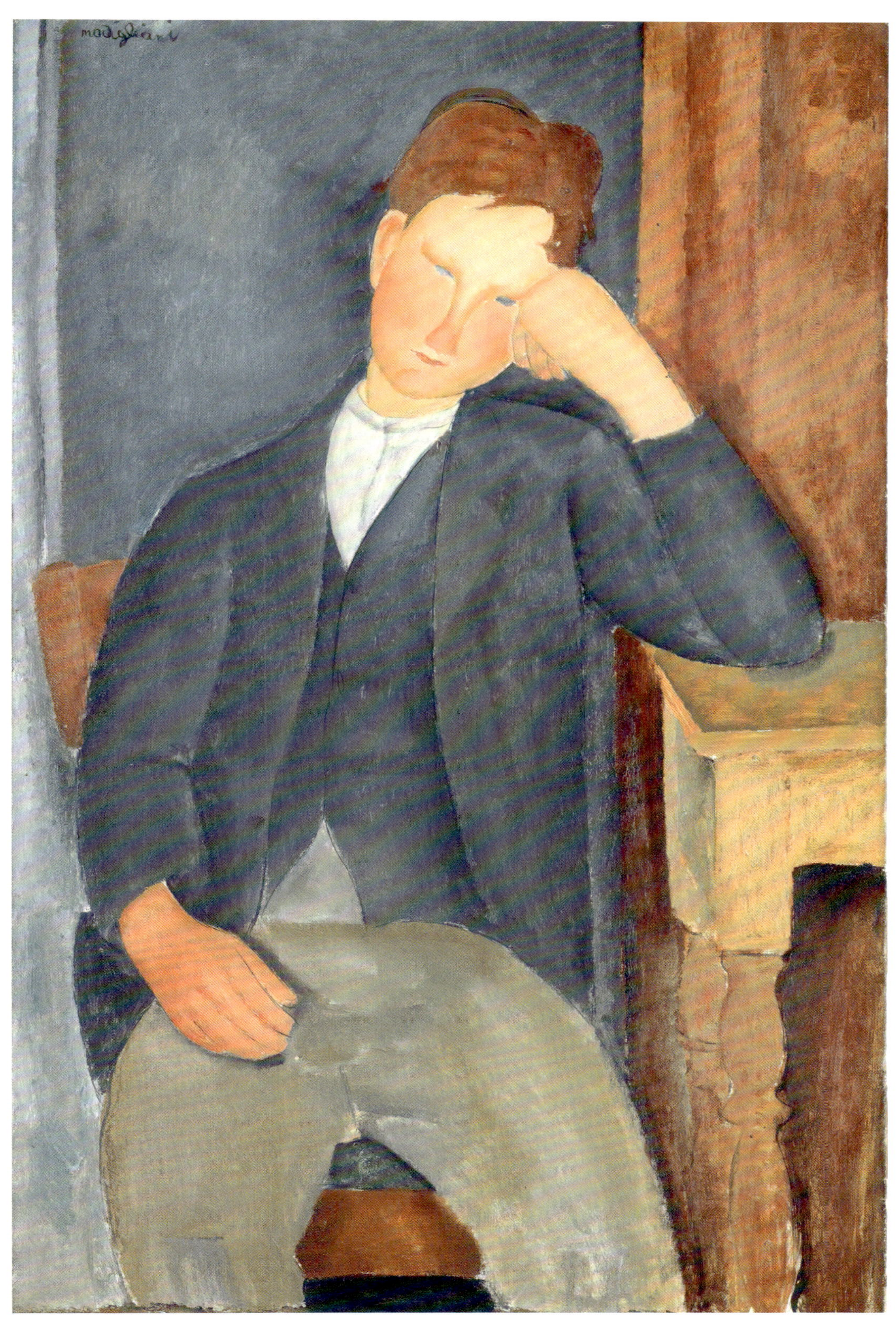

CAT. 40

Amedeo Modigliani (1884–1920)
The Young Apprentice, 1918–19

Oil on canvas, 100 × 65 cm

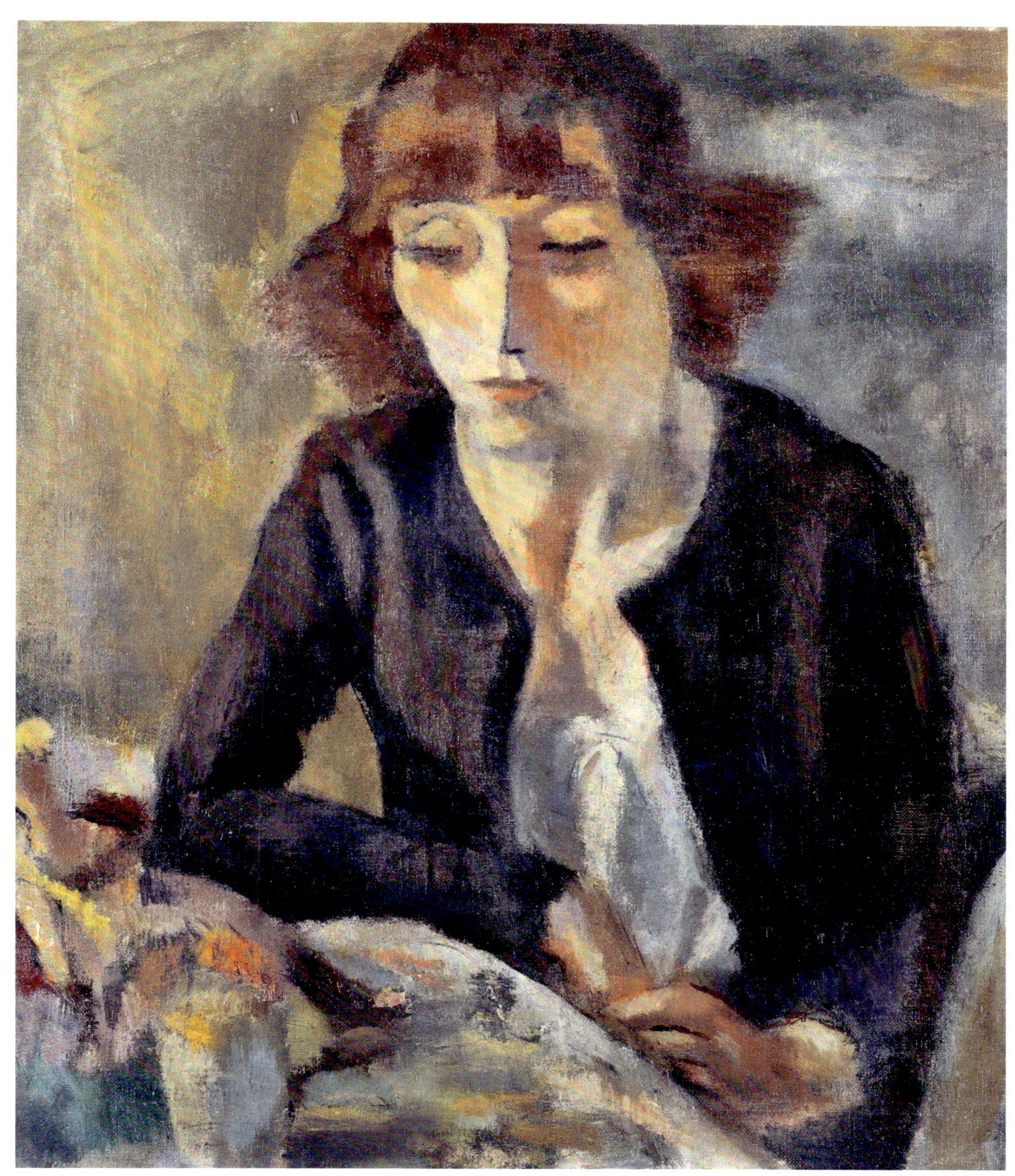

Jules Pascin (1885–1930)
Hermine David, 1918

Oil on canvas, 51 × 43 cm

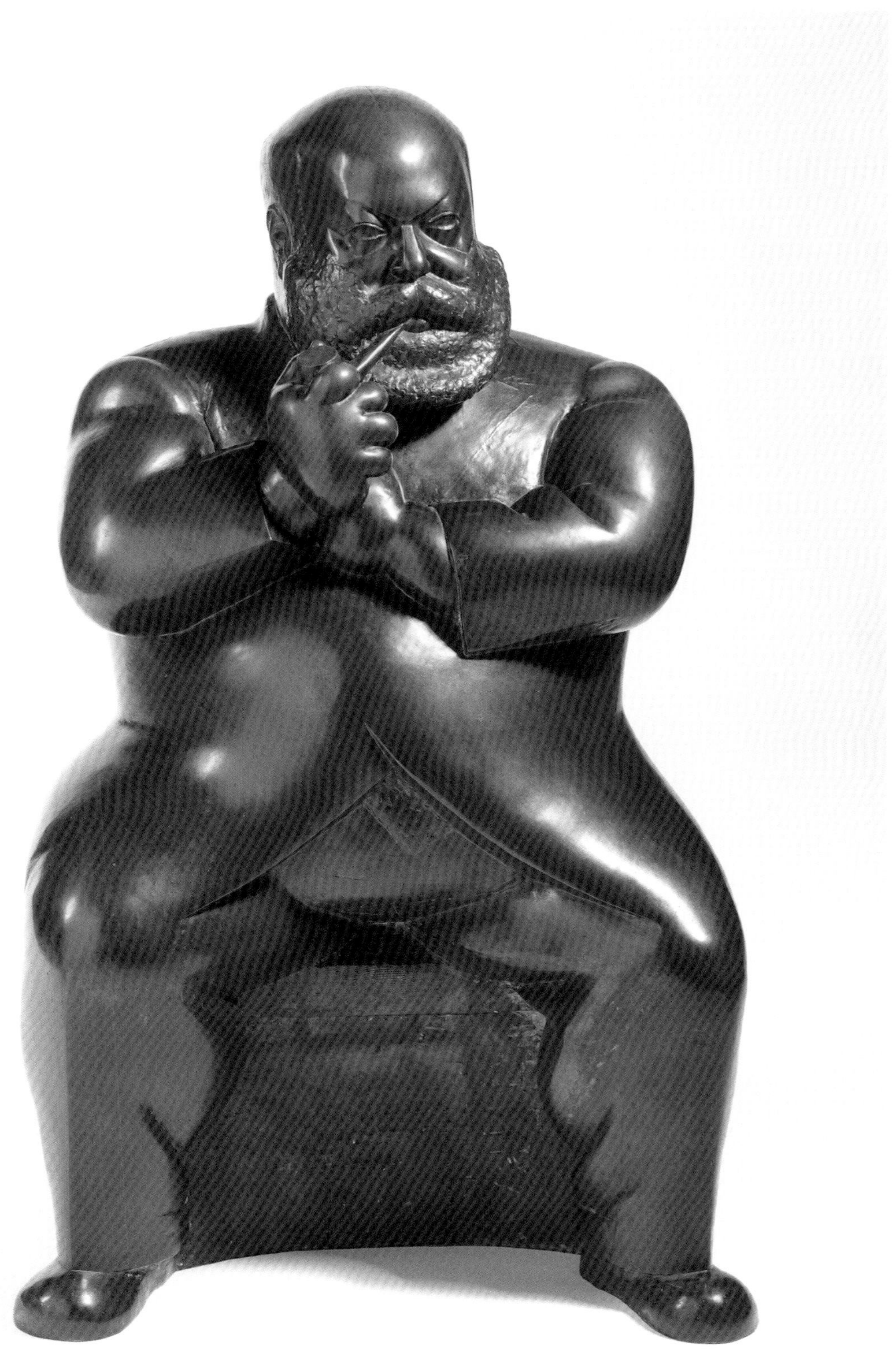

Chana Orloff (1888–1968)
Daniel O. Widhopff, 1923

Bronze, 106 × 61 × 54 cm

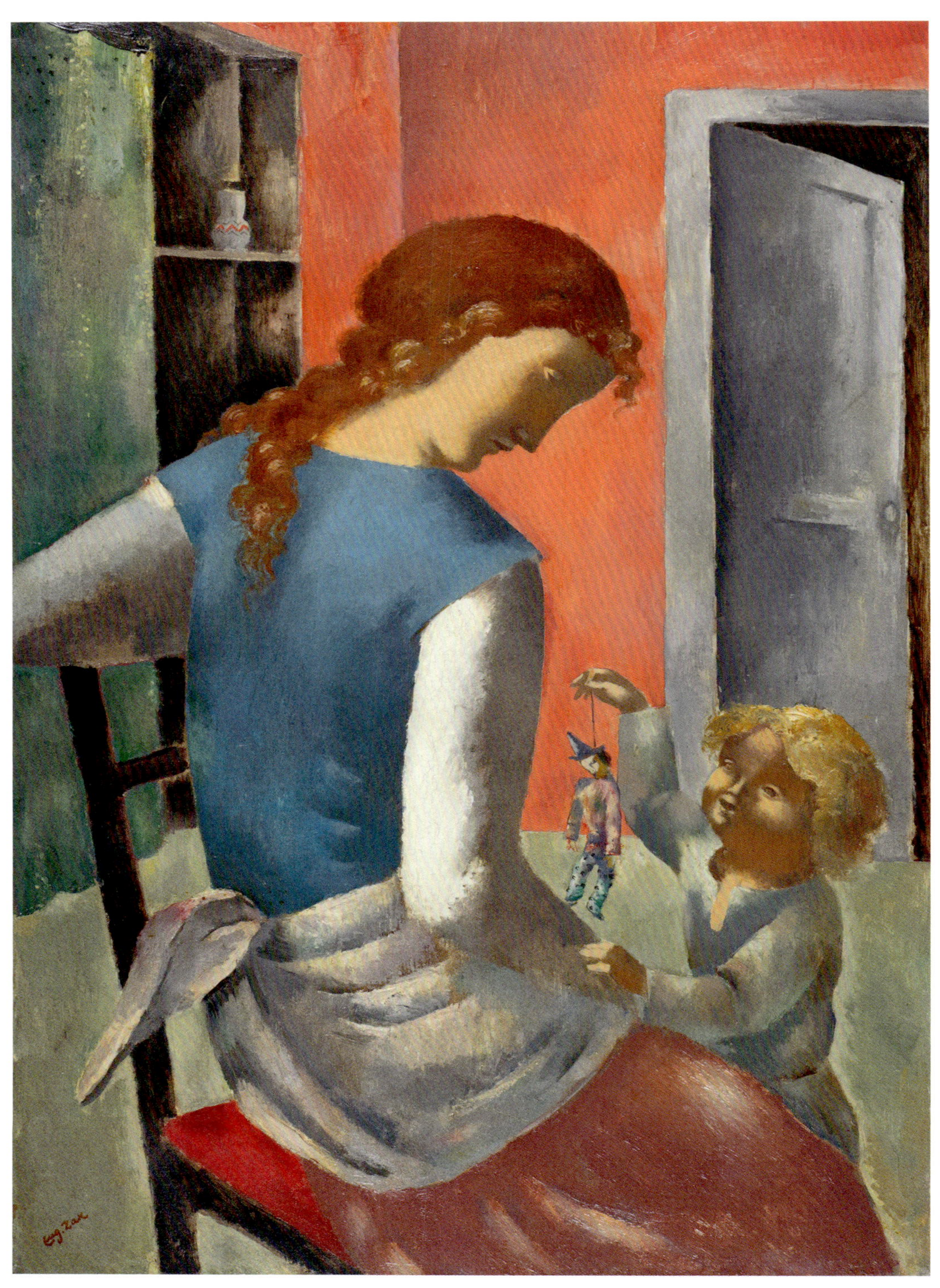

Eugène Zak (1884–1926)
The Toy, 1924

Oil on canvas, 92 × 65.7 cm

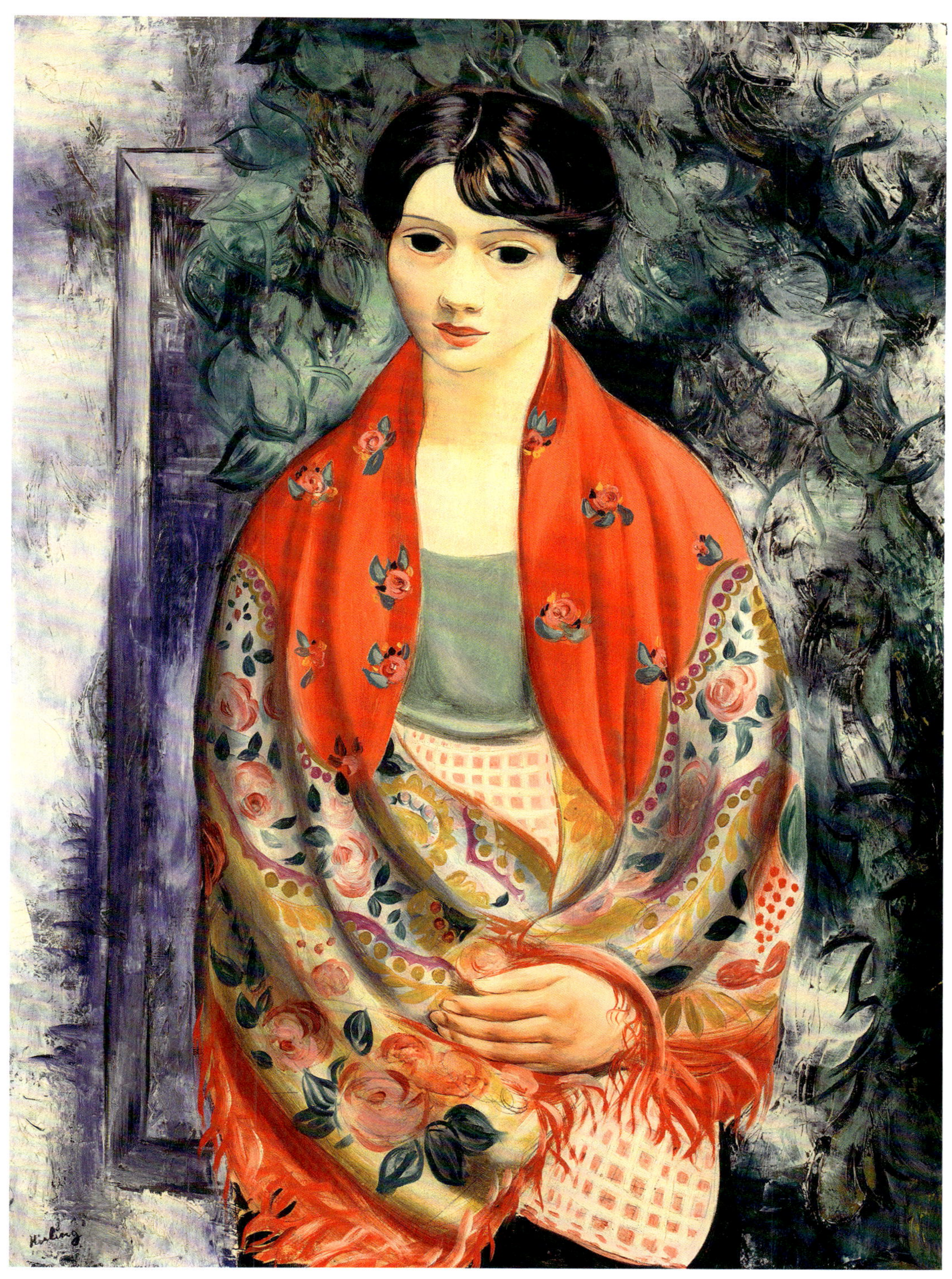

CAT. 44

Kisling (1891–1953)
Woman with a Polish Shawl, 1928

Oil on canvas, 100 × 72.5 cm

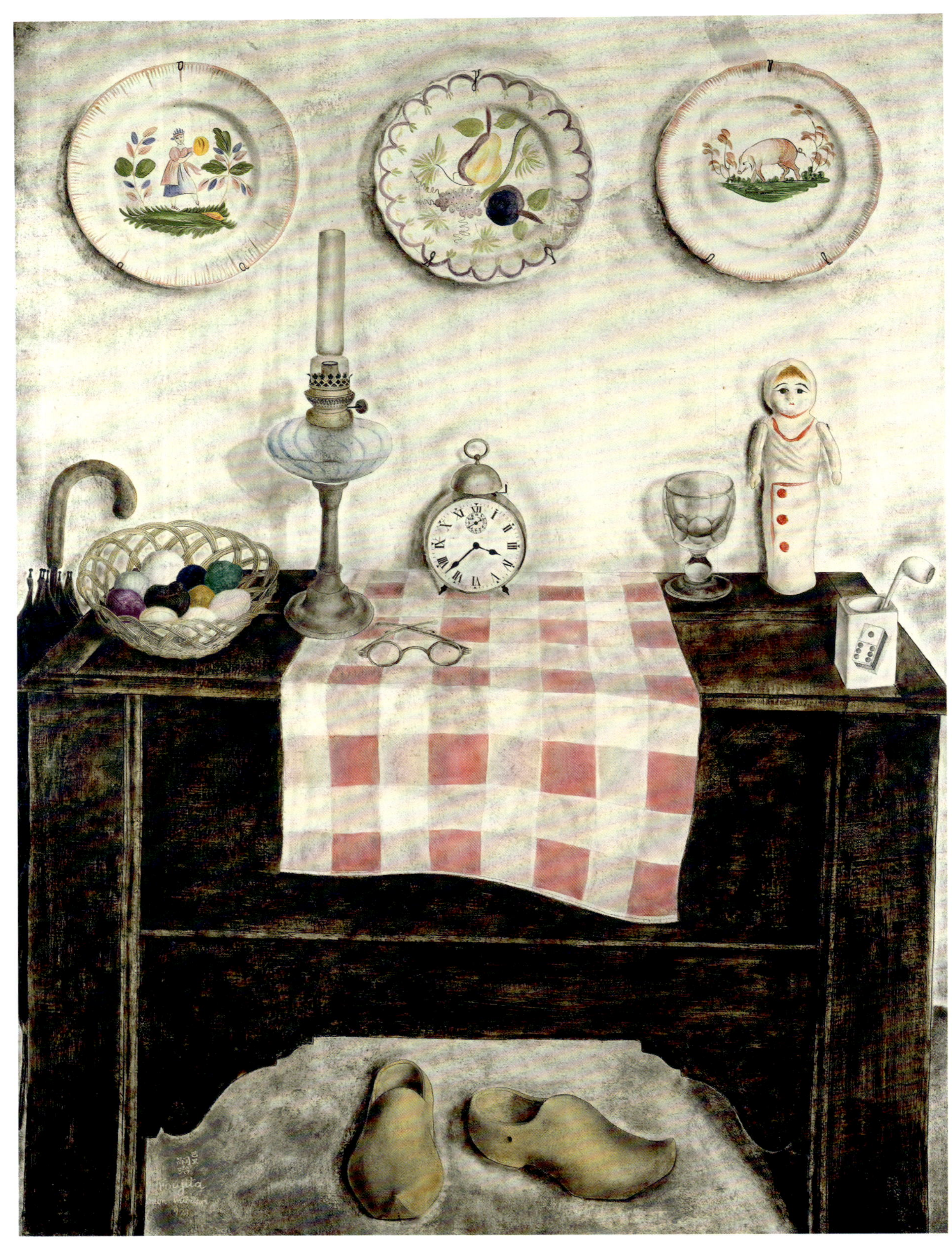

CAT. 45

Léonard Foujita (1886–1968)
My Interior, 1921

Oil on canvas mounted on wood panel, 130 × 97 cm

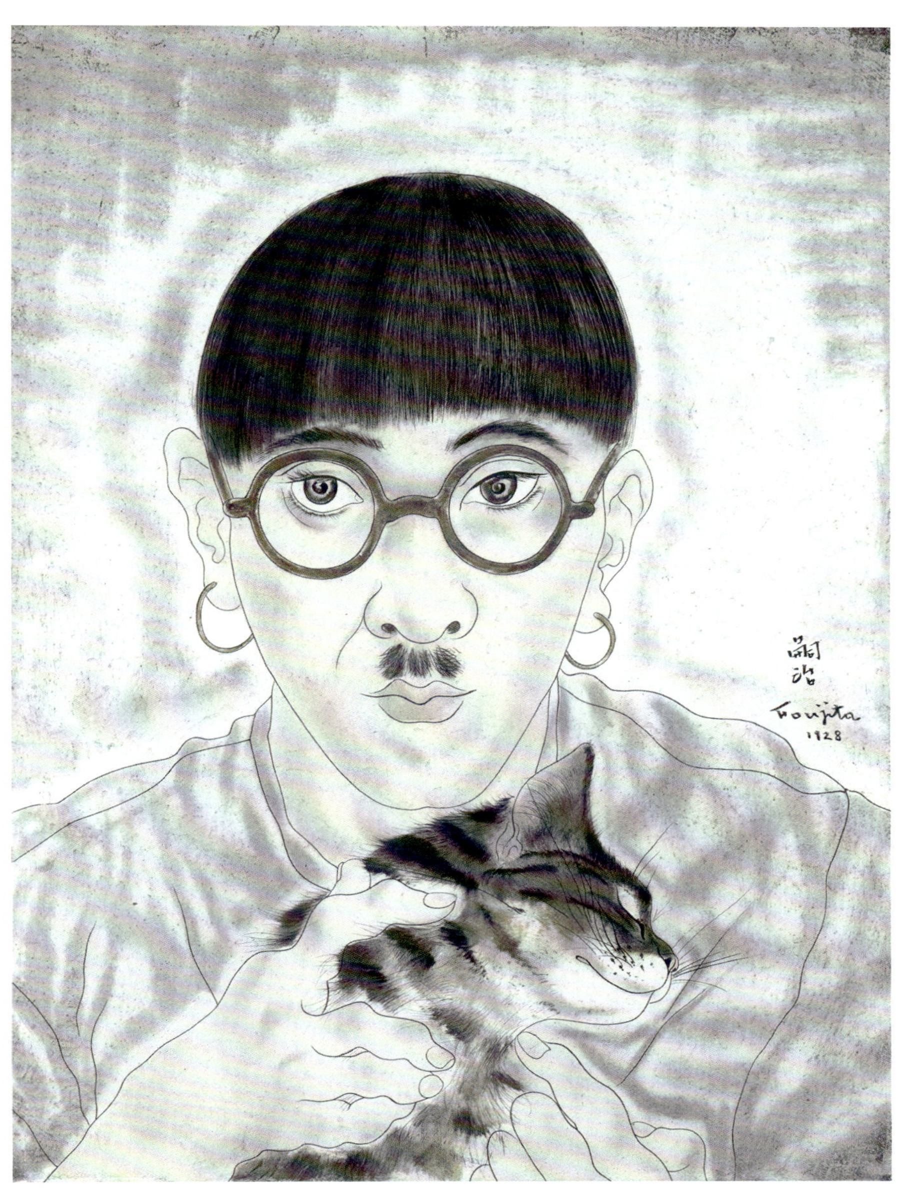

CAT. 46

Léonard Foujita (1886–1968)
Portrait of the Artist, 1928

Oil and gouache on canvas, 35 × 27 cm

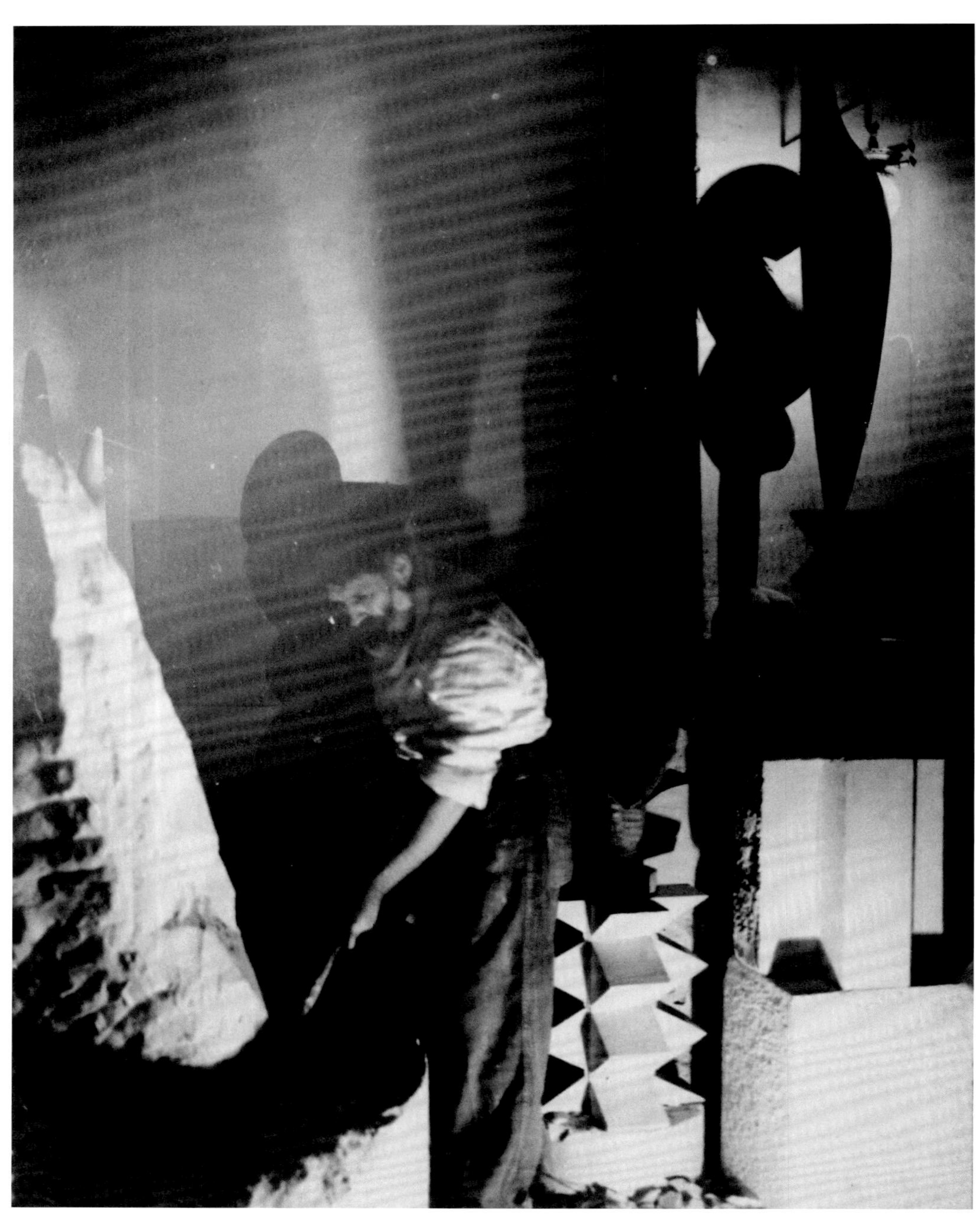

CAT. 47
Constantin Brancusi (1876–1957)
Brancusi Working at Night in his Studio, Impasse Ronsin, 1920

Silver gelatin print, 29.9 × 23.8 cm

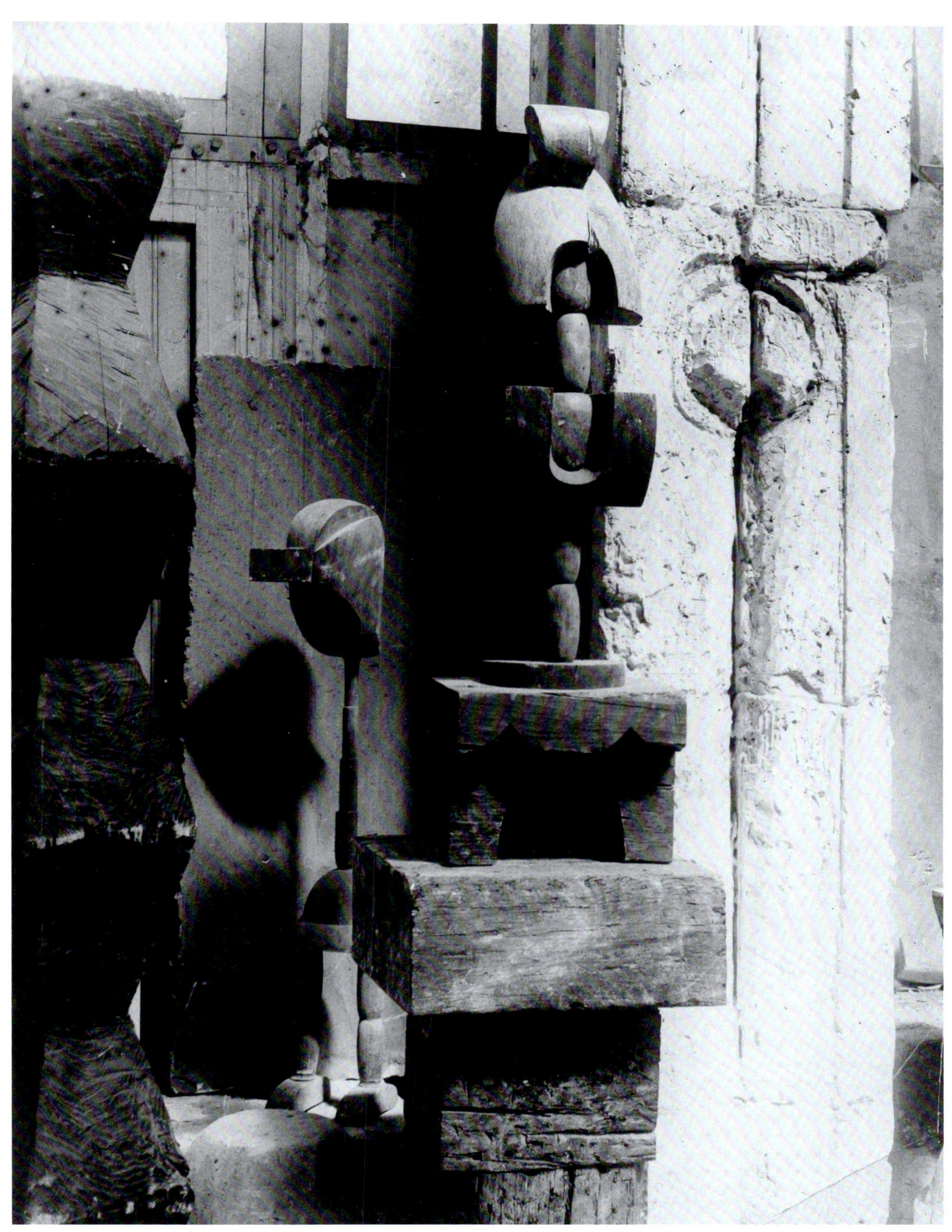

Constantin Brancusi (1876–1957)
Sculptures in the Studio, Impasse Ronsin,1920

Silver gelatin print, 39.8 × 29.8 cm

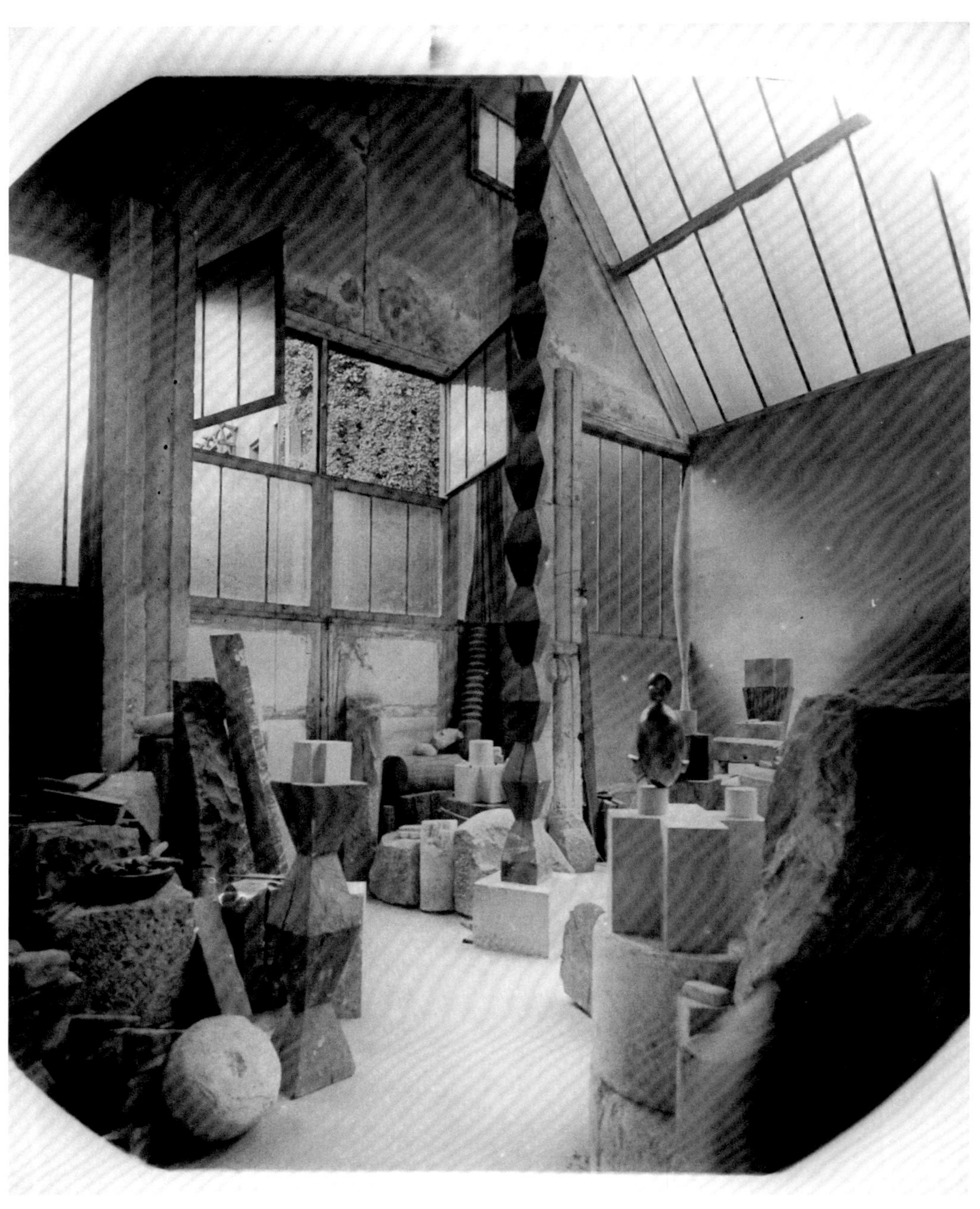

Constantin Brancusi (1876–1957)
The Studio Impasse Ronsin, 1926

Silver gelatin print, 29.7 × 23.7 cm

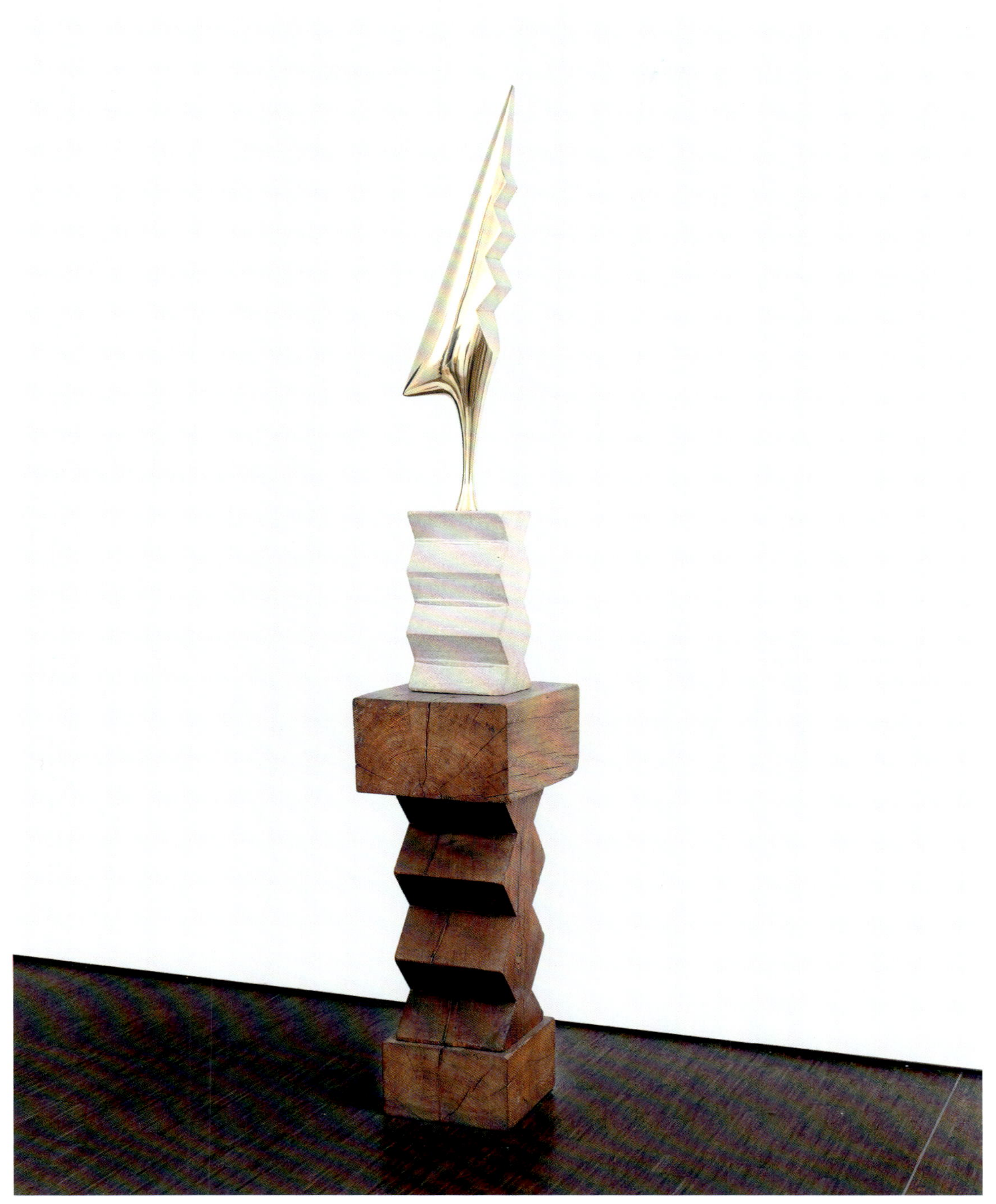

Constantin Brancusi (1876–1957)
The Cockerel, 1935

Polished bronze, limestone (?), wood, 103.4 × 12.1 × 29.9 cm (with plinths: 253.4 cm)

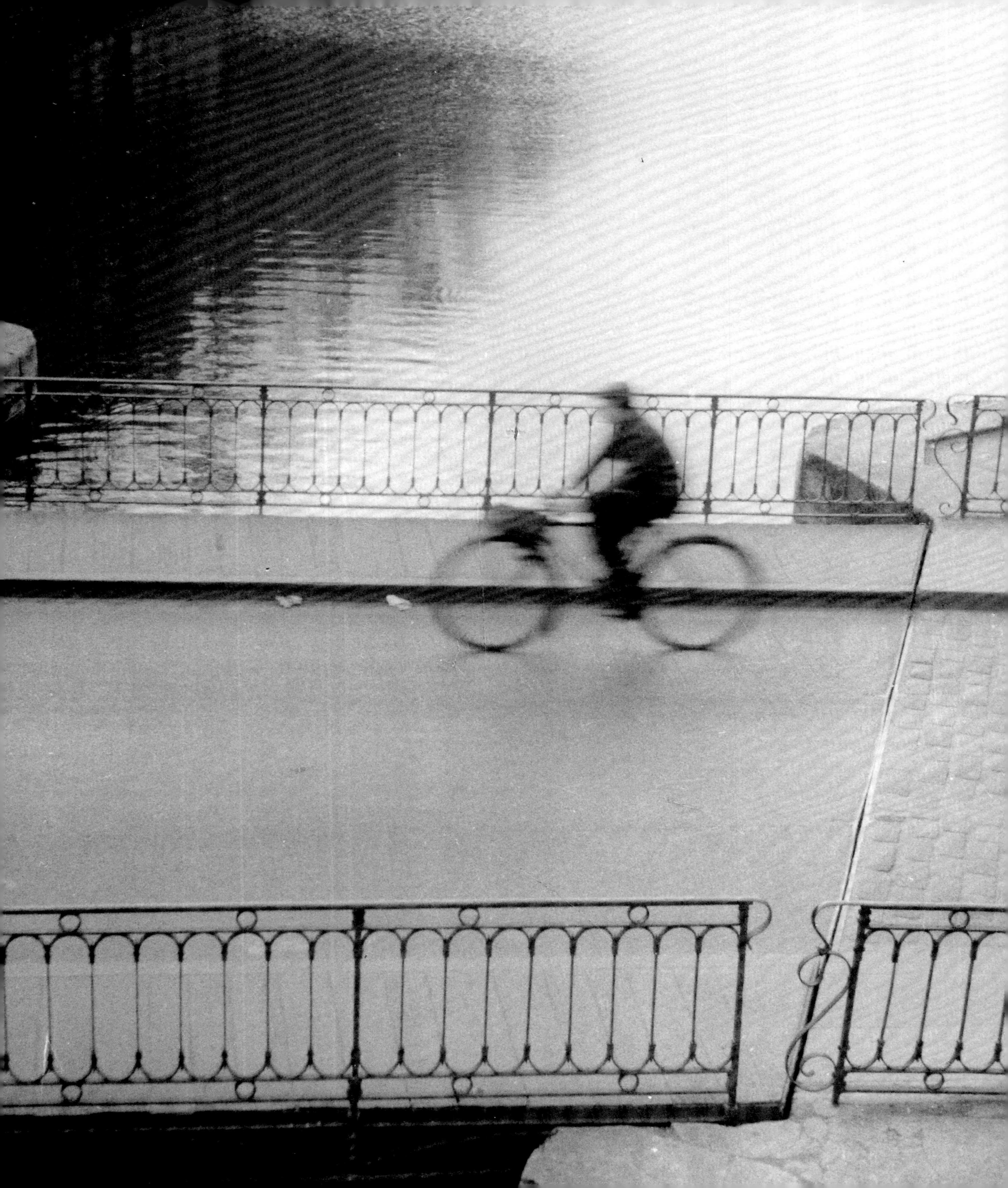

PARIS SEEN BY …

JULIE JONES

Paris, with its unique aura, attracted international photographers from an early stage, above all during the interwar period. They came in large numbers from all over the world – northern Europe, Italy, the USA, Japan, Germany, Hungary – and were often, like so many others, seeking refuge from difficult political and economic circumstances. Drawing on the avant-garde innovations of their countries of origin (in painting, film and photography), they contributed to the French capital's artistic vibrancy by helping to forge a cosmopolitan photographic modernism enriched by a wide range of influences.

These years between 1920 and 1930 were a turning point in the history of the photographic medium. Until this point, "art photography" was exclusively associated with pictorialist practices – its advocates sought to secure their medium's artistic status by harnessing it to traditional genres and pictorial styles. The new arrivals in Paris – photographers like André Kertész and François Kollar from Hungary, Germaine Krull, Marianne Breslauer and Ilse Bing from Germany, and the American Florence Henri – took a different stance, contributing to the development of a "new vision" of photography. Given their very diverse practices and careers, these international photographers cannot easily be grouped under the banner of a single "school". They nonetheless shared an avant-gardist spirit and iconographic culture that enabled them to invent new modes of representation adapted to the ongoing transformations of city life and the new experiences of contemporary individuals. As they sought to define their medium's unique attributes, each of these photographers in their own way defended a practice liberated from pictorial tradition. As such, they drew their subjects from the manifestations of the modern age – the new architecture, motorised vehicles, crowds – in a highly graphic style that often tended towards abstraction [CAT. 67, 68]. The city's unrelenting pace was captured in images by means of tilting and blurring effects, while architectural transformations offered new high-altitude perspectives [CAT. 55, 61, 70]. Another aspect of the capital's modernity was the persistence of a distinctively Parisian charm, celebrated by these photographers – Brassaï in particular – in scenes that documented daily life on the banks of the River Seine, or in intimate cafés and dance halls [CAT. 63–66]. This enduring picturesque quality, twinned with the newness of the city, often produced strange or even Surrealist-style visions [CAT. 71]. At the time, this rich iconography catered to a relatively limited audience of fans of avant-garde publications and exhibitions. Yet it also became more widely disseminated as numerous photographic agencies and popular magazines sprang into being, responding to the public's growing appetite for photo reportage.

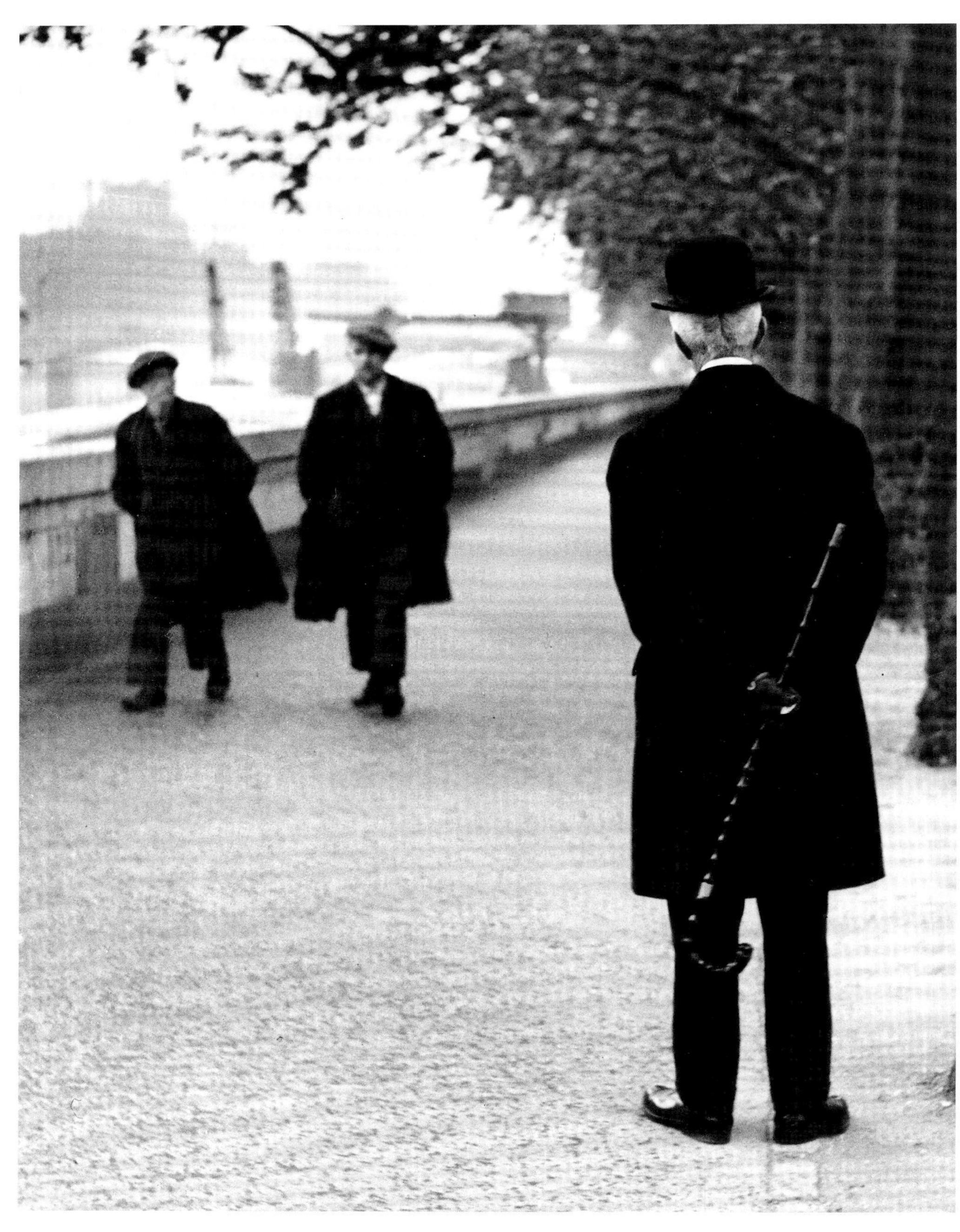

CAT. 51

André Kertész (1894–1985)
On the Quays, Paris, 1926

Silver gelatin print, 25.3 × 20.4cm

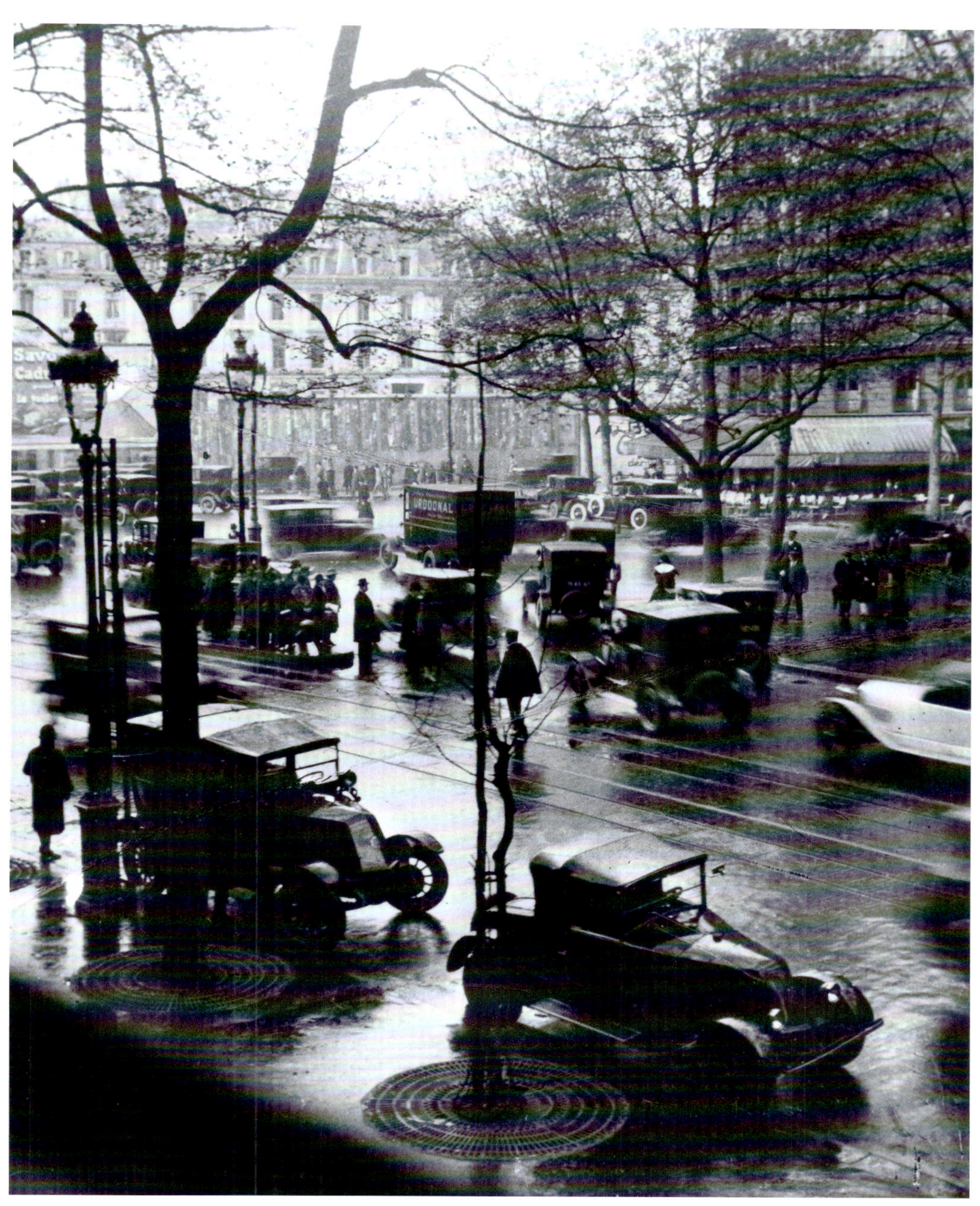

CAT. 52

André Kertész (1894–1985)
Boulevard Malesherbes at Midday, 1925

Silver gelatin print, 25.2 × 20.3 cm

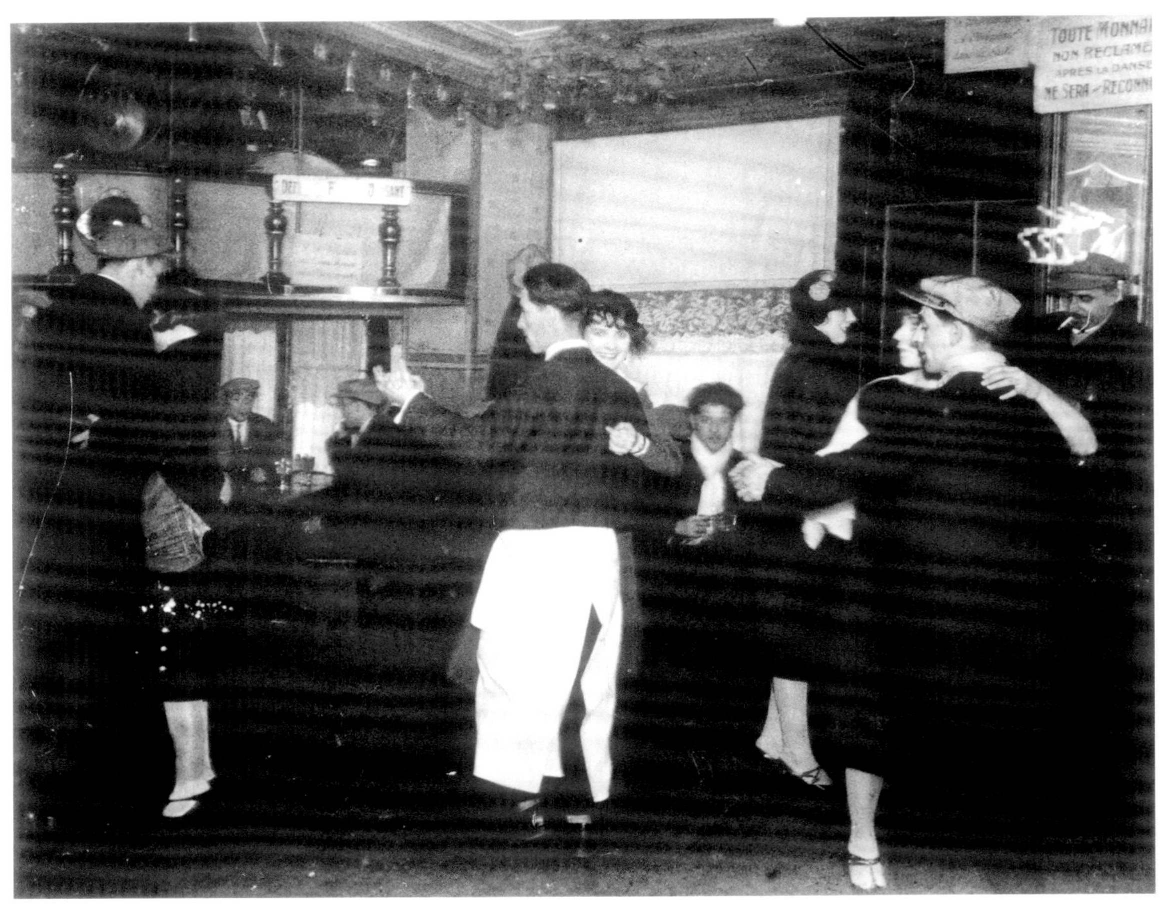

CAT. 53

André Kertész (1894–1985)
Bal Musette, Paris, 1926

Silver gelatin print, 20.3 × 25.3 cm

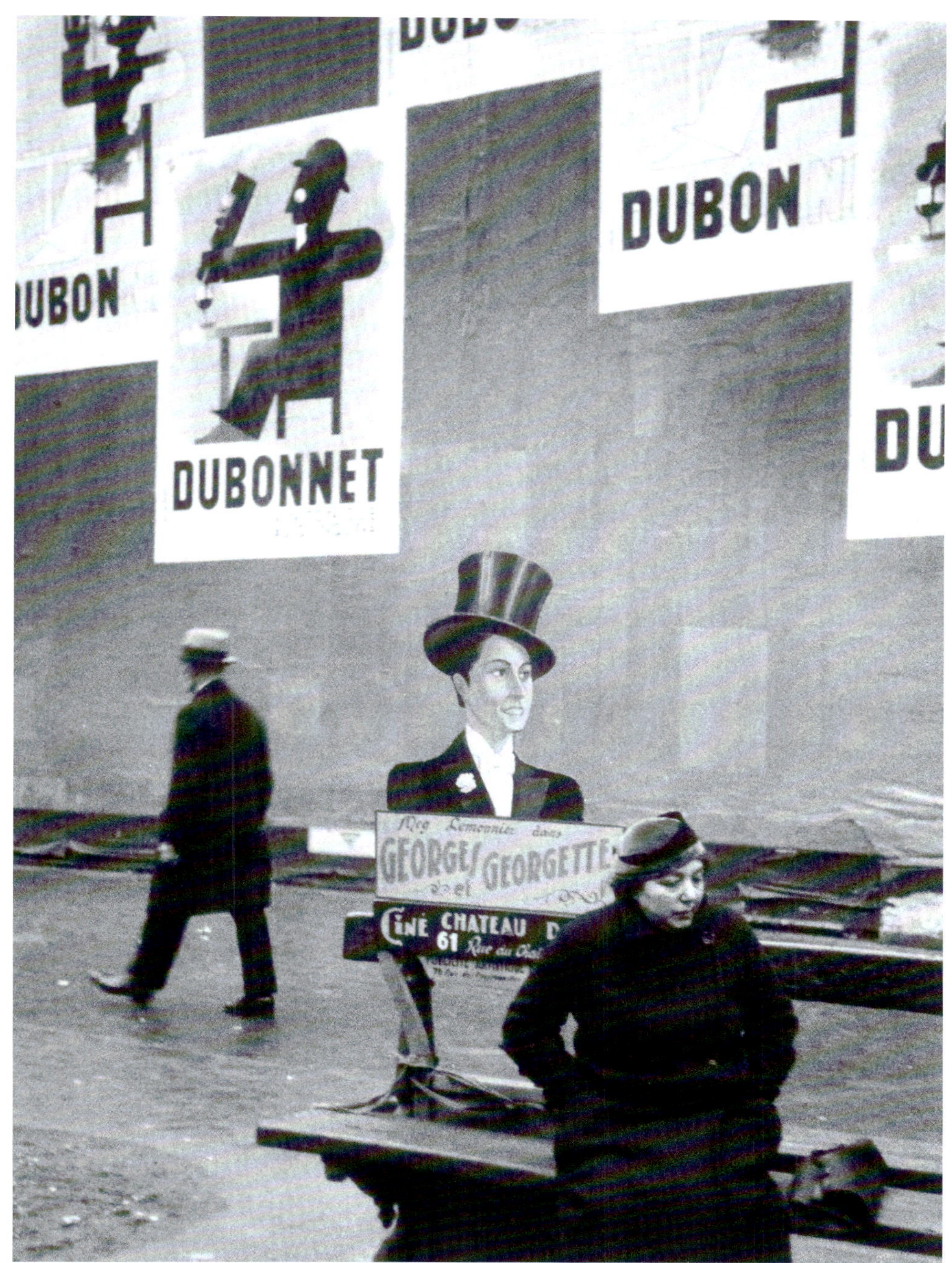

CAT. 54

André Kertész (1894–1985)
Dubo Dubon Dubonnet, 1934

Silver gelatin print, 25.3 × 20.3 cm

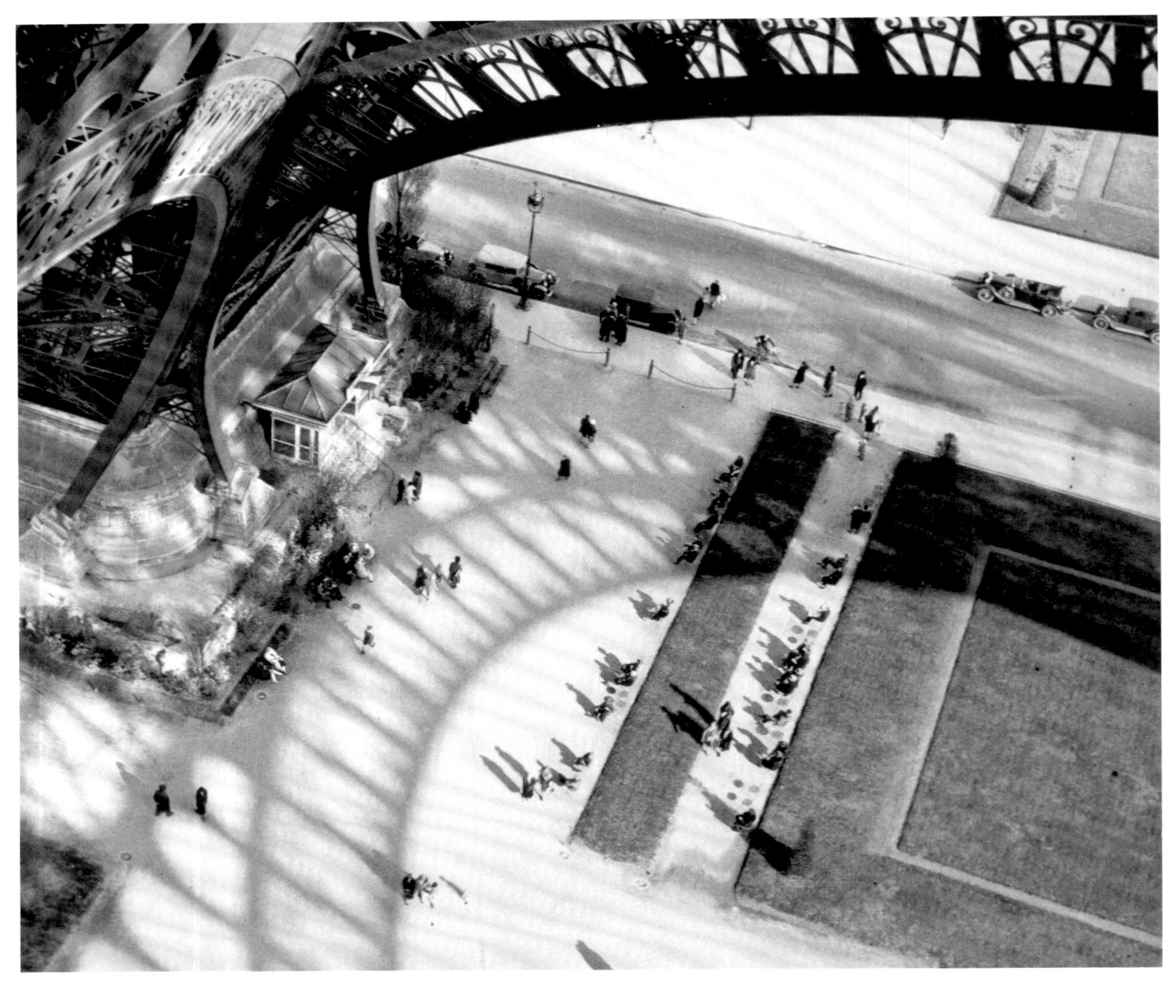

CAT. 55
André Kertész (1894–1985)
Shadow of the Eiffel Tower, 1929

Silver gelatin print, 20.4 × 25.3 cm

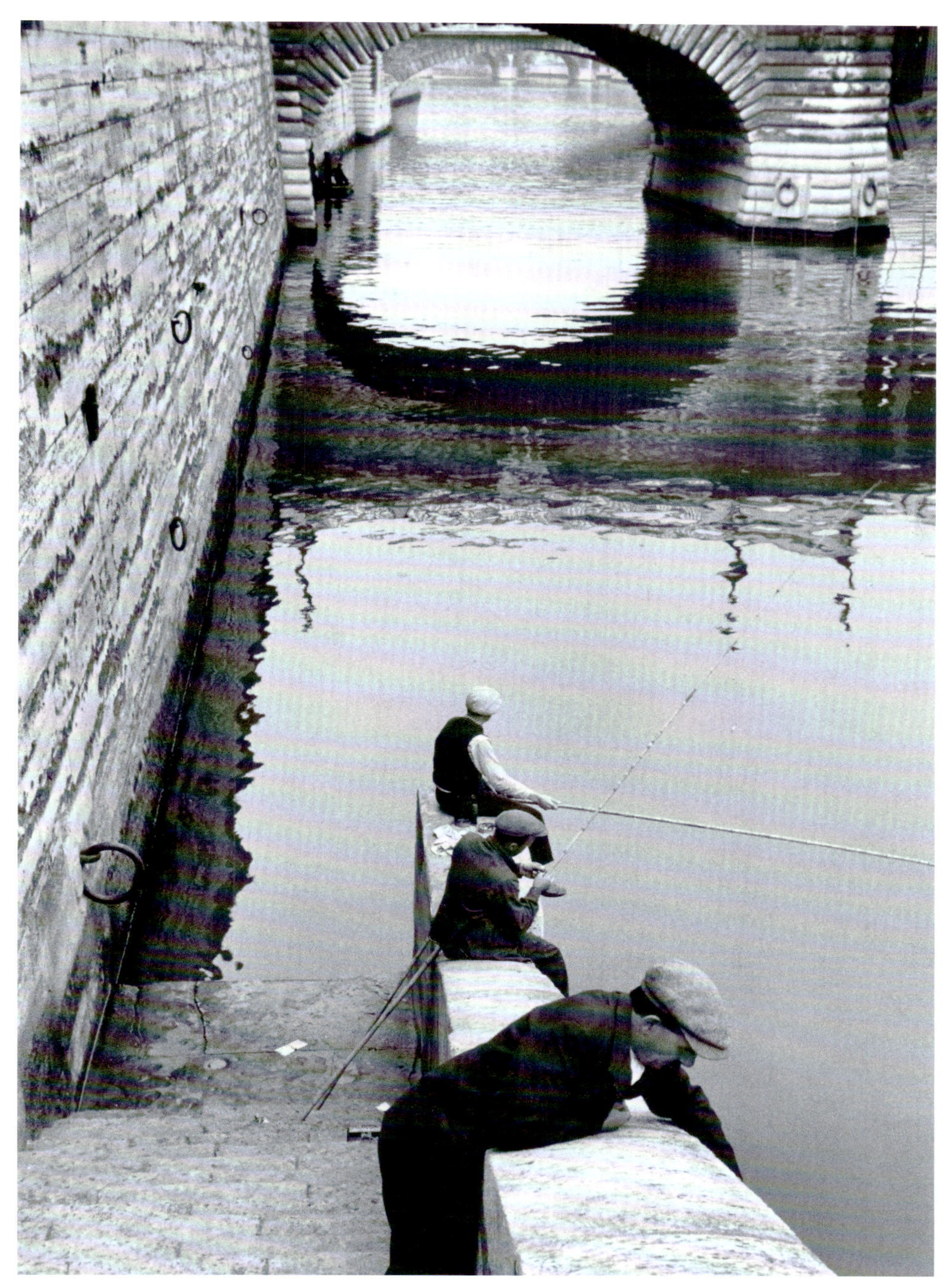

André Kertész (1894–1985)
Fishing, Paris, 1929

Silver gelatin print, 25.3 × 20.3 cm

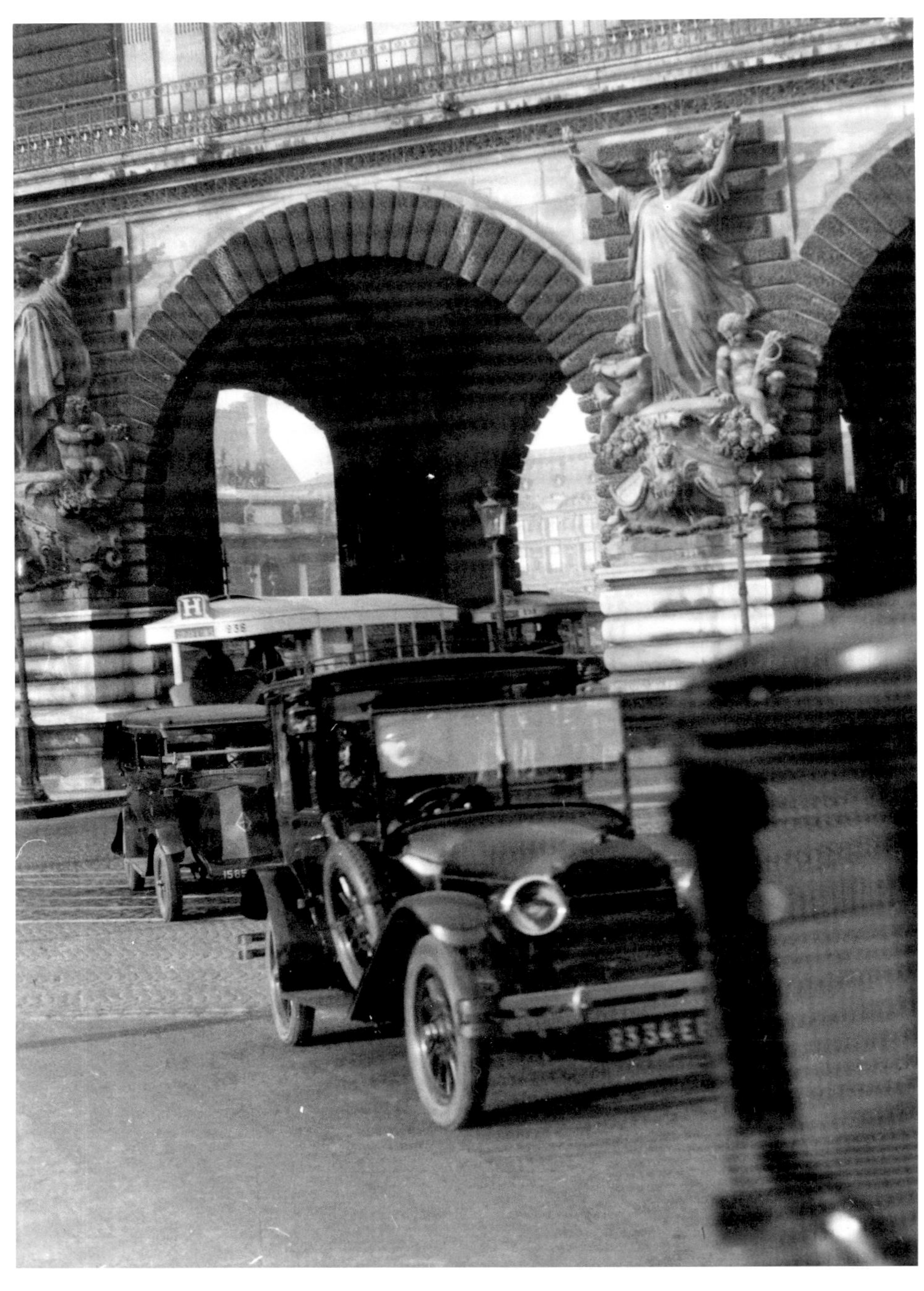

CAT. 57

Germaine Krull (1897–1985)
Traffic in front of the Louvre, Paris, 1926

Silver gelatin print, 16 × 11.6 cm

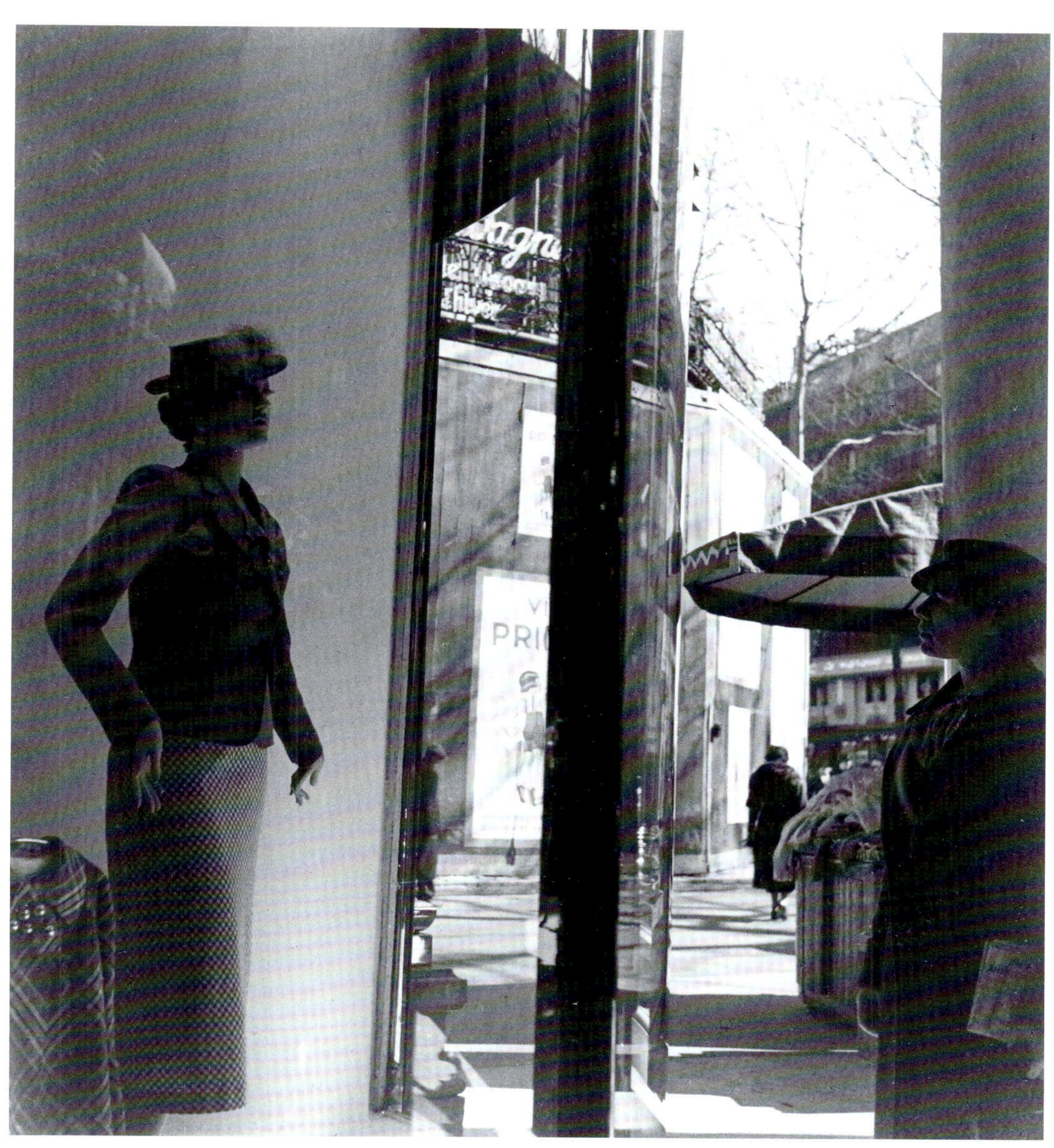

CAT. 58

Florence Henri (1893–1982)
Shop Windows, c. 1930

Silver gelatin print, 24.8 × 22.3 cm

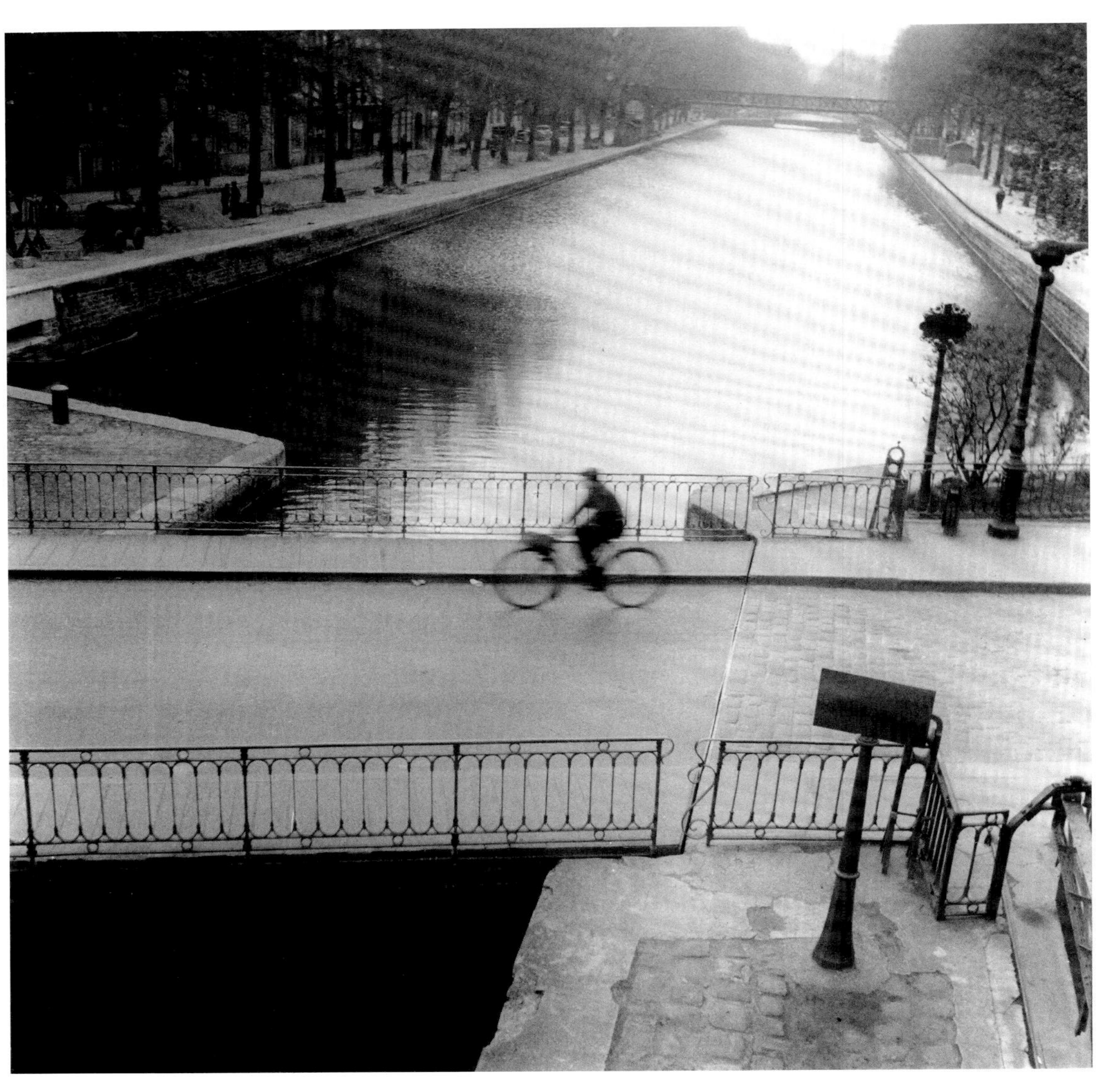

CAT. 59

Florence Henri (1893–1982)
Bridge over the Canal Saint-Martin, c. 1930–35

Silver gelatin print, 23 × 23 cm

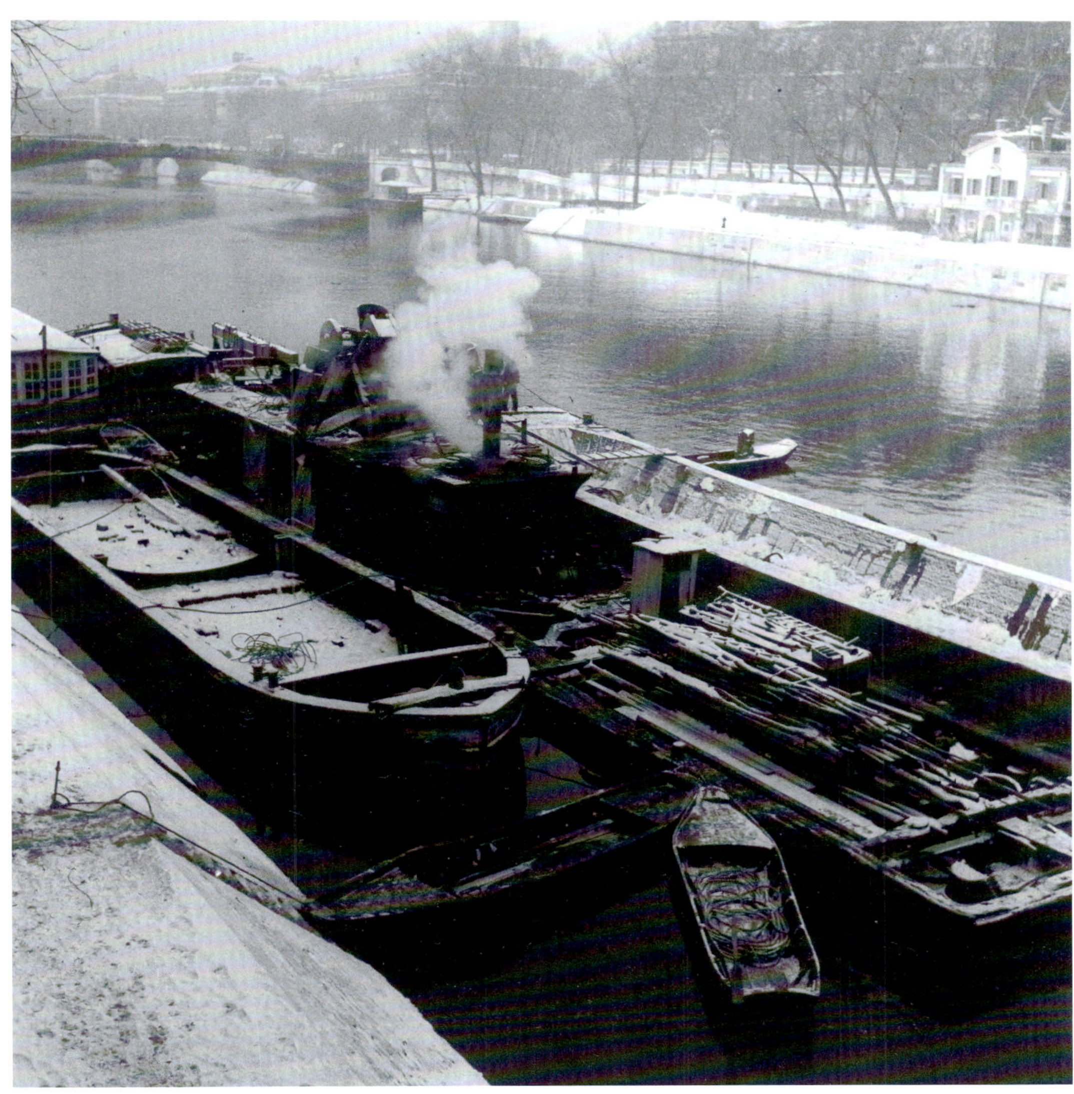

Florence Henri (1893–1982)
Barges on the Seine, c. 1930–35

Silver gelatin print, 24.6 × 23.9 cm

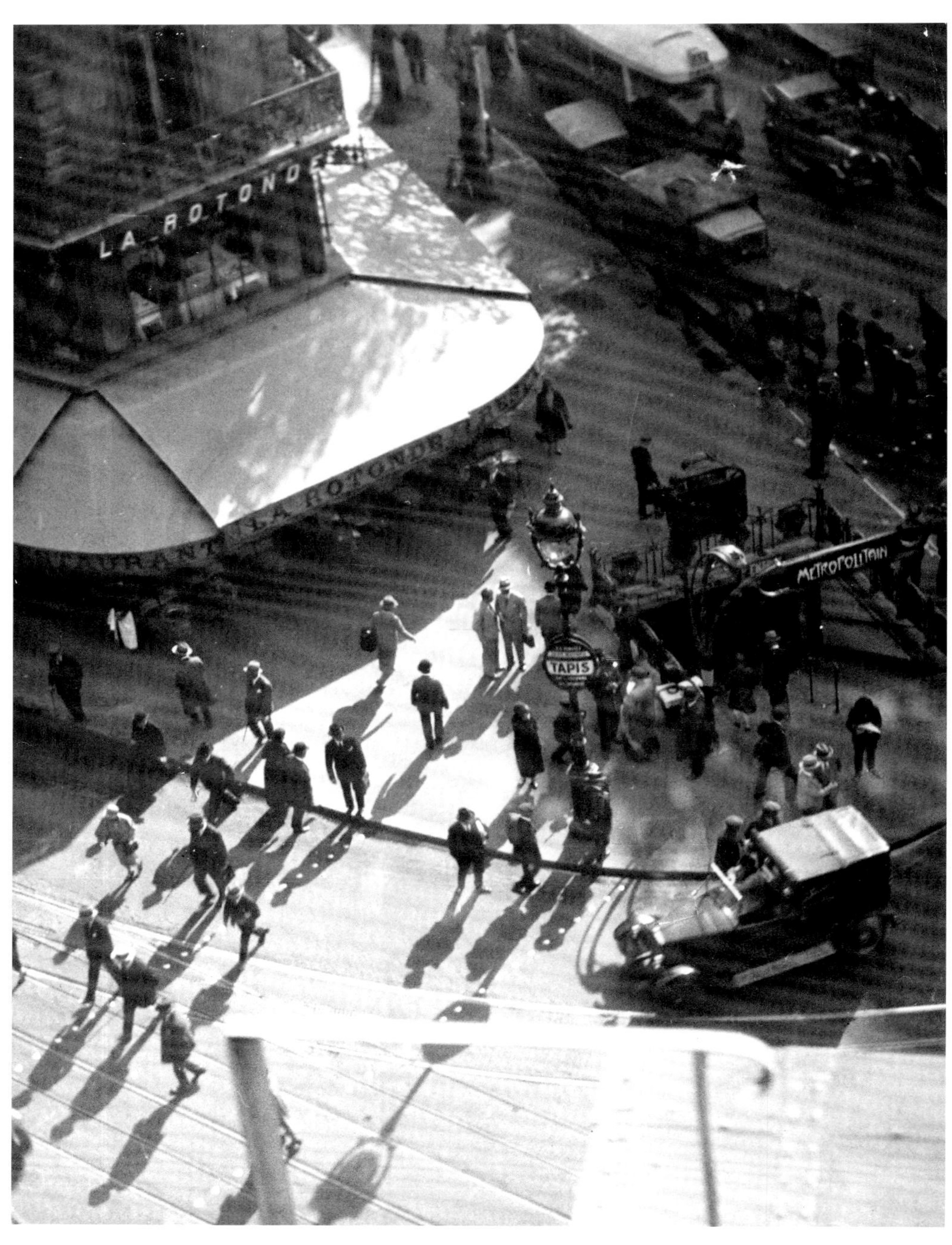

CAT. 61

Marianne Breslauer (1909–2001)
La Rotonde Seen from Above, 1929

Silver gelatin print, 23.7 × 17.8 cm, 23.3 × 17.6 cm (without margins)

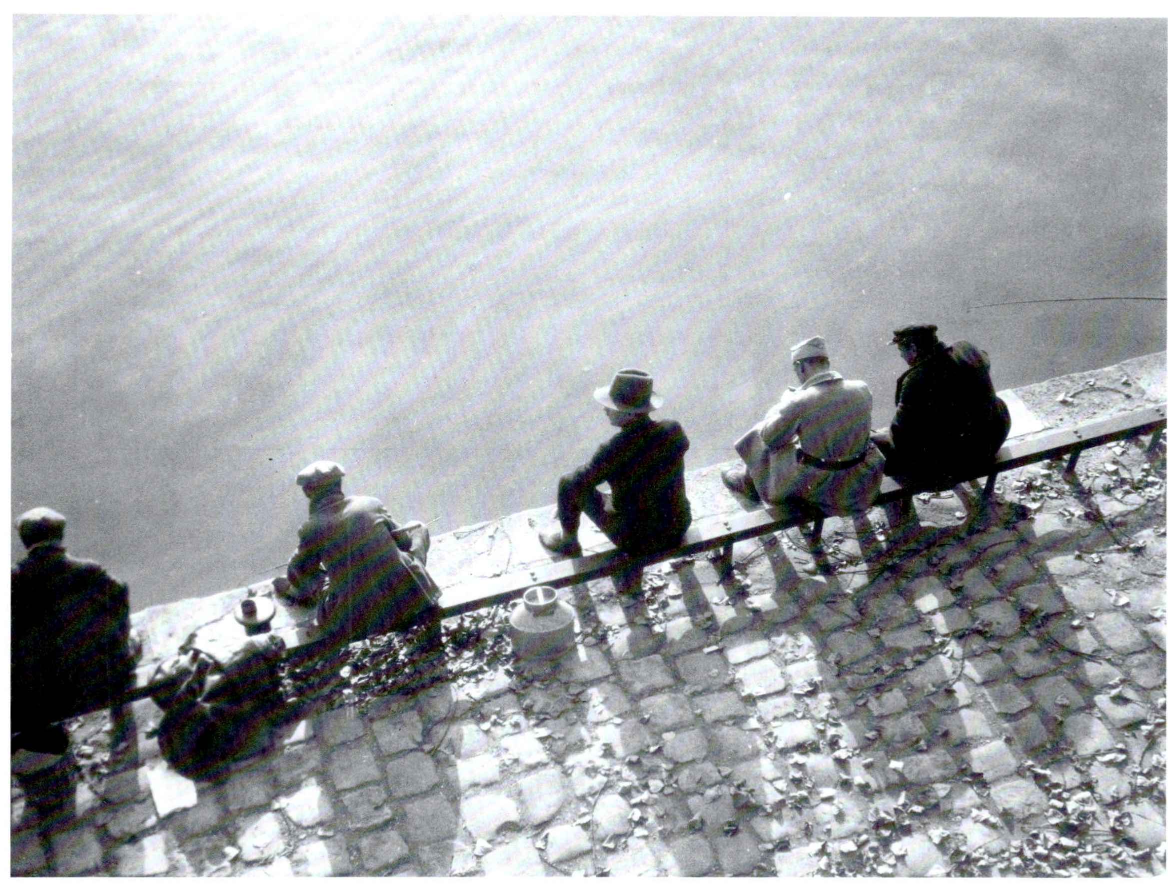

Marianne Breslauer (1909–2001)
Quays of the Seine, 1929

Silver gelatin print, 22.7 × 29.5 cm

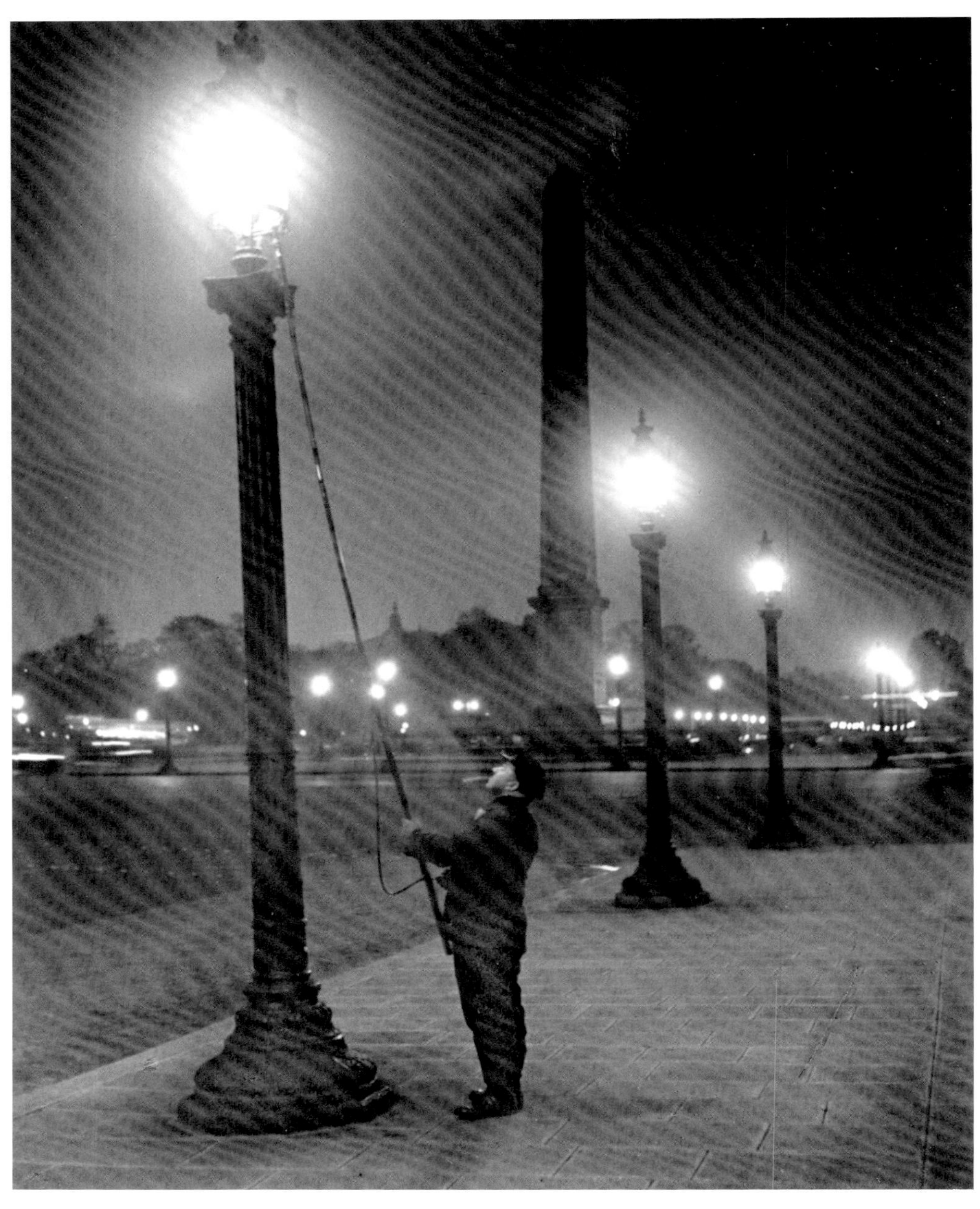

Brassaï (1899–1984)
Lamplighter, Place de la Concorde, c. 1930

Silver gelatin print, 29.7 × 23.5 cm

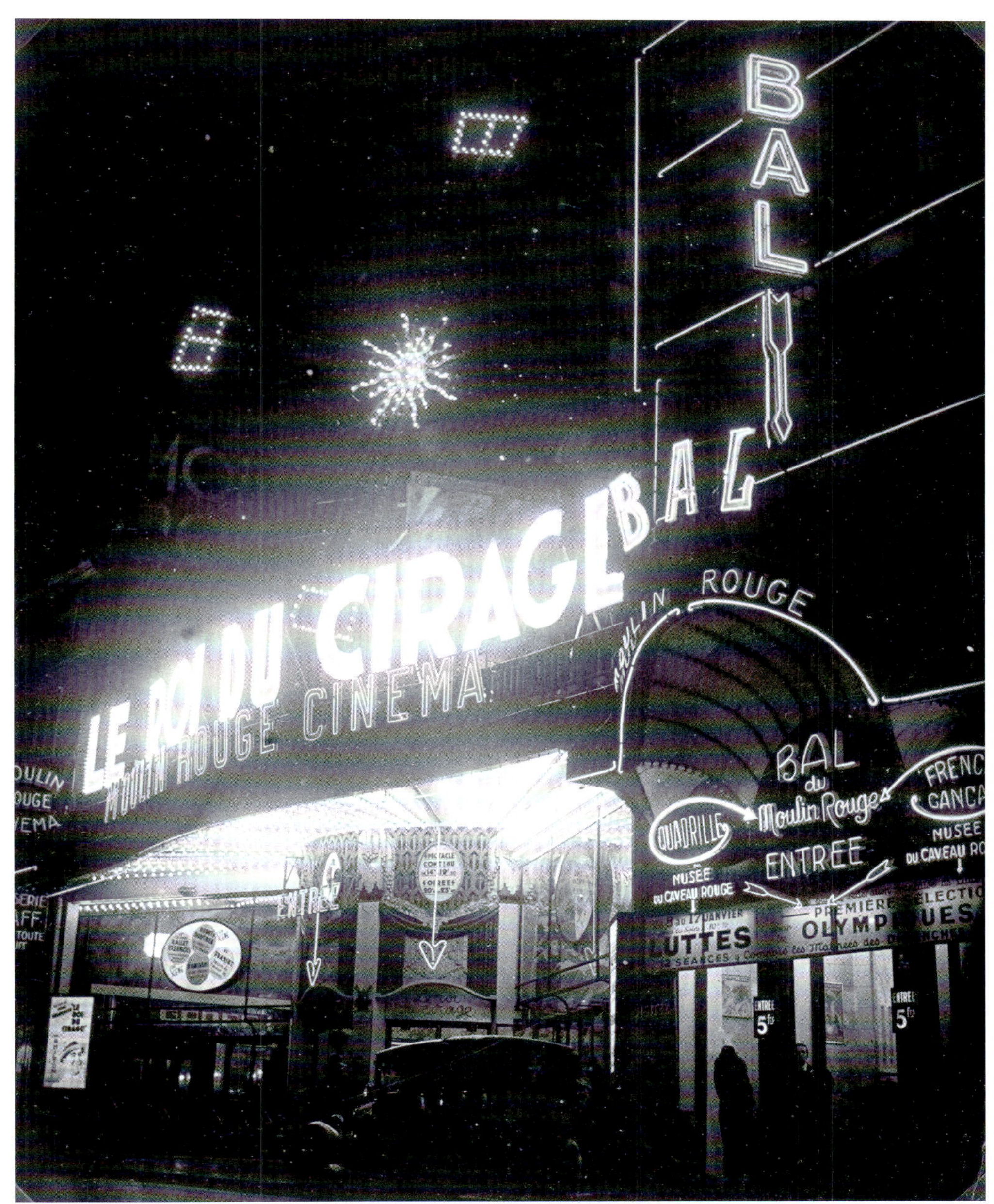

BAL
BAL
LE ROI DU CIRAGE
BAL
MOULIN ROUGE CINEMA
MOULIN ROUGE
MOULIN
ROUGE
CINEMA
BAL
du
Moulin Rouge
QUADRILLE
ENTREE
MUSÉE
DU CAVEAU ROUGE
FRENCH
CANCA
MUSÉE
DU CAVEAU R
ENTREE
PREMIÈRE
OLYMP
UES
LUTTES
ENTREE
5 frs
ENTREE
5 frs

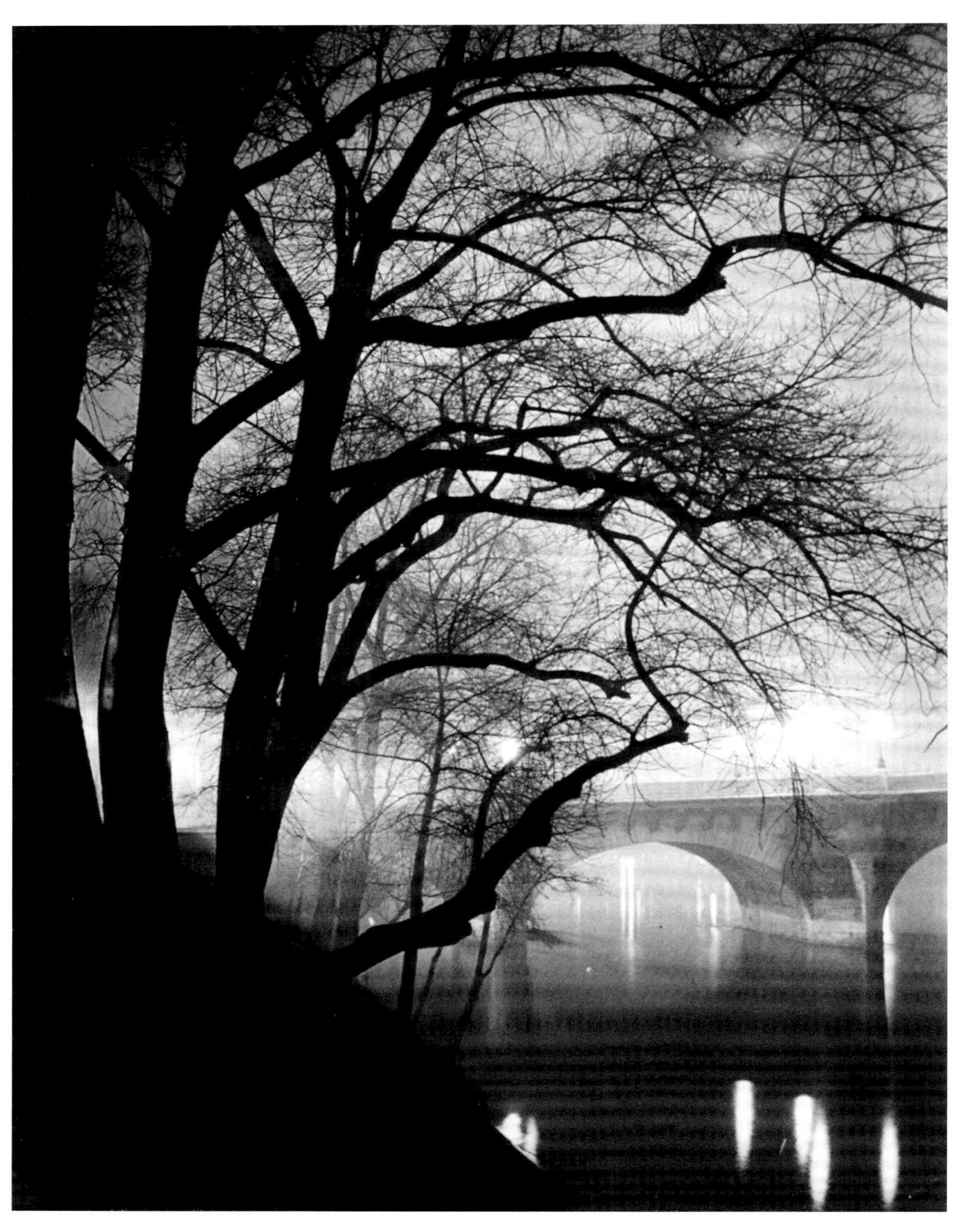

CAT. 65
Brassaï (1899–1984)
The Pont-Neuf at Night, c. 1932

Silver gelatin print, 30 × 22 cm

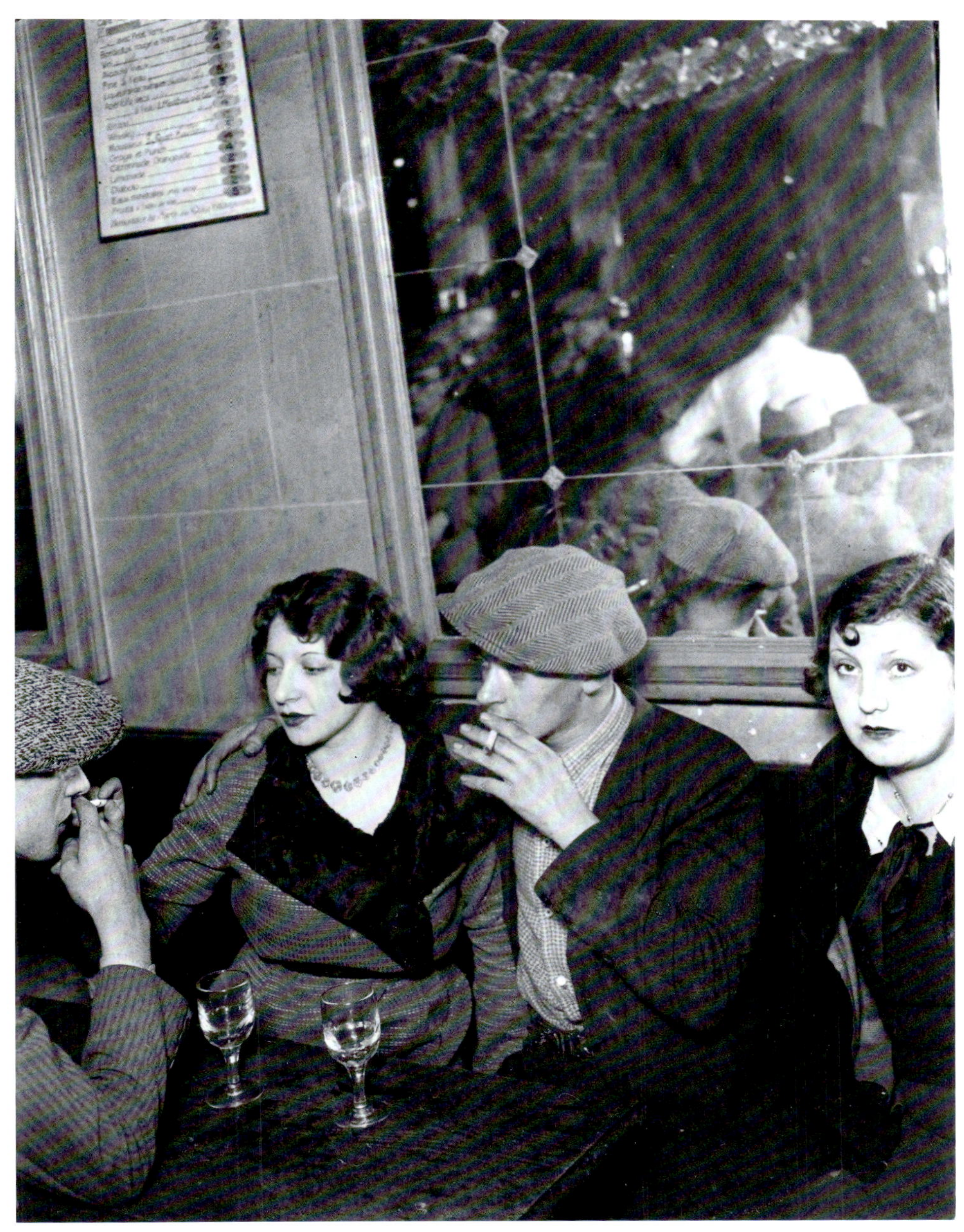

Brassaï (1899–1984)
The Quatre Saisons Bal Musette, Rue de Lappe, c. 1932

Silver gelatin print, 29 × 22 cm

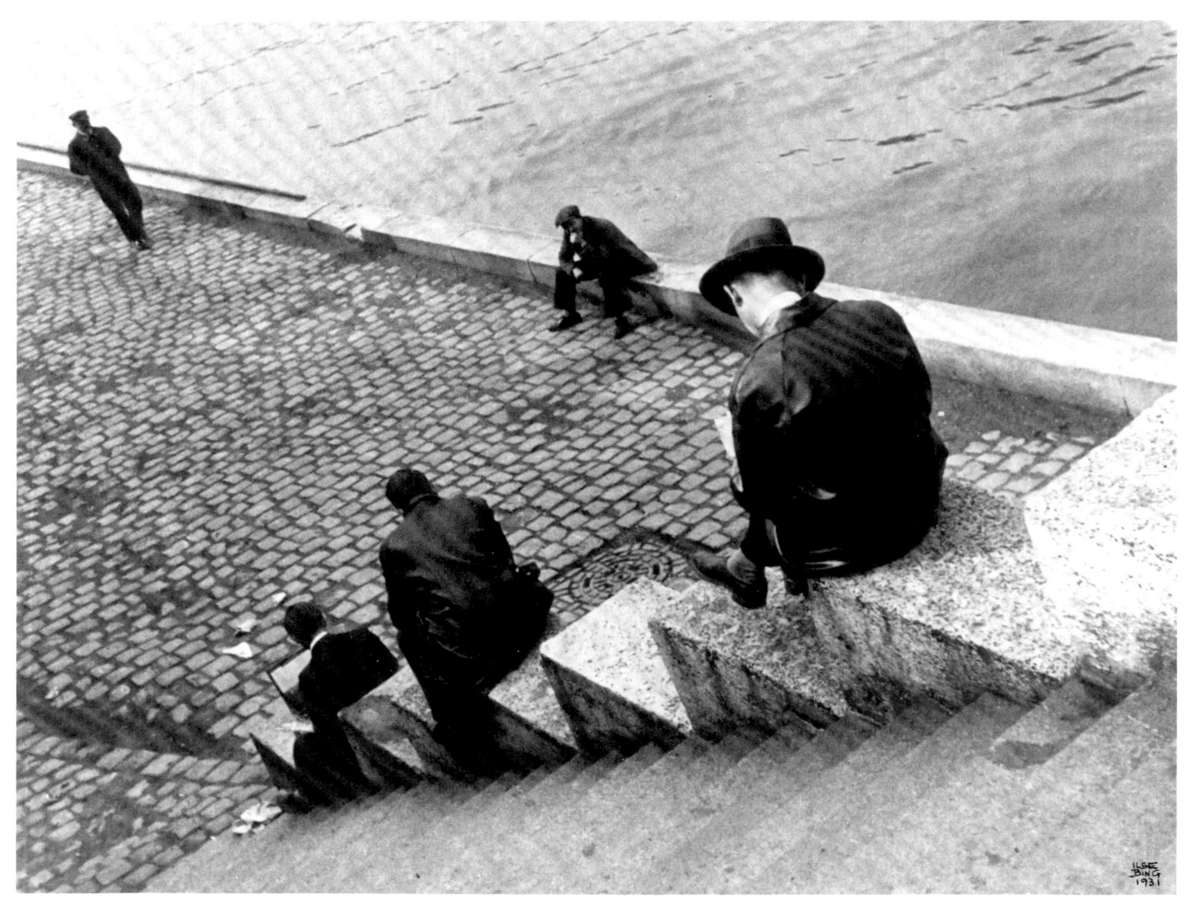

CAT. 67
Ilse Bing (1899–1998)
Paris, Three Men on Steps, 1931

Silver gelatin print, 27.8 × 35.5 cm

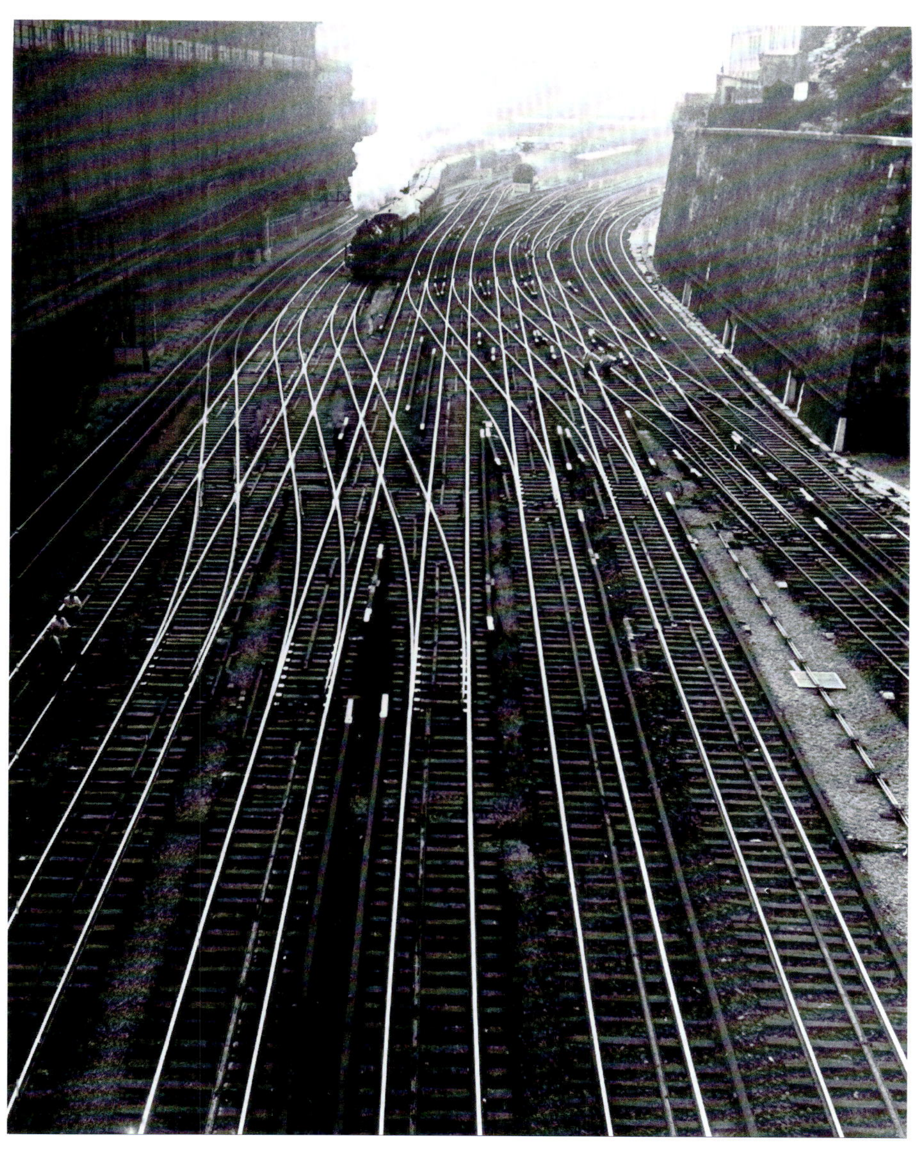

CAT. 68

Ergy Landau (1896–1967)
Saint-Lazare Railway Station, 1934

Silver gelatin print, 29 × 22.8 cm

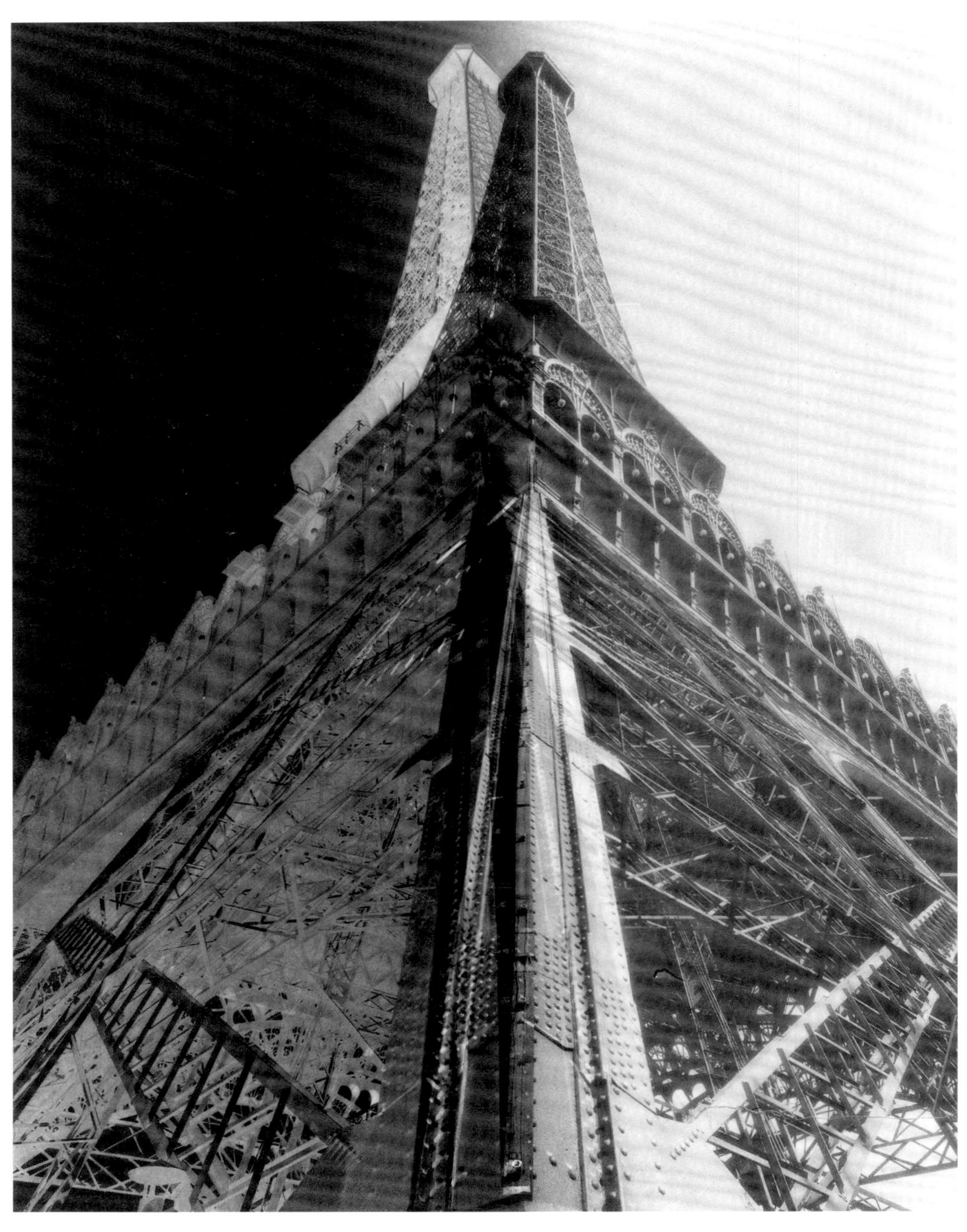

François Kollar (1904–79)
The Eiffel Tower, c. 1930

Silver gelatin print, 28.2 × 21.7 cm

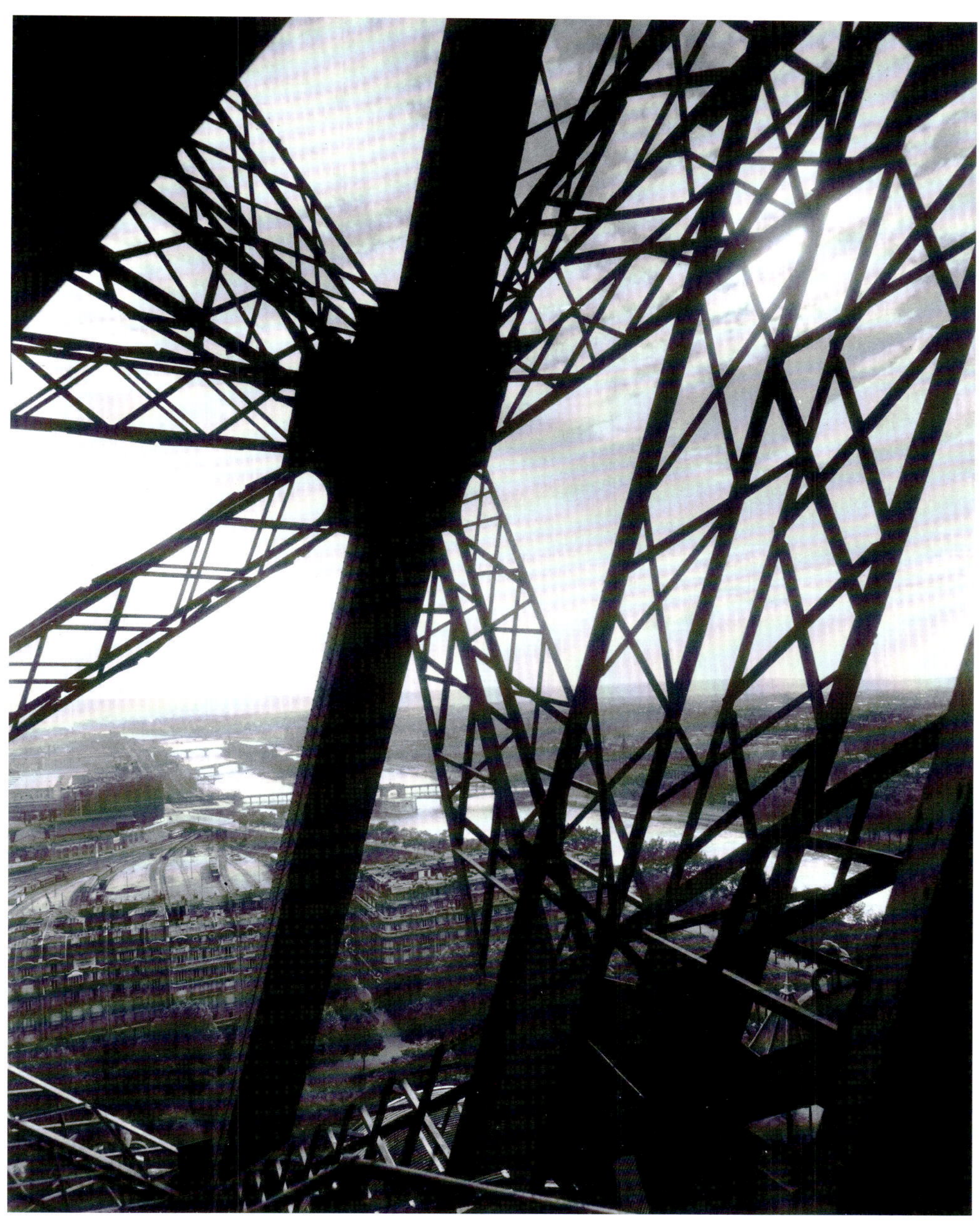

CAT. 70

François Kollar (1904–79)
Detail of the Structure of the Eiffel Tower, 1935

Silver gelatin print, 27.9 × 21.8 cm

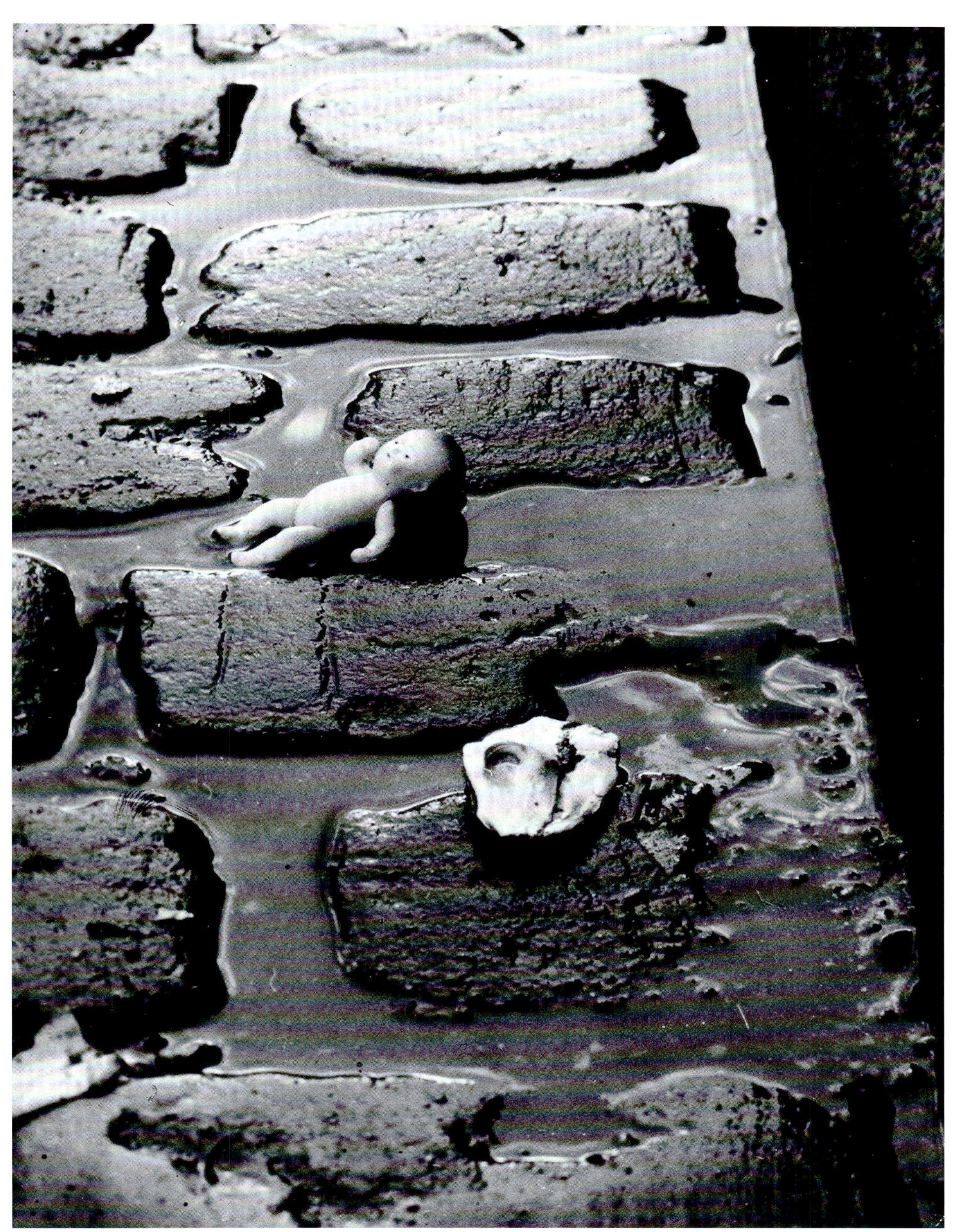

Wols (1913–51)
Doll on the Cobbles, 1938–39

Silver gelatin print, 23 × 17 cm

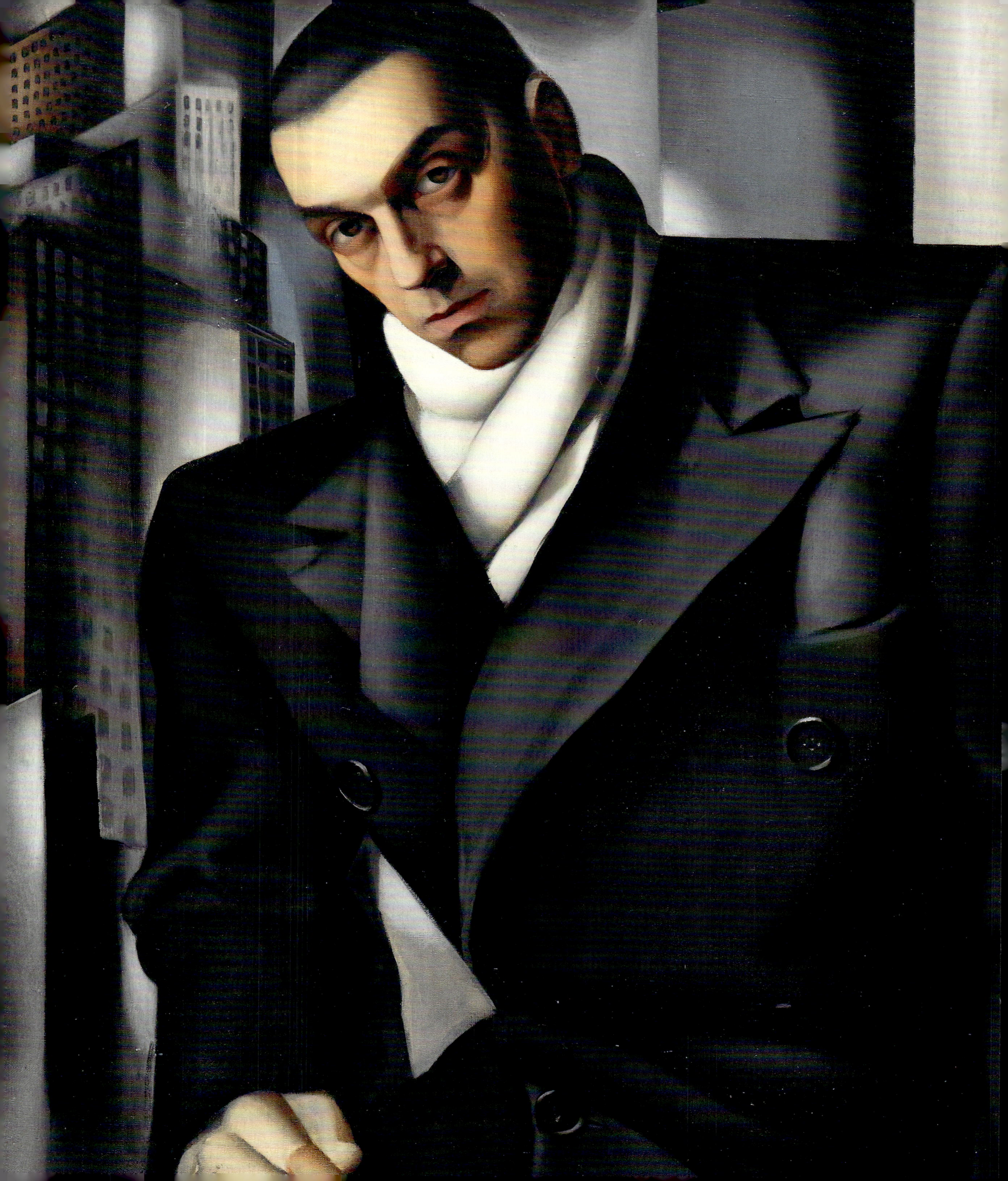

AROUND SOUTINE – PARISIAN PORTRAITS

Anna Hiddleston-Galloni

Many artists of the School of Paris dedicated their work to portraiture and figure studies. Drawn to the figure as a means of exploring notions of identity and selfhood, their interest in the pictorial genre was doubtless kindled by their feelings of displacement. Portraits by Soutine, Modigliani and Pascin also greatly contributed to a renewed treatment of the subject during this period which, depending on the artist, became a means of experimentation for a humanist expressionism, a refined stylisation or a more decorative mannerism.

An emblematic figure of the Montparnasse circle, Soutine often chose his models from the working classes, such as cooks, bell boys or waiters. His feverish expressionism depicted in restless brushstrokes and thick facture recalls portraits by Van Gogh, whose influence combined with Soutine's love for the Old Masters such as Rembrandt or El Greco he saw at the Louvre. Like the Mexican artist Diego Rivera in 1913 and Modigliani in 1916, Soutine chose to paint his friend the sculptor Oscar Miestchaninoff in 1923, also of Byelorussian origin, with whom he first lodged at the Cité Falguière when he arrived in Paris. In Soutine's painting, the subject with pouting mouth, fleshy face and distorted torso seems animated by an exaggerated expressivity [CAT. 72].

Pascin's portrait of his German dealer Alfred Flechtheim dressed as a toreador [CAT. 78] differs greatly in mood from this pictorial expressionism. It is both humorous and tender. The dealer's pinched mouth seems to hold back a laugh, and the pearly greys and ochres defy the garishness of his costume. Kees van Dongen's portraits offer yet another approach. He began his career as a fashion portrait painter after his encounter in 1916 with Jasmy Jacob, who worked as a model for the chic fashion house "Maison Jenny" on the Champs Élysées. Presented by Van Dongen at the Salon de la Société Nationale des Beaux-Arts in 1920, this monumental portrait of the woman who was to become his lover [CAT. 80] portrays her wearing a dress glittering with jewels and sequins applied in blobs of paint straight from the tube. Her expression is cold and inspires little empathy, her hand rests like a claw against her hip. It indicates, perhaps, the former anarchist's implicit criticism of the world she embodied.

At the end of the 1920s, the Polish artist Tamara de Lempicka endowed the genre with an Art-Deco feel. Though loosely tied to the geometrical aesthetic of Cubism – she was taught by André Lhote at the Académie de la Grande-Chaumière shortly after arriving in Paris in 1916 – her portrait of her daughter, Kizette, *Girl in a Green Dress*, 1927 [CAT. 81], transforms the young girl's mannerist silhouette into that of a sculpted goddess, a symbol of modern woman's recent independence.

Finally, in 1933, the same year Adolf Hitler rose to power, Max Beckmann rendered a rather ironic and caricatured portrait of a Frenchman [CAT. 83] decked out with pipe and moustache. Painted from memory in his Frankfurt studio, this anonymous man he met on the train led to a painting that reveals the artist's mixed feelings about his stay in the French city he had just left – without a penny in his pocket.

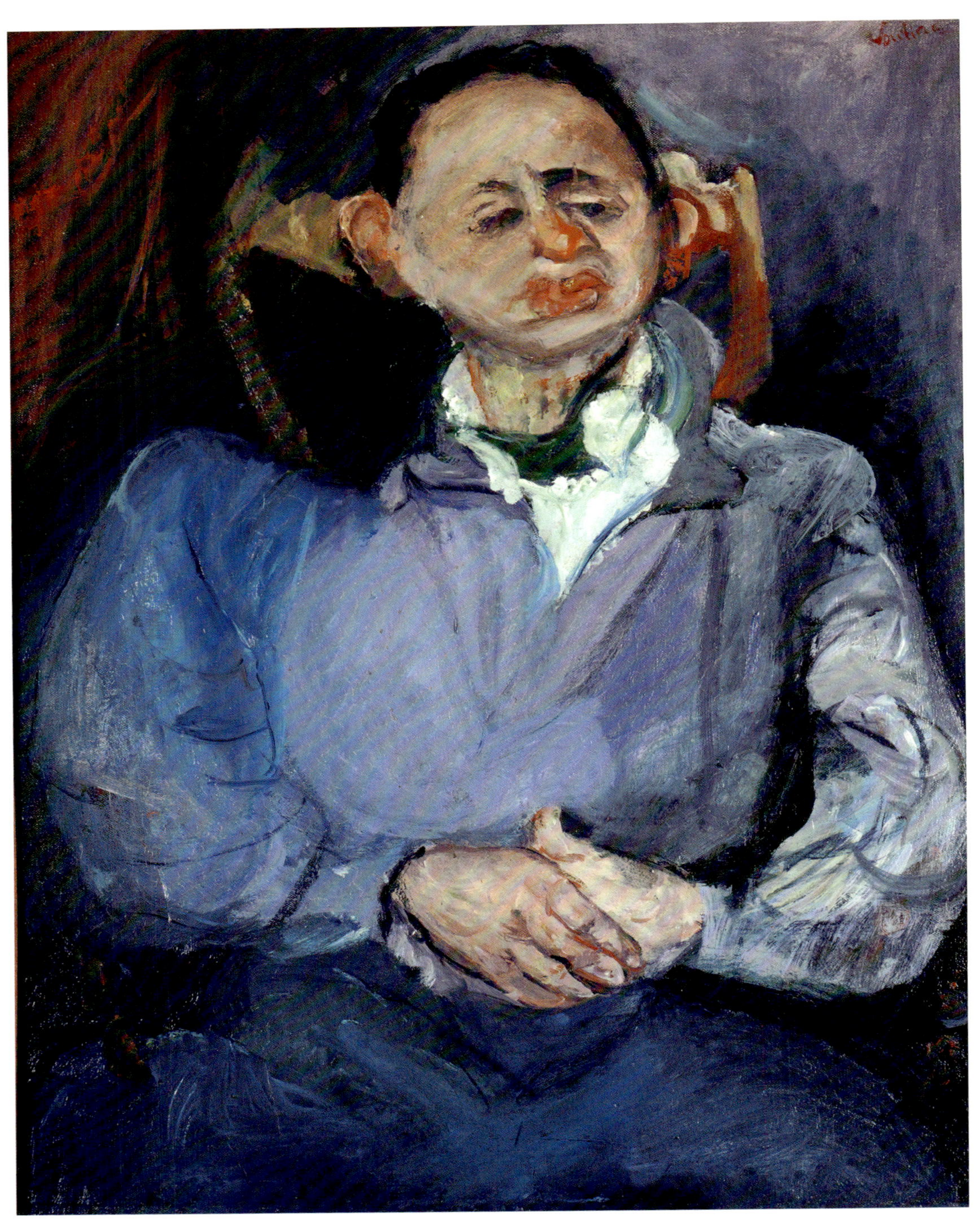

CAT. 72
Chaïm Soutine (1893–1943)
The Sculptor Oscar Mieſtchaninoff, 1923–24

Oil on canvas, 83 × 65 cm

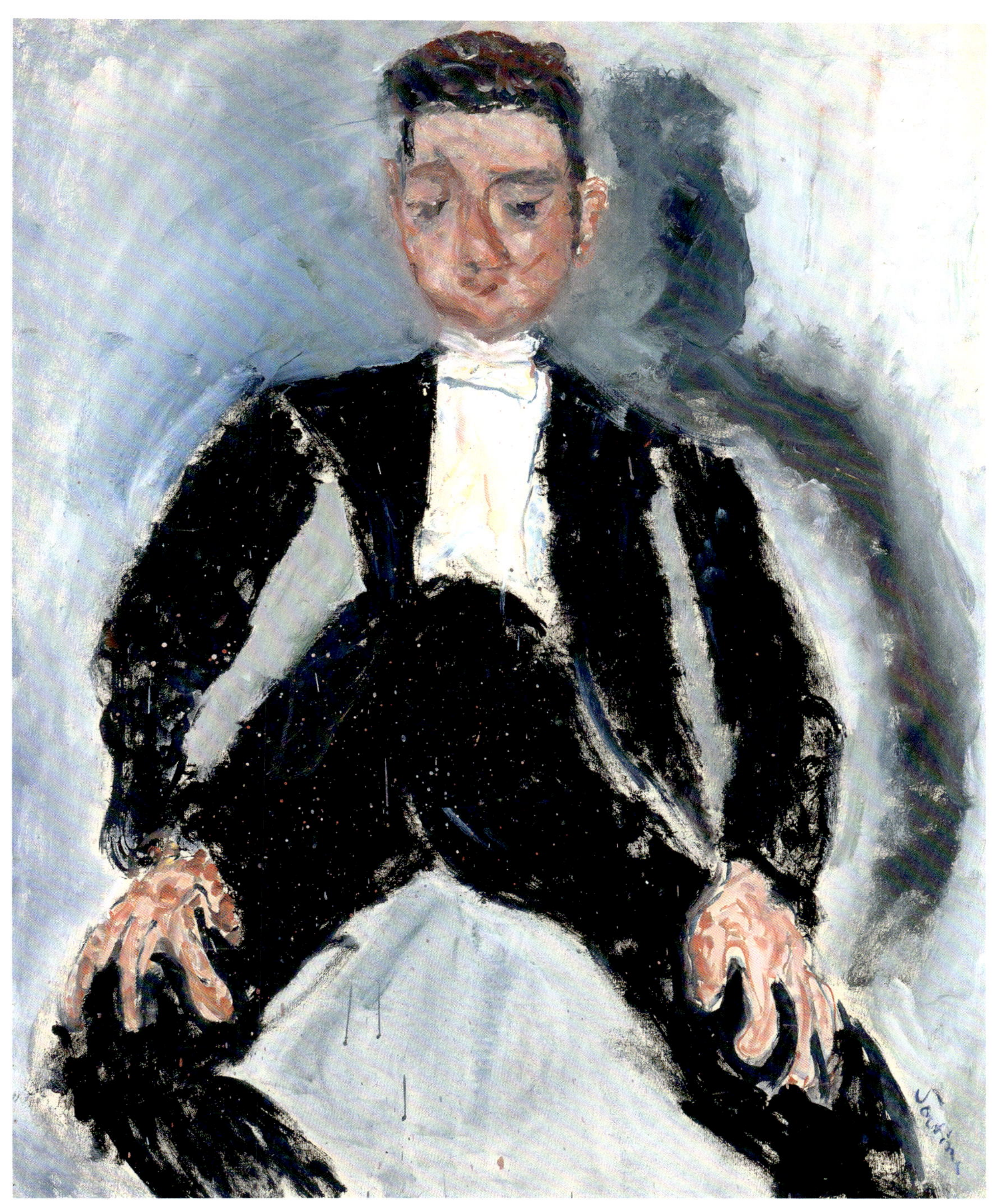

CAT. 73

Chaïm Soutine (1893–1943)
The Best Man, 1924–25

Oil on canvas, 100 × 81 cm

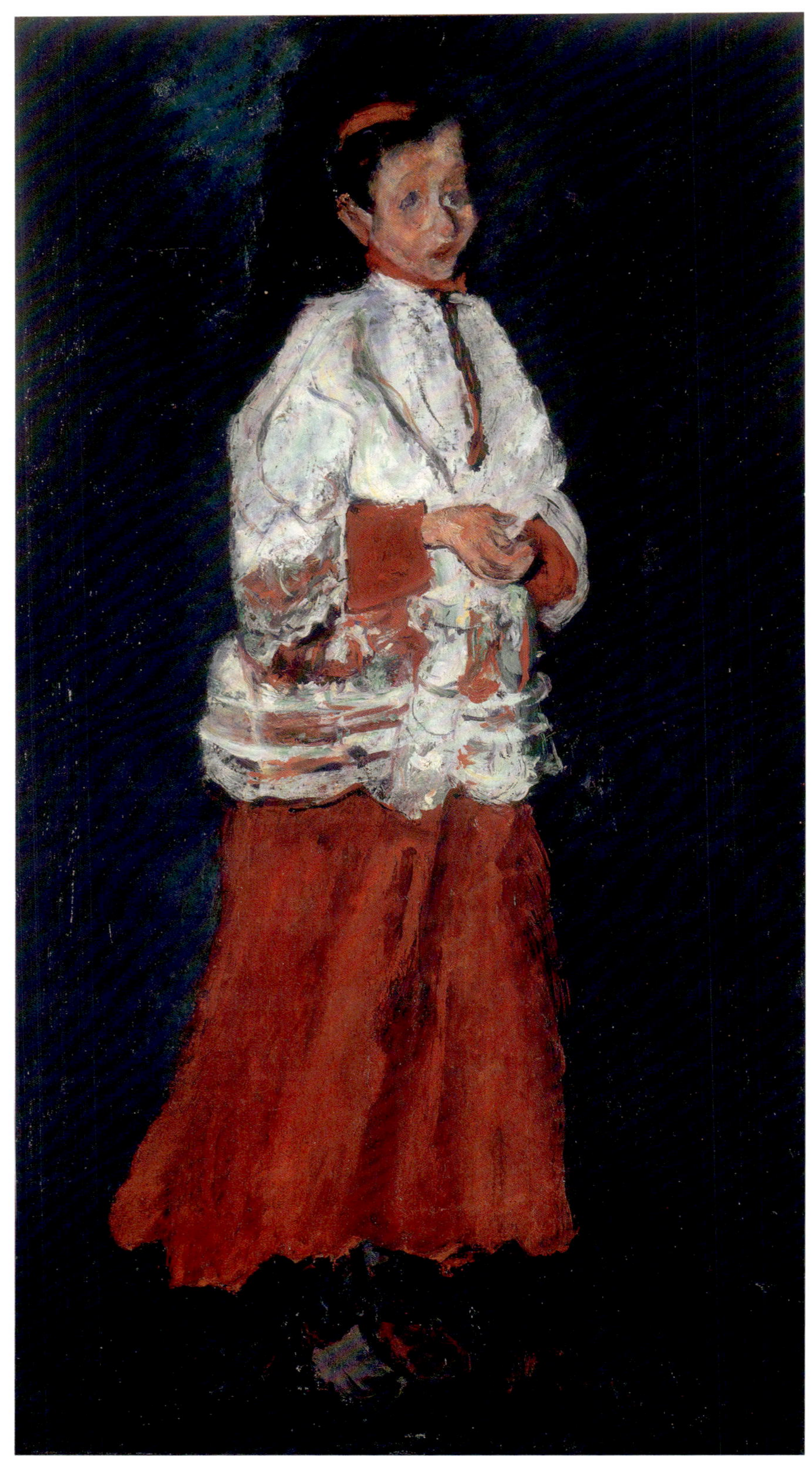

CAT. 74
Chaïm Soutine (1893–1943)
The Head Altar Boy, 1925

Oil on canvas, 100 × 55.9 cm

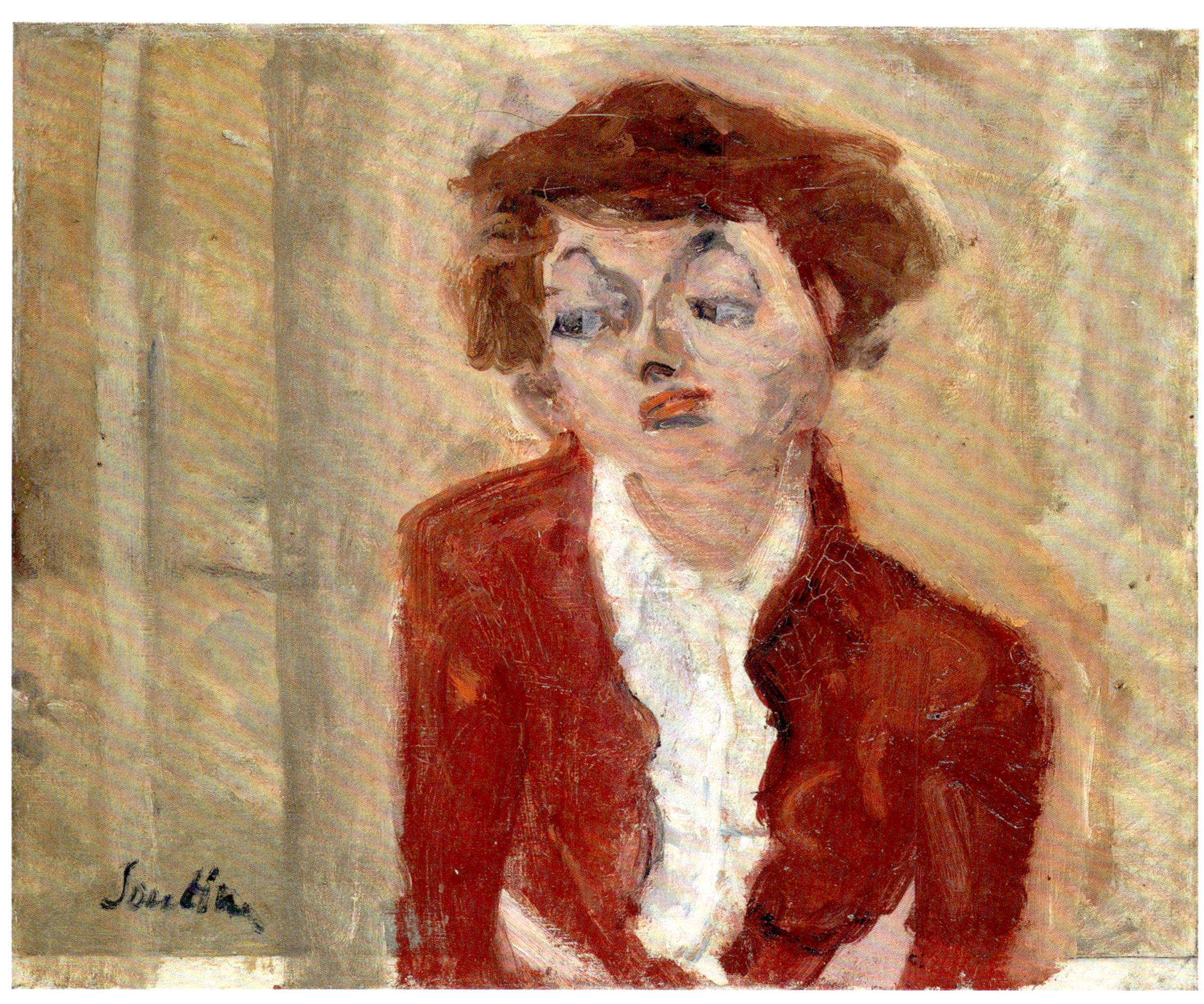

CAT. 75

Chaïm Soutine (1893–1943)
The Young English Girl, c. 1934

Oil on canvas, 46 × 65 cm

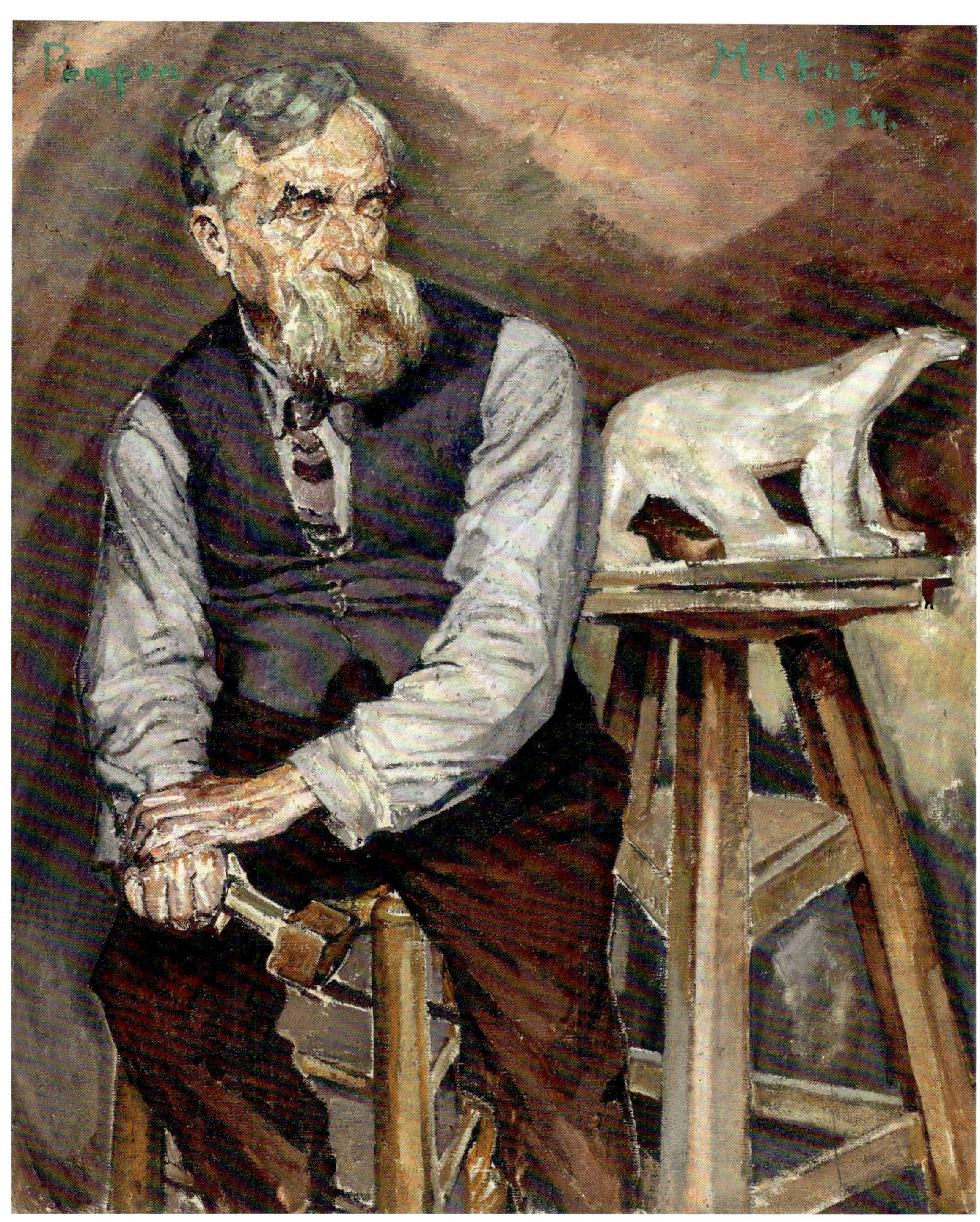

CAT. 76

Mela Muter (1876–1967)
The Sculptor François Pompon, 1924

Oil on canvas, 146 × 114 cm

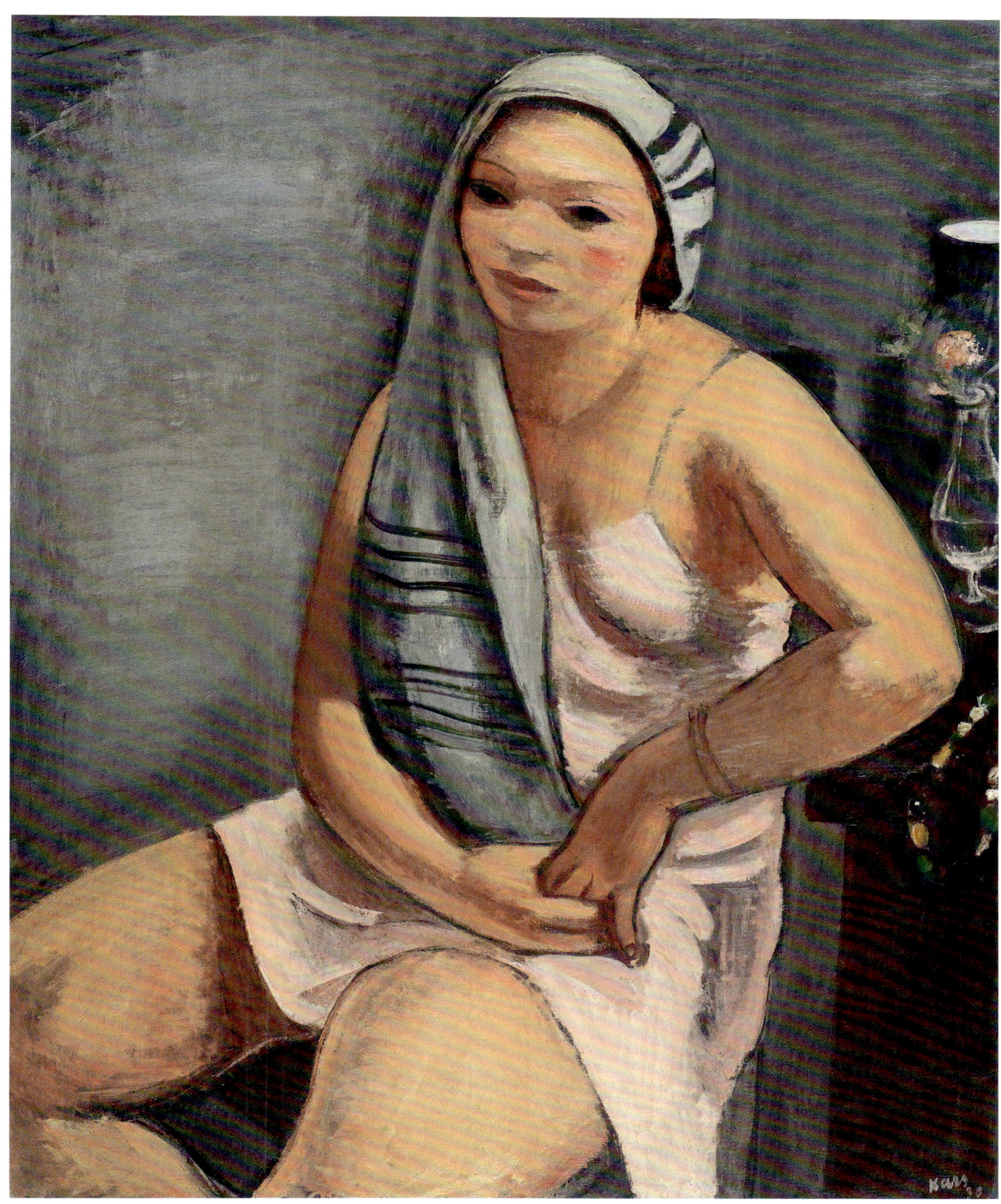

CAT. 77

Georges Kars (1882–1945)
Woman with a Grey Shawl, 1930

Oil on canvas, 100 × 81 cm

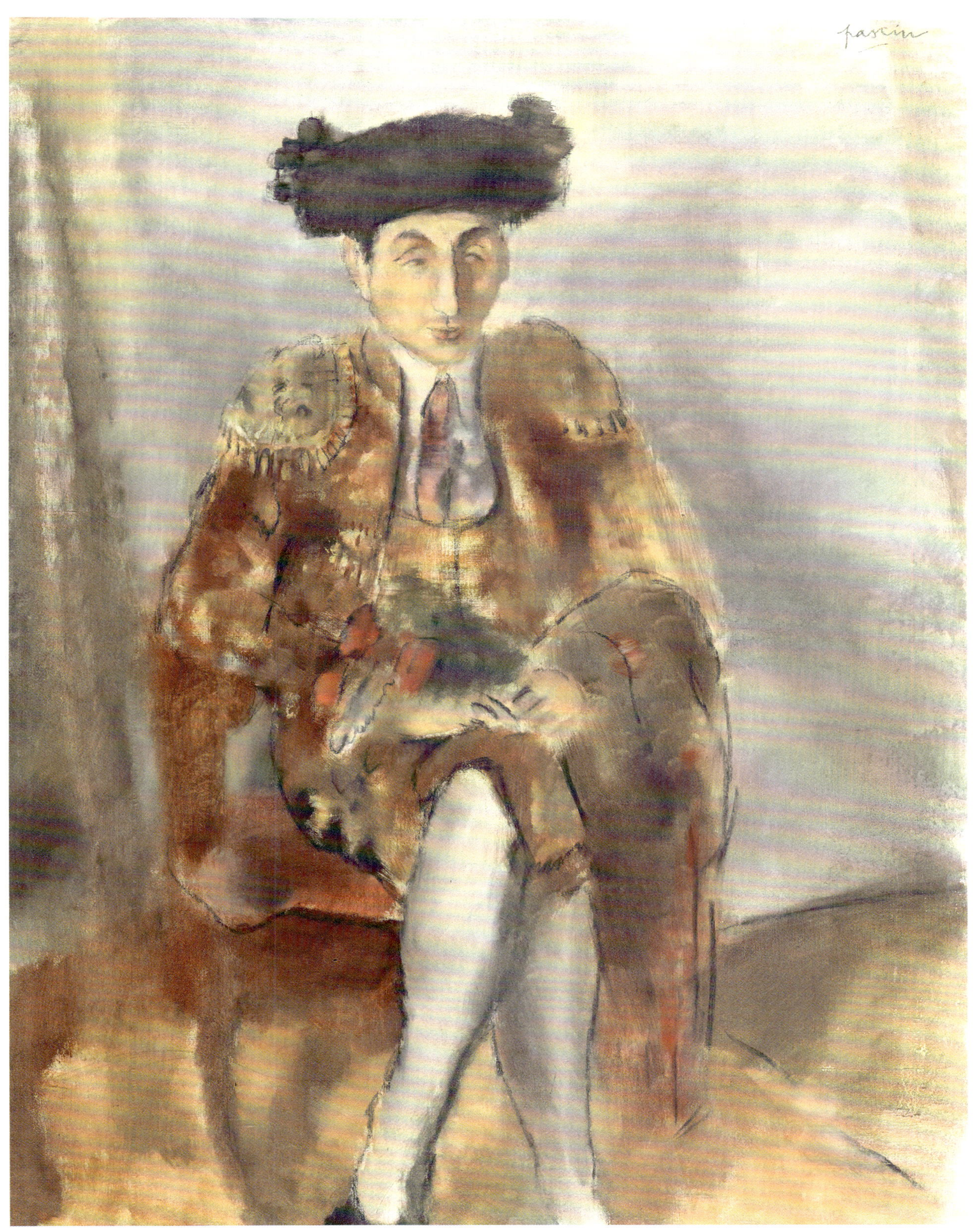

CAT. 78

Jules Pascin (1885–1930)
Alfred Flechtheim Dressed as a Toreador, 1925

Oil on canvas, 104 × 80 cm

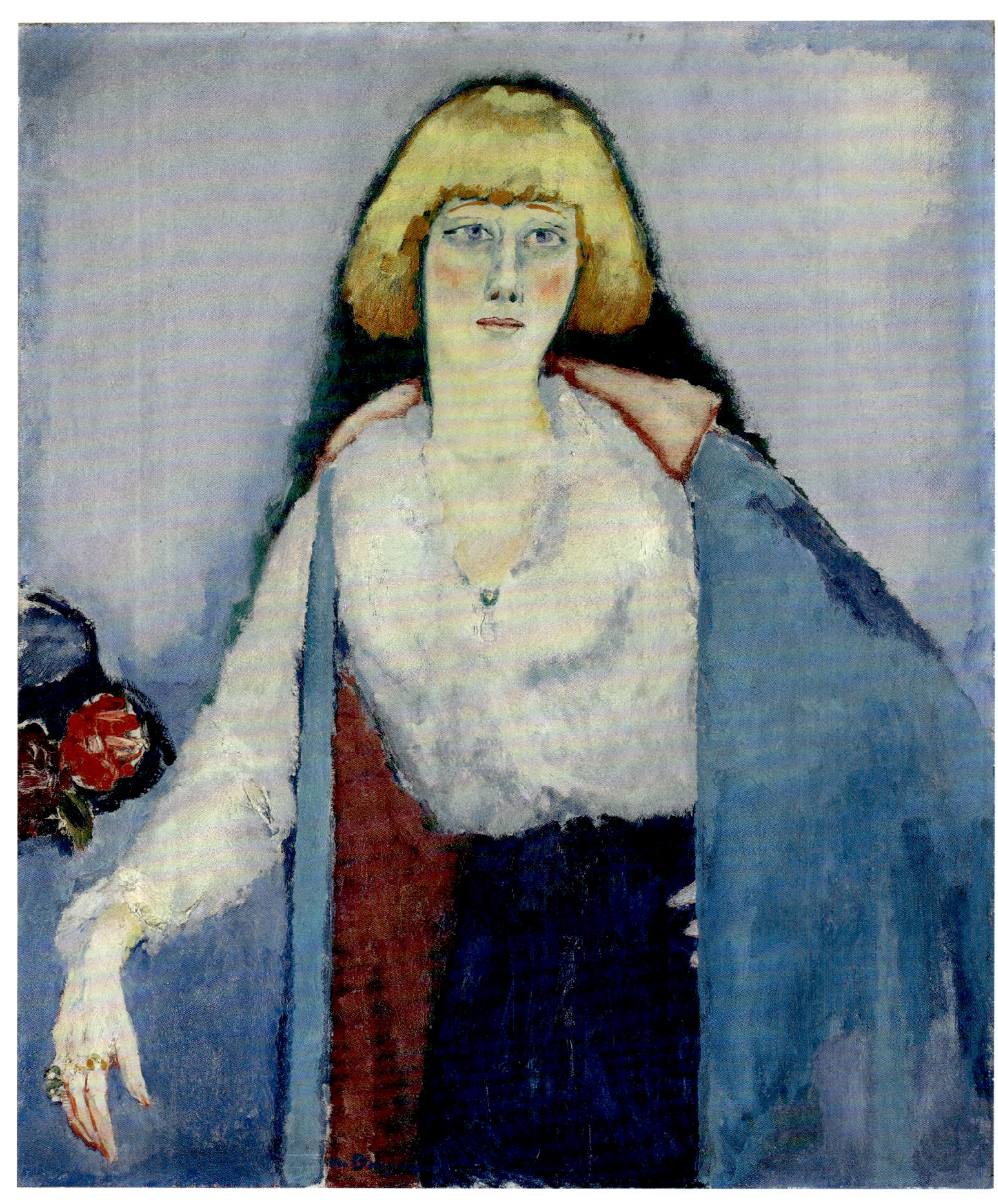

CAT. 79
Kees van Dongen (1877–1968)
Billy, c. 1920

Oil on canvas, 100 × 81 cm

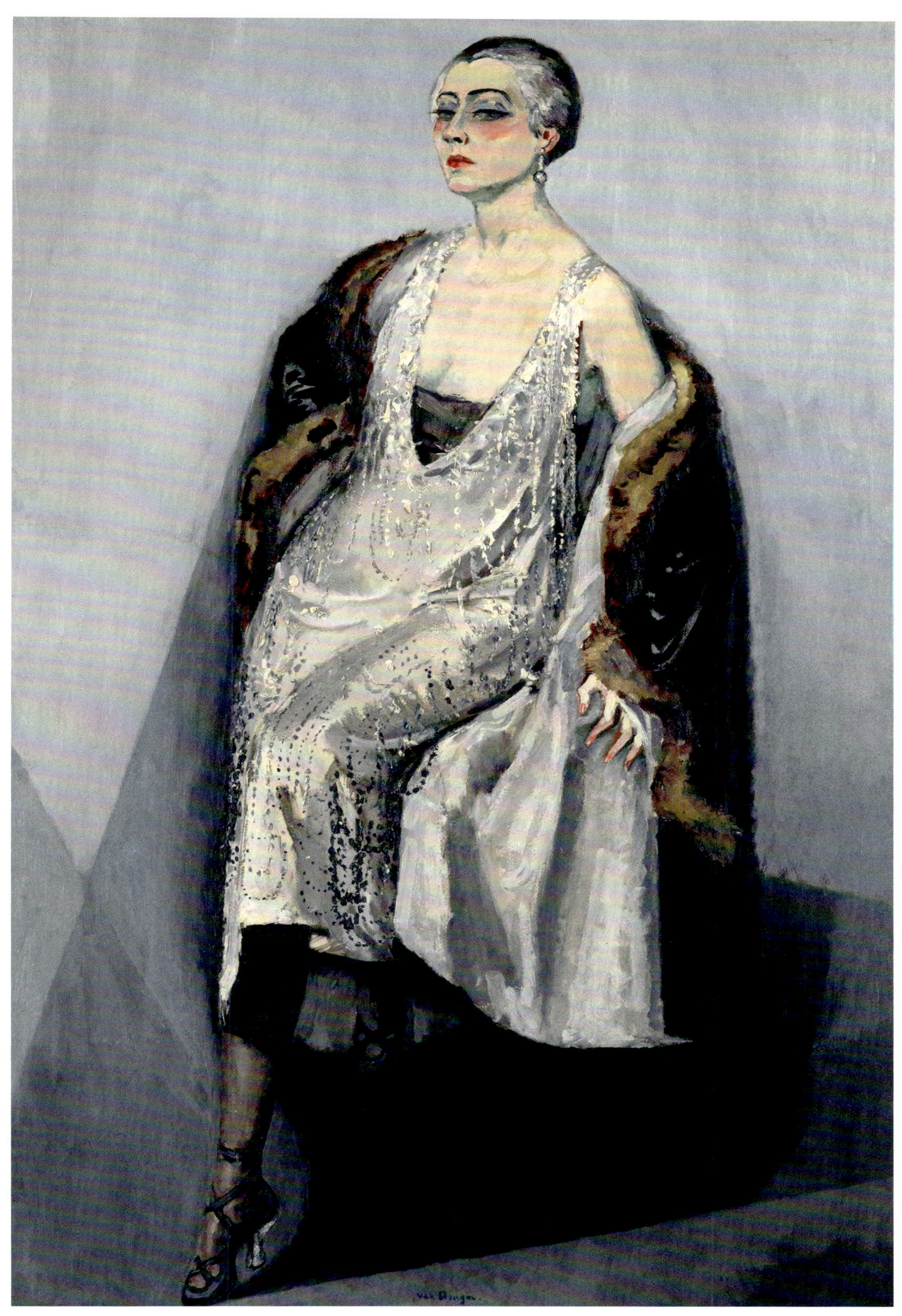

CAT. 80
Kees van Dongen (1877–1968)
Jasmy Jacob, 1920

Oil on canvas, 195 × 131.5 cm

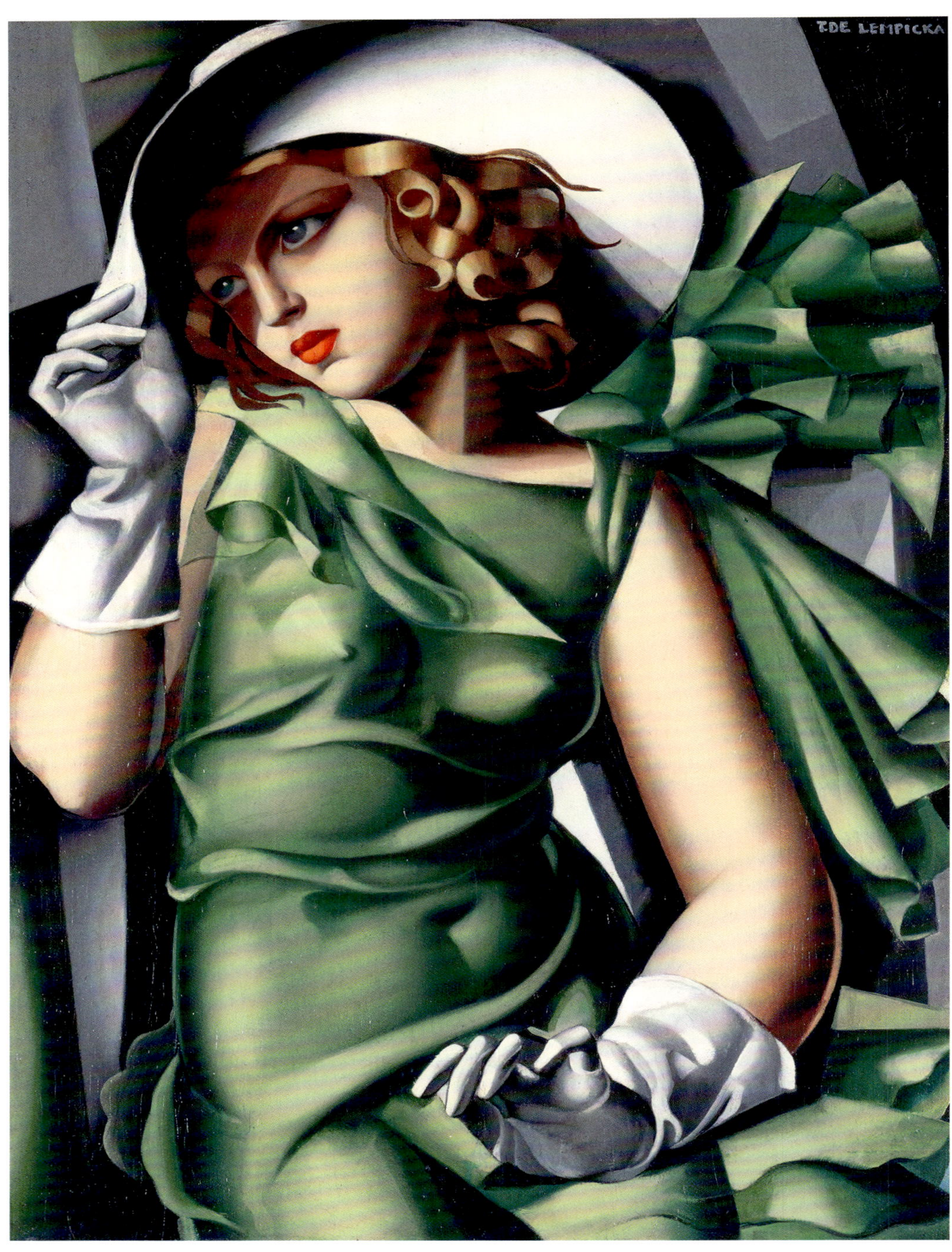

CAT. 81

Tamara de Lempicka (1898–1980)
Girl in a Green Dress, 1927–30

Oil on wood, 61.5 × 45.5 cm

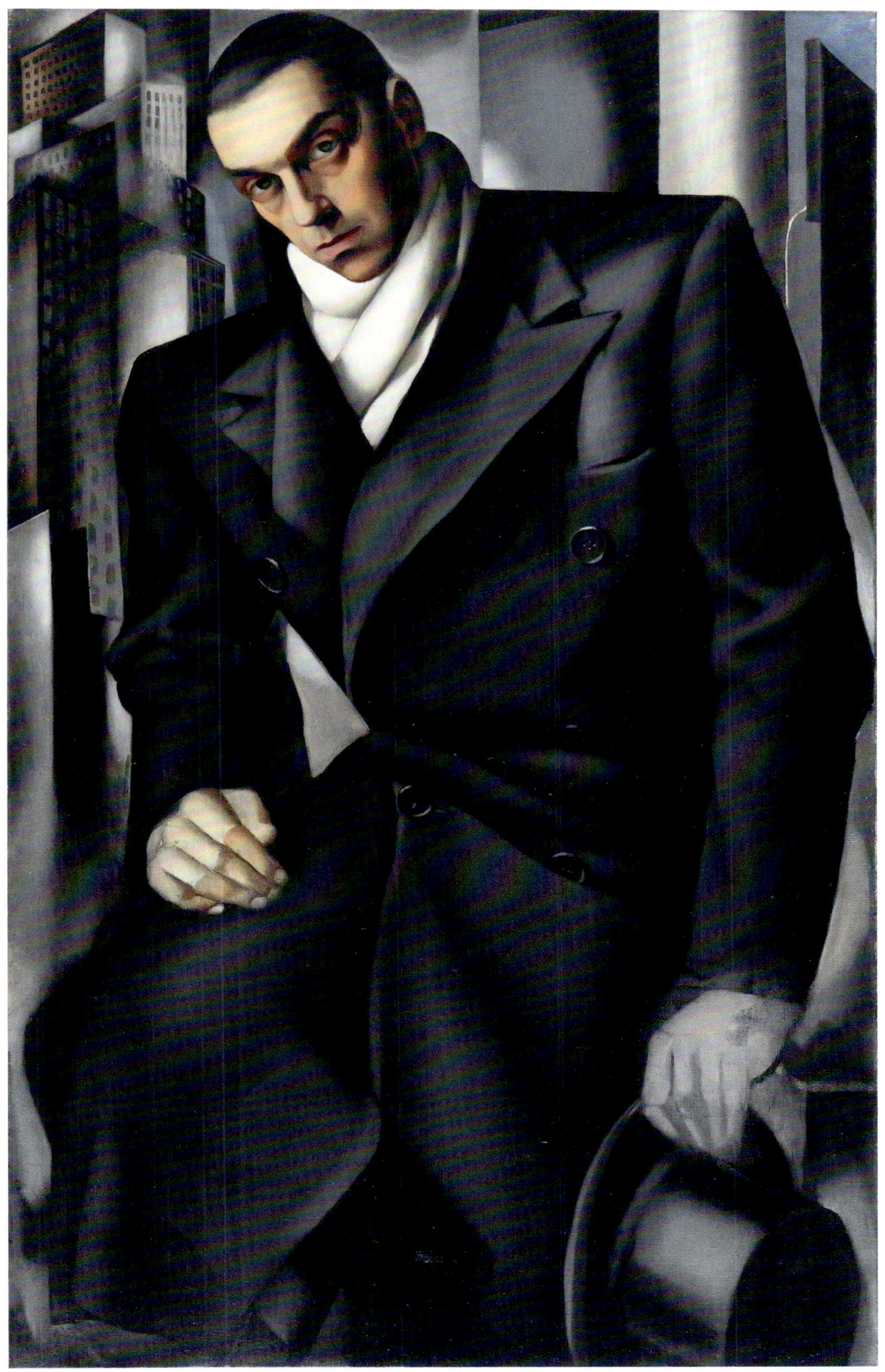

CAT. 82

Tamara de Lempicka (1898–1980)
Thadeus Lempicki, 1928

Oil on canvas, 130 × 80.5 cm

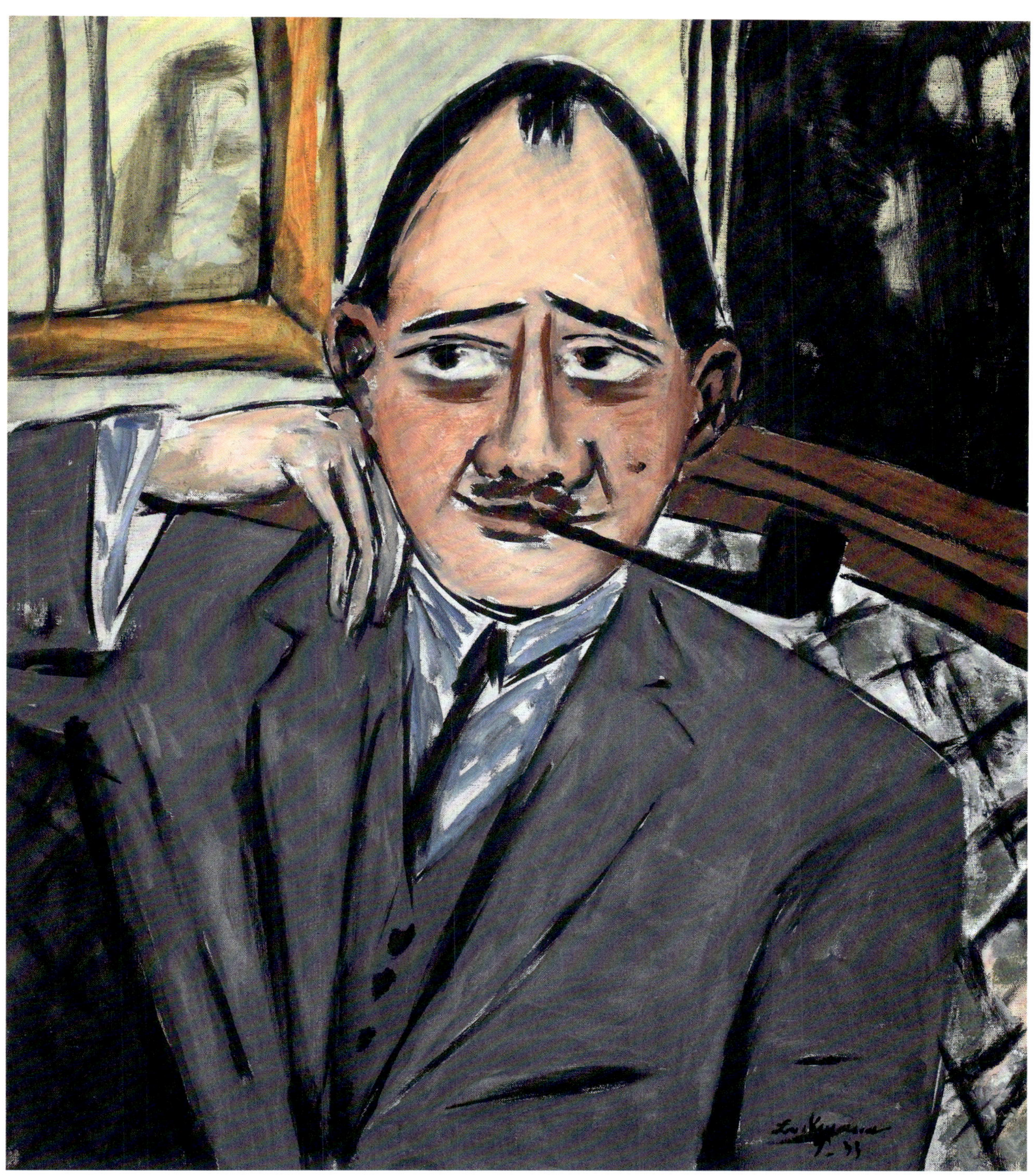

Max Beckmann (1884–1950)
Portrait of a Frenchman, 1933

Oil on canvas, 70 × 60 cm

APPENDICES

CHRONOLOGY

NATHALIE ERNOULT

WITH THE ASSISTANCE OF INÈS LASSALE

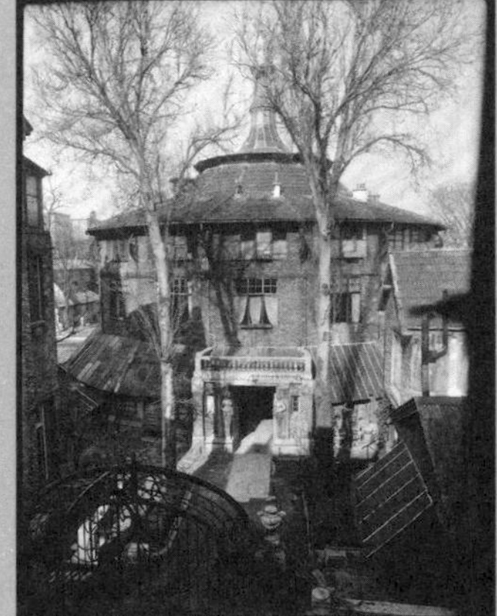

La Ruche, 1968
Photograph by Walter Limot
Paris, Musée Carnavalet, Ph 15410

1900

- **October:** the Paris World's Fair (Exposition Universelle) sees Pablo Picasso make his first visit to Paris.
- **October:** the Dutch painter Kees van Dongen, who first visited Paris in 1897 and settled there in 1899, does all the drawings for an issue of satirical weekly picture magazine *L'Assiette au beurre*, entitled "Petite histoire pour petits et grands nenfants [*sic*]", recounting the sad fate of an unmarried mother.
- **Autumn:** the Académie de La Palette art school opens in Montparnasse.
- **December:** Van Dongen moves to the Impasse Girardon in Montmartre.
- Russian painter Serge Férat and his cousin Baroness Hélène d'Oettingen arrive in Paris after visiting Florence.

1901

- **May:** Picasso visits Paris a second time.
- **June:** Picasso's first exhibition in Paris, with Spanish painter Francisco Iturrino, at Galerie Ambroise Vollard, 6 Rue Lafitte, Paris IX.
- The Cité des Fourneaux, a cul-de-sac of artists' studios adjacent to the Institut Pasteur, is renamed Cité Falguière; many foreign artists are among the tenants.
- Polish painter Mela Muter moves to Paris.
- Wealthy Americans also settle in Paris, enticed by the quality of life as well as its reputation for luxury, fashion and the arts.

NOTE

This chronology focuses on foreign artists in Paris, specifically on those who feature in the exhibition. Russian artists are identified by their region of origin when it corresponds today to a country other than Russia.

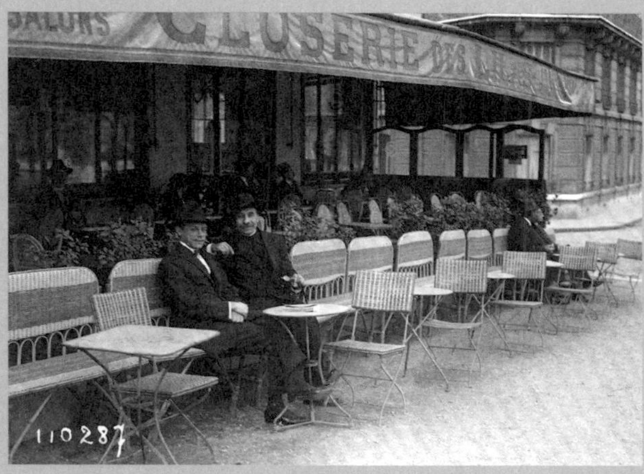

Paul Fort (right) on the terrace at La Closerie des Lilas, 1920
Photograph by Maurice-Louis Branger
Roger-Viollet, BRA-110287

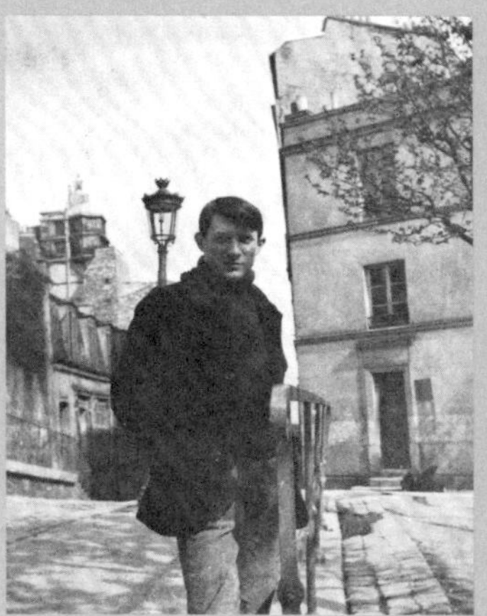

Pablo Picasso on the Place Ravignan in Montmartre, 1904
Unknown photographer
Paris, Musée National Picasso-Paris
Paris, Musée National Picasso-Paris, APPH15301

1902

- **January:** Czech painter František Kupka, living in Paris since 1896, illustrates an entire issue of *L'Assiette au beurre*.
- **December:** American art collector Leo Stein moves into an apartment at 27 Rue de Fleurus, Paris VI. He is joined a few months later by his sister, the writer Gertrude Stein.
- Sculptor Alfred Boucher opens the La Ruche studio complex on Passage Dantzig in the Vaugirard neighbourhood; the very cheap rents allow penniless foreign artists to gain a foothold in Montparnasse.
- The young German banker Daniel-Henry Kahnweiler moves to Paris and becomes a gallerist.
- Polish painter Eugeniusz Zak arrives in Paris to study under academic painter Jean-Léon Gérôme at the École Nationale des Beaux-Arts (National School of Fine Art).

1903

- **April:** the unsolved murder of a Christian boy prompts three days of anti-Jewish rioting in Kishinev in then Bessarabia, leaving hundreds killed and injured. The first of a long series of pogroms that takes place in the Pale of Settlement and elsewhere in the Russian Empire between 1905 and 1907. These events sees many Jews forced into exile.
- **October:** establishment of the Salon d'Automne, first held at the Petit Palais and then at the Grand Palais. Like the Salon des Indépendants founded in 1884, this annual exhibition openly embraces modernism.
- Café La Rotonde opens at 105 Boulevard du Montparnasse.
- La Closerie des Lilas reopens in a building recently constructed at 171 Boulevard du Montparnasse. The cafe will soon be frequented by many of the leading figures of the artistic community, particularly the literary circle of Paris, who gather around the poet and dramatist Paul Fort.
- Arrival in Paris of Polish painter Ludwig Markus (who will take the name Louis Marcoussis in 1912) and German painter Max Beckmann.

1904

- **February:** Van Dongen participates in the Salon des Indépendants for the first time; he will also exhibit at the Salon d'Automne later in the year.
- **April:** Picasso moves into the Bateau-Lavoir, a building converted to studios on the Butte Montmartre.
- **July:** arriving in Paris, Romanian sculptor Constantin Brancusi takes a studio at 9 Cité Condorcet, Paris IX.
- **November:** Van Dongen has his first solo show in Paris at Galerie Ambroise Vollard.
- German art dealer Wilhelm Uhde moves to the French capital and he buys works by Picasso and Georges Braque, as well those of the self-taught painter Henri Rousseau, known as Douanier Rousseau.
- Swiss painter Martha Stettler founds the Académie de la Grande-Chaumière, near Montparnasse, attended by many foreign artists.

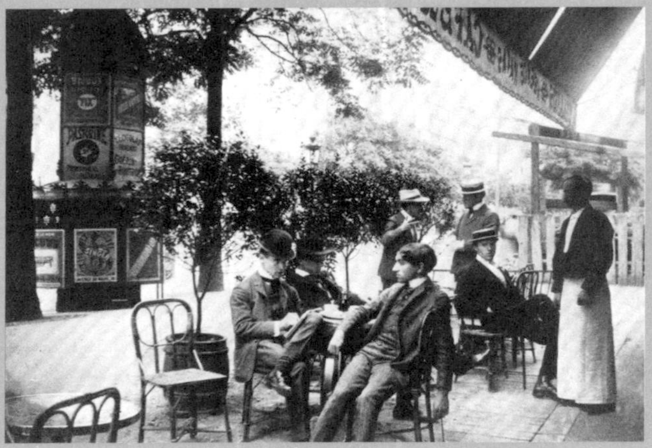

Jules Pascin (front) on the
terrace at Le Dôme,
Paris, 1906
Unknown photographer
Paris, Centre Pompidou,
MNAM-CCI, Bibliothèque
Kandinsky

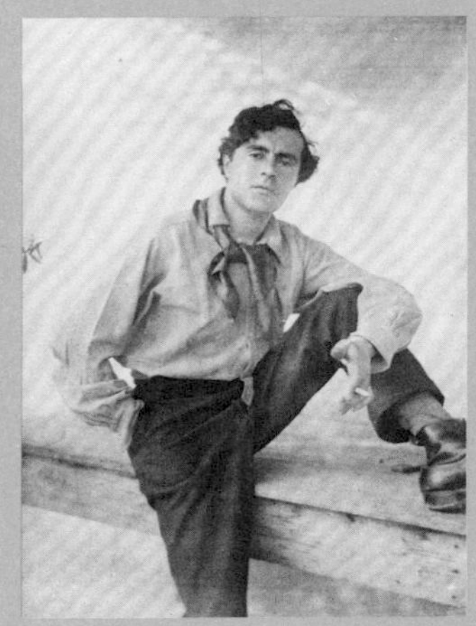

Amedeo Modigliani in his studio
in Montparnasse, around 1909
Unknown photographer
Paris, Centre Pompidou, MNAM-
CCI, Bibliothèque Kandinsky,
Fonds Marc Vaux

1905

- **22 January:** revolution breaks out in Russia after Czar Nicholas II's troops fire on a huge demonstration demanding social and political reforms. When the protest is shut down by military force, many rebels (Lenin among them) take refuge in Paris, mainly in the XIIIth and XIVth arrondissements.
- **March:** Serge Férat participates in the Salon des Indépendants for the first time, under the name of Roudnieff; Mela Muter is another first-time exhibitor.
- **October:** Marcoussis participates in the Salon d'Automne for the first time, where the work of the Fauves – Van Dongen among them – causes a scandal.
- **Autumn:** Polish-Italian poet Guillaume Apollinaire meets Picasso for the first time at the Bateau-Lavoir.
- **December:** arriving in Paris from Munich, the Bulgarian painter Jules Pascin finds accommodation on Rue Delambre in Montparnasse. He frequents the café Le Dôme, opened in 1898, a meeting point for German-speaking artists and intellectuals.
- The Hungarian painter Alfred Reth, newly arrived from Budapest, takes up residence in Montparnasse.

1906

- **January:** arriving from Venice, the Livorno-born painter and sculptor Amedeo Modigliani rents a studio on Rue Caulaincourt in Montmartre.
- **March:** Marcoussis participates in the Salon des Indépendants for the first time.
- **June:** the Russian artist Vassily Kandinsky settles in Sèvres, near Paris, with his partner, the German painter Gabriele Münter.
- **September:** the Spanish artist Juan Gris arrives in Paris and takes a room at the Hôtel Caulaincourt in Montmartre.
- **October:** Kupka, Brancusi and the still Moscow-based Russian artist Natalia Goncharova exhibit for the first time in the Salon d'Automne. Goncharova comes to Paris for the Salon.
- **Autumn:** Ukrainian artist Sonia Terk (the future Sonia Delaunay) arrives in Paris to settle there permanently.
- **November:** on arriving in Paris, the Portuguese painter and draughtsman Amadeo de Souza-Cardoso rents a live-in studio in Montparnasse.
- Arrival in Paris of Byelorussian sculptor Oscar Miestchaninoff, who takes a studio in the Cité Falguière.
- Picasso paints the *Portrait of Gertrude Stein* (New York, The Metropolitan Museum of Art). Stein has begun to form what will become a substantial collection of modern paintings.

1907

- **May:** German art dealer Daniel-Henry Kahnweiler opens a gallery on Rue Vignon, near the Madeleine, acquiring his first works by Braque, Vlaminck and Van Dongen at the Salon des Indépendants.
- **July:** visitors to the Bateau-Lavoir, Kahnweiler among them, get a preview of Picasso's *Les Demoiselles d'Avignon* (New York, The Museum of Modern Art).
- **October:** Modigliani and the painter Gino Severini, his fellow Italian who arrived in Paris the previous year, participate for the first time in the Salon d'Automne, which features a major retrospective of Paul Cézanne. This proves to be an opportunity for many artists to discover his work, which will be an important influence on the Cubist painters.
- Arrival in Paris of Polish artist Henri Hayden.
- Brancusi moves to a new studio at 54 Rue du Montparnasse.
- Moïse Kisling leaves Kraków for Paris, where he finds accommodation in Montmartre before moving on to Montparnasse.

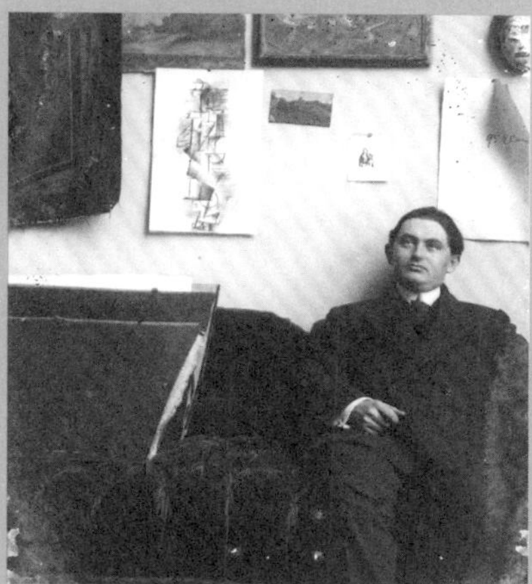

Daniel-Henry Kahnweiler
in Picasso's studio at
11, Boulevard de Clichy,
autumn 1910
Photograph by Pablo Picasso
Paris, Musée National
Picasso-Paris, APPH17382

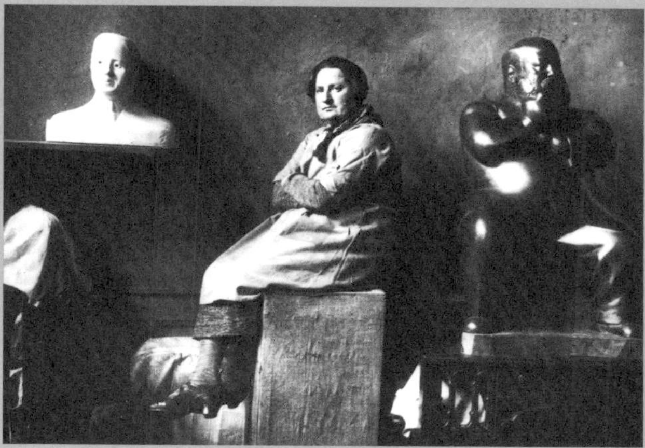

Chana Orloff in her studio
on Rue d'Assas, 1925
Photograph by Thérèse Bonney
Collection Ateliers-
Musée Chana Orloff

1908

- **January:** with the support of the Steins, Henri Matisse opens an art school of his own in the former Couvent des Oiseaux on Rue de Sèvres, Paris VII, attended by many foreigners.
- **March:** Modigliani and Severini participate in the Salon des Indépendants for the first time.
- **March:** German painter and sculptor Otto Freundlich makes his first visit to Paris, renting a studio at the Bateau-Lavoir.
- **Summer:** Hungarian sculptor Joseph Csáky and Czech painter Georges Kars move to Paris.
- **September:** Pascin participates in the Salon d'Automne for the first time.
- **October:** painter Paul-Élie Ranson opens the Académie Ranson on Rue Henri-Monnier, Paris IX. Kisling and Gino Severini teach there.
- **December:** in London, Sonia Terk enters a marriage of convenience with Wilhelm Uhde, thus escaping family pressures.
- The Russian painter Marie Vassilieff, who arrived in Paris in 1904, opens the Académie Russe in Montparnasse.
- Arrival in Paris of Ukrainian sculptor Alexander Archipenko, who takes a studio at La Ruche.
- Sonia Terk's first solo show in Paris, organised by Uhde at Galerie Notre-Dame-des-Champs in Montparnasse, where she meets the painter Robert Delaunay.
- At the Bateau-Lavoir, Gris moves into the studio vacated by Van Dongen.

1909

- **February:** Italian artist Filippo Tommaso Marinetti sends his "Futurist Manifesto" to Severini, who has it published in the daily newspaper *Le Figaro*.
- **June:** Kandinsky and Münter return to Germany.
- **August:** Russian painter Léopold Survage arrives in Paris, where he will settle permanently.
- **October:** arriving in Paris, the Lithuanian sculptor Chaïm Jacob Lipchitz takes a studio at La Ruche.
- **Autumn:** sculptor Antoine Bourdelle starts to teach at the Académie de la Grande-Chaumière, where he will influence many foreign artists.
- **November:** Van Dongen signs a seven-year contract with Galerie Bernheim-Jeune, 15 Rue Richepance, Paris I.
- Picasso and his companion, Fernande Olivier, leave the Bateau-Lavoir for the Boulevard de Clichy, just below Montmartre.
- Kahnweiler publishes Apollinaire's first volume, *The Rotting Magician*, illustrated with woodcuts by André Derain.

1910

- **15 March:** Kupka moves to Puteaux in the inner suburbs of the French capital.
- **March:** Brancusi, Archipenko, Hayden and Pascin all participate in the Salon des Indépendants for the first time.
- **August:** on arriving in Paris, Ukrainian sculptor Chana Orloff takes a studio on Rue d'Assas, Paris VI.
- **Autumn:** Byelorussian sculptor Ossip Zadkine arrives in Paris; he takes a studio at La Ruche the following year.
- **5 November:** the Nord-Sud underground railway company opens a Métro (subway) line that connects Montmartre and Montparnasse.
- **15 November:** having divorced Uhde, Sonia Terk marries Robert Delaunay.

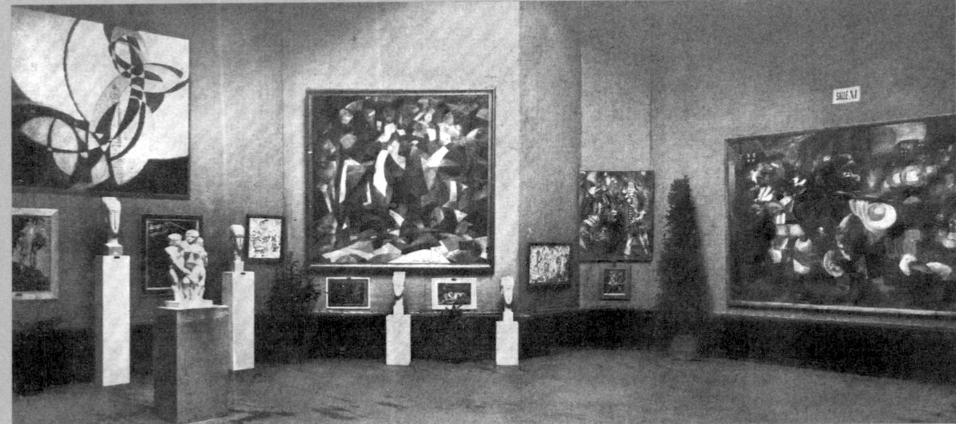

View of Room XI
at the Salon d'Automne of
1912, from *L'Illustration*,
12 October 1912
Archives *L'Illustration*

1911

1912

1913

- **5 March:** Modigliani and Souza-Cardoso stage a first private exhibition of their own works at the latter's studio.
- **April:** Kupka, Zadkine and Souza-Cardoso all make their first appearance at the Salon des Indépendants, where artists grouped in Room 41 provoke a scandal with their first public presentation of Cubist paintings.
- **May:** having arrived in Paris in late 1910, the Byelorussian painter Marc Chagall takes a studio at La Ruche.
- **October:** Archipenko and Survage participate in the Salon d'Automne for the first time.
- **November:** Marie Vassilieff leaves the Académie Russe to open the Académie Vassilieff in her own studio at 21 Rue du Maine, Paris XIV.
- **December:** arrival in Paris of Dutch painter Piet Mondrian.
- **End of the year:** the Académie Ranson, until now located close to Montmartre, moves to 7 Rue Joseph-Bara in Montparnasse.
- First solo shows in Paris by Zak and then Hayden at Galerie Druet, 20 Rue Royale, Paris VIII.
- In response to a commission, Brancusi creates a version of his sculpture *The Kiss* for the tomb of a young Russian exile in the Cimetière du Montparnasse.
- Architect André Arfvidson builds a block of apartments with studios on Rue Campagne-Première, Montparnasse.

- **January:** establishment of the Académie Moderne at 86 Rue Notre-Dame-des Champs in Montparnasse. Scandinavian, Polish, Russian and Romanian artists will attend.
- **5 February:** first Italian Futurist exhibition in Paris at Galerie Bernheim-Jeune.
- **February:** supported financially by Baroness d'Oettingen, Apollinaire and Férat take over the editorship of the magazine *Les Soirées de Paris* (*Paris Nights*).
- **March:** first participation in the Salon des Indépendants of Gris and Chagall, the latter notably exhibiting *To Russia, Asses and Others* [CAT. 25].
- **March:** Mondrian takes a studio at 33 Avenue du Maine, near the Gare Montparnasse.
- **Spring:** Swiss poet Blaise Cendrars settles in Paris and makes contact with the artistic milieu of Montparnasse.
- **10–30 October:** the Salon de la Section d'Or takes place at Galerie La Boétie, Paris VIII, notably featuring the work of Cubist artists – Archipenko, Marcoussis and Kupka among them.
- **October:** Chagall, Souza-Cardoso and Kisling participate in the Salon d'Automne for the first time.
- **October:** accompanied by his new partner, Eva Gouel, who has left Marcoussis for him, Picasso moves to a new studio at 242 Boulevard Raspail, near Montparnasse.
- Byelorussian painter Pinchus Krémègne crosses the Russian–German frontier illegally to come to Paris. His friend and compatriot, the painter Michel Kikoïne, joins him.
- Kisling signs a contract with art dealer Adolphe Basler.

- **February:** Gris signs a contract with art dealer Daniel-Henry Kahnweiler.
- **March:** Kisling and Survage participate in the Salon des Indépendants for the first time.
- **May:** Serge Diaghilev's Ballets Russes premiere *The Rite of Spring* at the Théâtre des Champs-Élysées. Dramatically innovative in their disregard for established convention, the music of Igor Stravinsky and the choreography of Vaslav Nijinsky cause a scandal, challenging the standards of classic dance.
- **July:** joining fellow Byelorussians Kikoïne and Krémègne in Paris, the painter Chaïm Soutine is hosted by Miestchaninoff in his studio at the Cité Falguière.
- **August:** Japanese painter Tsuguharu Foujita disembarks in Marseille before travelling to Paris. He takes up residence in Montparnasse, where he meets Picasso.
- **August:** Severini marries Jeanne, daughter of poet Paul Fort. Apollinaire acts as witness.
- **October:** Italian artist Giorgio de Chirico exhibits some thirty paintings at his own studio in Montparnasse.
- **November:** Lipchitz, Orloff and Zadkine participate in the Salon d'Automne for the first time.
- **November:** a nude by Van Dongen exhibited at the Salon d'Automne – *The Spanish Shawl* (Paris, Centre Pompidou, Musée National d'Art Moderne) – is taken down by the police on the grounds of obscenity.
- **Autumn:** Picasso moves to a new studio at 5 bis, Rue Victor-Schœlcher, still in the Montparnasse neighbourhood.
- Kisling moves his studio to 3 Rue Joseph-Bara, also in Montparnasse.
- First stay in Paris of Ukrainian painter Mané-Katz, who studies under academic painter Fernand Cormon at the École Nationale des Beaux-Arts.
- Pascin meets the young Martiniquan woman Aicha Goblet, who becomes one of his principal models.

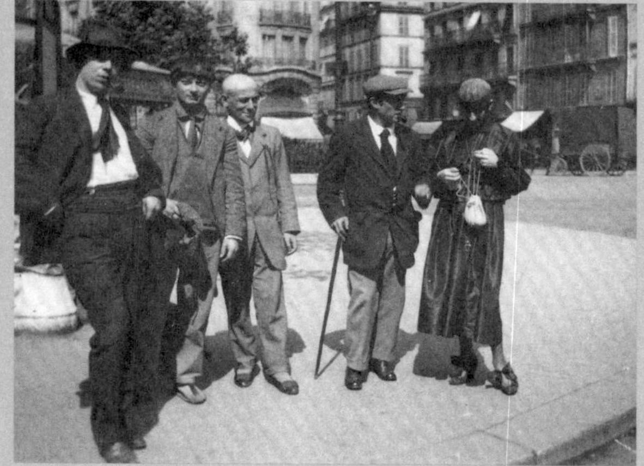

Manuel Ortiz de Zárate,
Kisling, Max Jacob, Pablo
Picasso and Pâquerette in
front of the café de la Rotonde,
Boulevard de Montparnasse,
12 August 1916
Photograph by Jean Cocteau
Paris, Musée National
Picasso-Paris, *MP2003-15

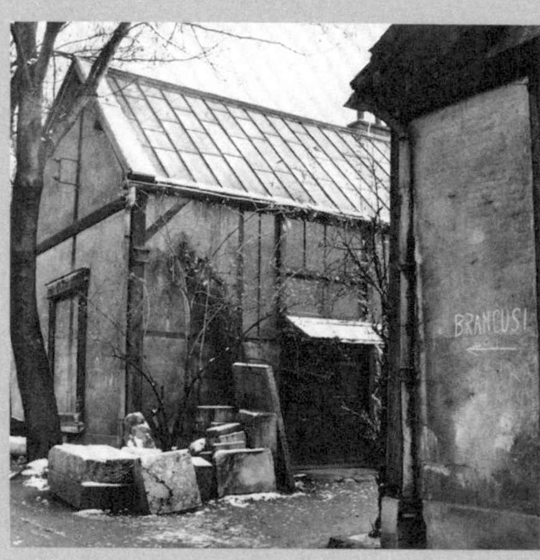

Exterior view of
Constantin Brancusi's
studio on Impasse Ronsin,
around 1948
Photograph by
Florence Homolka
Paris, Centre Pompidou
– Musée National d'Art
Moderne, bequest of
Constantin Brancusi, 1957

1914

- **February:** Reth has his first solo show in Paris at Galerie Berthe Weill, Rue Victor-Massé, Paris IX.
- **February:** opening of Galerie Paul Guillaume on Rue du Faubourg-Saint-Honoré, Paris VIII. After the war, many foreign artists will exhibit here including Modigliani, Picasso, Soutine and Van Dongen.
- **March:** Sonia Delaunay participates in the Salon des Indépendants for the first time.
- **April:** Russian artists Michel Larionov and Natalia Goncharova pay a brief visit to Paris. Galerie Paul Guillaume will go on to stage their first exhibition in the French capital in June.
- **June:** Hayden signs a contract with art dealer Léonce Rosenberg.
- **3 August:** in Sarajevo, a Serb nationalist assassinates Archduke Franz-Ferdinand, heir to the Austro–Hungarian throne. This leads to the outbreak of the First World War as interlocking alliances come into play and France declares war on Germany.
- Shortly after the declaration of war, Soutine volunteers, but must soon leave the army on account of ill health; Vassilieff and Foujita nurse the sick and wounded for the French Red Cross; Apollinaire, Cendrars, Csáky, Kisling, Kupka and Marcoussis enlist in the Foreign Legion; Archipenko leaves Paris for Nice, as does Survage, discharged due to ill health; Lipchitz extends his visit to Spain, where Sonia and Robert Delaunay also take up residence, while Souza-Cardoso, visiting Portugal, does not return to Paris; learning in Vitebsk of the outbreak of war, Chagall decides to remain in Russia; in October, Pascin goes to New York (obtaining American citizenship in 1920).
- **December:** Kahnweiler takes refuge in Switzerland; his gallery stock is seized as "enemy property" by the French government. Uhde sees his collection confiscated on the same grounds.
- Having arrived from Warsaw, Polish poet and art dealer Léopold Zborowski is present in Paris.

1915

- **January:** Marie Vassilieff opens a canteen on Rue du Maine, Paris XIV, allowing numbers of foreign artists to eat their fill for very little money.
- Discharged after being wounded in action, Kisling returns to Montparnasse and obtains French citizenship.
- Lipchitz returns to Paris, taking over Brancusi's studio in Montparnasse.
- Soutine signs a contract with art dealer Leopold Zborowski.
- **End of the year:** Cendrars and the painter Émile Lejeune establish the Lyre et Palette club in Montparnasse to support Russian artists and intellectuals in France.

1916

- **January:** Zadkine joins the Foreign Legion.
- **July:** art critic André Salmon organises an important exhibition of "Modern Art in France" at the Salon d'Antin, at which Picasso's *Les Demoiselles d'Avignon* is shown in public for the first time.
- **Winter:** Lipchitz signs a contract with the Léonce Rosenberg's gallery, which buys his entire past and future output.
- After visiting the city twice – in 1908 and 1911 – the Spanish painter Maria Blanchard settles in Paris, near the Gare Montparnasse, joining her friend Juan Gris.
- Back in Paris after being declared unfit for service, Brancusi sets up studio on Impasse Ronsin, Paris XV.
- To replace French workers sent to the front, the government organises campaigns to recruit foreigners: 225,000 Europeans (Spanish, Italian, Portuguese, Greek, Bulgarian) arrive to work in France.

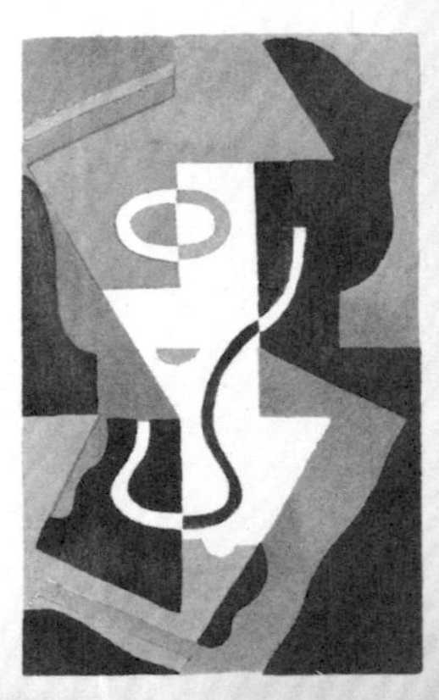

Invitation to solo show by Juan Gris
at Galerie L'Effort Moderne, 1919
Paris, Centre Pompidou, MNAM-CCI,
Bibliothèque Kandinsky,
Fonds Léonce Rosenberg

1917

- **21 January:** Apollinaire organises Survage's first exhibition, at the home of Germaine Bongard, sister of the couturier Paul Poiret, also a courturier and an artist.
- **January:** Foujita moves to 5 Rue Delambre in Montparnasse.
- **March–April:** Modigliani meets the painter Jeanne Hébuterne at the Académie de la Grande-Chaumière.
- **May:** the Ballets Russes premiere *Parade* at the Théâtre du Châtelet, with script by Jean Cocteau, music by Erik Satie, costumes and stage design by Picasso and choreography by Léonide Massine.
- **June:** Foujita's first solo show in Paris at Galerie Chéron, 56 Rue La Boétie, Paris VIII, with which he signs a contract.
- **4 June:** formation in France of a Polish army to fight in the name of an independent Poland under the French high command. Poles will arrive from across Europe and America to enlist.
- **October:** having overthrown the Czar's government, the Bolshevik party takes power in Russia, establishing a communist regime. As a result, many Russian artists and intellectuals take refuge in France.
- **December:** Modigliani's first solo show in Paris at Galerie Berthe Weill. Madame Weill hangs female nudes in the window, prompting the police to interrupt the opening and take down the paintings on the grounds of indecency.
- Fleeing the Russian Revolution, the Polish artist Tamara de Lempicka takes up residence on Rue du Montparnasse.

1918

- **January:** taking over Kahnweiler's role in promoting the Cubists, Léonce Rosenberg opens Galerie L'Effort Moderne at 19 Rue de la Baume, Paris VIII, showing works by Gris, Picasso and Lipchitz.
- **15 February–2 March:** Mela Muter's first solo show in Paris at Galerie Chéron.
- **25 October:** in Portugal, Souza-Cardoso dies of the Spanish flu.
- **11 November:** the signing of the armistice between France and Germany marks the end of the First World War.
- **18 November:** Apollinaire dies of the Spanish flu.
- Mané-Katz obtains French citizenship.
- Archipenko leaves Paris to live in Berlin.
- To compensate for losses to the labour force due to the war, the French government signs agreements with Poland, Italy and Czechoslovakia allowing their nationals to come and work in French industry and agriculture.

1919

- **5 April:** Gris has his first solo show in Paris at Galerie L'Effort Moderne.
- **5 May:** after spending six months in the Nièvre in central France, Goncharova and Larionov decide to settle in the French capital, at 43 Rue de Seine, Paris VI.
- **June:** the signing of the Treaty of Versailles officially establishes the defeat of Germany and the Austro-Hungarian Empire.
- **Summer:** after the failure of the Hungarian Soviet Republic, the counter-revolution turns on its supporters, particularly on the artists and intellectuals among them, forcing some into exile.
- **September:** signing of the Treaty of Saint-Germain-en-Laye, which declares the dissolution of the Austro-Hungarian Empire: Poland, Czechoslovakia, Hungary and Yugoslavia are recognised as independent countries.
- **November:** re-opening of the Salon d'Automne, where Foujita exhibits for the first time.
- Establishment of the Association des Artistes Scandinaves at the Maison Watteau, 6 Rue Jules-Chaplain, Paris VI, which acts as cultural centre and exhibition space.
- Soutine leaves Paris for Céret in the eastern Pyrenees mountains.
- Survage leaves Nice for Paris.
- Blanchard has his first solo show in Paris at Galerie L'Effort Moderne.
- Kikoïne's first solo show in Paris at Galerie Chéron.
- Kisling's first solo show in Paris at Galerie Druet.

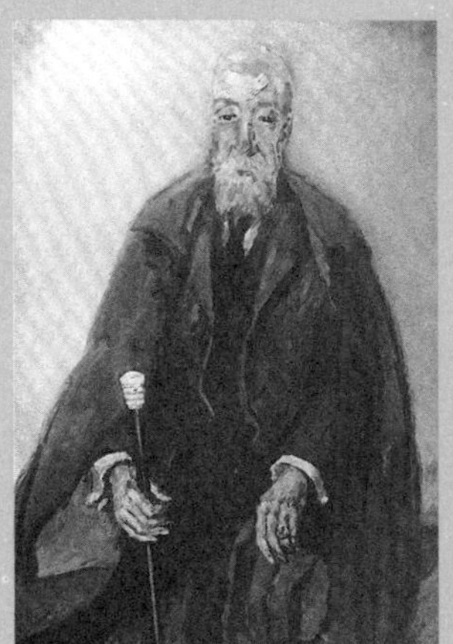

Kees van Dongen,
Portrait of Anatole France, 1921
Location unknown

1920

- **24 January:** death of Amedeo Modigliani, followed by the suicide of Jeanne Hébuterne.
- **28 January:** re-opening of the Salon des Indépendants, where Blanchard and Foujita exhibit for the first time.
- **January:** Romanian poet Tristan Tzara moves to Paris.
- **January:** Lipchitz has his first solo show in Paris at Galerie L'Effort Moderne.
- **February:** Kahnweiler returns to Paris.
- **March:** the second Salon de la Section d'Or is held at Galerie La Boétie.
- **March:** the Spanish painter Joan Miró arrives in Paris and immediately pays a visit to Picasso.
- **16 May–2 June:** Zadkine stages his first solo show at his own studio on Rue Rousselet, Paris VII.
- **October:** Rolf de Maré forms the Ballets Suédois, resident at the Théâtre des Champs-Élysées.
- **Autumn:** Kahnweiler opens Galerie Simon at 29 bis, Rue d'Astorg, Paris VIII, re-establishing relations with his artists (with the exception of Picasso).
- **December:** Csáky has his first solo show in Paris at Galerie L'Effort Moderne.

1921

- **January:** Lipchitz, Kars and Orloff participate in the Salon des Indépendants for the first time.
- **April:** Van Dongen's portrait of writer Anatole France is exhibited at the Salon of the Société Nationale des Beaux-Arts; it causes a scandal, being considered disrespectful.
- **30 May:** Uhde's collection, confiscated during the war, is sold at auction.
- **13–14 June:** first of four auctions at which the government sells off the gallery stock confiscated from Kahnweiler.
- **June:** the American photographer Man Ray settles in Paris.
- **June:** Kupka's first solo show in Paris at Jacques Povolozky's gallery at 17 Rue des Beaux-Arts and 13 Rue Bonaparte, Paris VI.
- **November:** the American novelist Ernest Hemingway takes up residence in the Latin Quarter.
- Zadkine obtains French citizenship.
- **End of the year:** the Delaunays move back to France for good.

1922

- **28 January:** art critic Jean Robiquet declares that there are too many foreign artists at the Salon des Indépendants. The committee decides to arrange the next salon by nationality.
- **January:** the Swiss sculptor Alberto Giacometti takes a hotel room in Montparnasse before renting Archipenko's former studio.
- **March:** Orloff's first solo show in Paris at Jacques Povolozky's gallery.
- **March:** Csáky obtains French citizenship.
- **29 October:** King Victor-Emmanuel III of Italy appoints fascist leader Benito Mussolini as head of government. Persecuted and driven out of employment, many trade unionists and anti-fascist activists seek refuge in Paris.
- **November:** Lempicka participates in the Salon d'Automne for the first time.
- The American millionaire collector Albert C. Barnes visits Paris buying numerous works by Lipchitz, Modigliani, Pascin, Picasso and particularly Soutine.
- Kars has his first solo show in Paris at Galerie La Licorne, 110 Rue La Boétie, Paris VIII.
- On the terrace of the café La Rotonde, Foujita meets Lucie Badoud, whom he nicknames Youki; she becomes his partner and muse. They take an apartment at 17 Avenue Henri-Martin, Paris XVI.

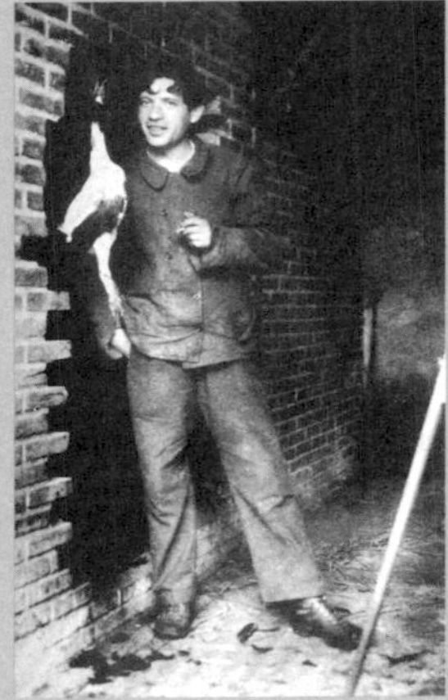

Chaïm Soutine, 1925
Unknown photographer

1923

- **February:** Lempicka participates in at the Salon des Indépendants for the first time.
- **29 April:** the Russian cultural association Tcherez organises an exhibition of Russian artists at Galerie La Licorne with Sonia Delaunay, Survage and Zadkine.
- **5 May:** Mané-Katz's first solo show in Paris at Galerie Percier, 38 Rue La Boétie, Paris VIII.
- **May:** Dutch artist Theo van Doesburg moves to Paris.
- **Spring:** painter Albert Besnard organises the first Salon des Tuileries, in which Foujita, Hayden, Kars, Kisling and Zadkine take part.
- **24 July:** following the Treaty of Lausanne, which puts an end to hopes of an independent Armenia, 60,000 Armenian refugees arrive in France.
- A "Society of Friends of Jewish Culture" is formed in Paris, organising lectures and concerts. Now back in the French capital, Chagall takes part in its activities.
- The Hungarian photographer Ergy Landau moves to Paris.
- Archipenko ultimately leaves Paris to live in New York.
- The architect Le Corbusier builds houses with studios for sculptors Lipchitz and Miestchaninoff in Boulogne-sur-Seine, not far from Paris.

1924

- **January:** Hungarian photographer Gyula Halász, known as Brassaï, arrives in Paris to work as a journalist.
- **February:** the decision to arrange artists by nationality at the Salon des Indépendants is met with widespread objections. Many foreign artists – Csáky, Foujita, Lipchitz, Muter, Van Dongen and Zadkine among them – give up their membership in protest.
- **Spring:** Chagall, Van Dongen and Lipchitz participate in the Salon des Tuileries for the first time.
- **17 October–8 November:** Pascin's first solo show in Paris at Galerie Pierre Loeb, 13 Rue Bonaparte, Paris VI.
- **1 November–14 December:** Mané-Katz participates in the Salon d'Automne for the first time.
- Opening of Le Select, the first bar in Montparnasse to stay open all night. It becomes the meeting point for American writers.
- The German photographer Florence Henri arrives in Paris and attends the Académies Montparnasse and Moderne.
- The young Slovak François Kollar moves to Paris hoping to become a professional photographer.
- Ergy Landau opens his own studio at 17 Rue Lauriston, Paris XVI, taking portrait photographs.
- Kikoïne obtains French citizenship.
- Paris becomes the European capital of anti-fascism in exile. The number of anti-fascist refugees is estimated at around 15,000 (2 per cent of the Italian population in France).

1925

- **27 January:** taking up a coinage of Roger Allard's, the critic André Warnod publishes in *Comœdia* an article entitled "L'École de Paris existe" ("The Paris School Exists"). He follows this the same year with *Les Berceaux de la jeune peinture* (*The Cradles of Young Painting*).
- **22 April–early May:** Marcoussis' first solo show in Paris at Pierre Chareau's interior design shop, 3 Rue du Cherche-Midi, Paris VI.
- The Hungarian photographer André Kertész arrives in Paris and takes up residence in Montparnasse.
- Soutine moves to 8 Rue du Saint-Gothard in Montparnasse.

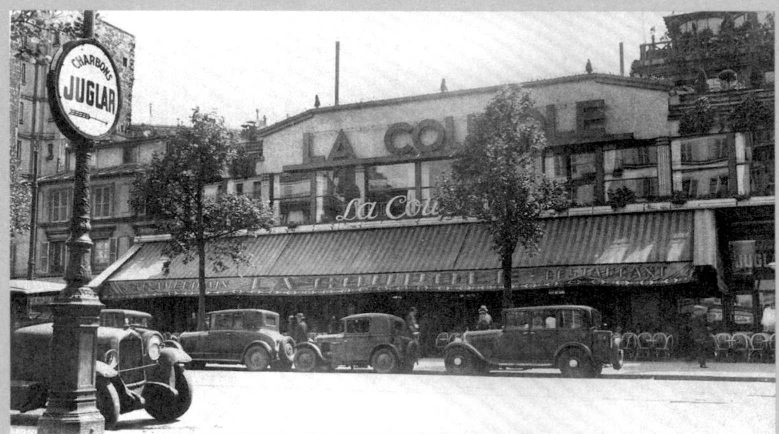

Brasserie La Coupole, around 1930
Unknown photographer
Roger-Viollet, RV-358814

1926

- **January:** death of Eugène Zak.
- **December:** Giacometti takes a studio at 46 Rue Hippolyte-Maindron in Montparnasse.
- **End of the year:** Chagall signs a contract with Galerie Bernheim-Jeune.
- Swedish painters Per Lasson Krohg and Otte Sköld open the Académie Scandinave in Montparnasse.
- Spanish painter and sculptor Salvador Dalí visits Paris for the first time.
- Orloff obtains French citizenship and has Auguste Perret build him a house with a studio at 7 bis, Villa Seurat, Paris XIV.
- Opening of La Coupole, the first café-brasserie in Montparnasse with a dance floor. La Coupole will become a meeting place for many artists.
- The German photographer Germaine Krull moves to Paris, where she opens a fashion photography studio.

1927

- **14–24 March:** Kertész has his first solo show in Paris at Galerie Au Sacre du Printemps, 5 Rue du Cherche-Midi, Paris VI.
- **11 May:** death of Juan Gris.
- **June:** Soutine's first solo show in Paris at Galerie Bing, 20 bis, Rue La Boétie, Paris VIII.
- **December:** Eugène Zak's widow, Hedwige Zak, opens Galerie Zak on Rue de l'Abbaye in the Saint-Germain-des-Prés neighbourhood.
- Kikoïne leaves La Ruche for a studio in Montrouge, in the southern Parisian suburbs.
- Chagall and Survage obtain French citizenship.

1928

- **March:** Hemingway leaves Paris to return to the United States.
- **24 May:** opening of the first annual independent photography exhibition, known as the "Salon de l'escalier", at the Théâtre des Champs-Élysées. All but one of the photographers exhibited are foreigners, among them Man Ray, Krull and Kertész.
- Soutine meets his future patrons, Marcellin and Madeleine Castaing.
- Zadkine moves into a new studio at 100 Rue d'Assas, in Montparnasse (now home of the Zadkine Museum).

1929

- **15–31 January:** Kandinsky's first solo show in Paris at Galerie Zak.
- **June:** Alice Prin, nicknamed "Kiki de Montparnasse", model for a number of foreign artists established in Paris, including Kisling, Man Ray and Modigliani, publishes her memoirs.
- **19 August:** death of Serge Diaghilev in Italy followed by the dissolution of the Ballets Russes.
- **September:** Beckmann divides his life between Berlin and Paris, where he rents a studio at 23 bis, Boulevard Brune, Paris XIV.
- **October:** the Wall Street Crash provokes an unprecedented economic crisis forcing a number of American artists and intellectuals to return to the United States.
- **October:** Lempicka leaves Paris for New York.
- The German photographer Marianne Breslauer moves to Paris, where she meets Man Ray.
- Pascin signs a contract with Galerie Bernheim-Jeune.
- Florence Henri opens her own photography studio – Studio Henri at 8 Rue de Varenne, Paris VII.
- Van Dongen obtains French citizenship.

1930

- **January:** Foujita and Youki return to Paris after visiting Japan and the United States.
- **March:** Beckmann's first solo show in Paris at Galerie de la Renaissance, 11 Rue Royale, Paris II.
- **March–April:** Florence Henri's first solo show in Paris at Studio 28, 10 Rue Tholozé, Paris XVIII.
- **May:** Lempicka's first solo show in Paris at Galerie Colette Weill, 71 Rue La Boétie, Paris VIII.
- **June:** Pascin commits suicide.
- **28 November:** first screening at Studio 28 of Spanish filmmaker Luis Buñuel's *L'Âge d'or*, financed by Charles and Marie-Laure de Noailles.
- **November:** Picasso participates in the Salon d'Automne for the first time.
- **November:** German photographer Ilse Bing moves to Paris where she works as a photojournalist.

1931

- **March:** Blanchard signs a contract with Galerie Vavin, 28 Rue Vavin, Paris VI.
- **May–November:** believing the International Colonial Exhibition in the Bois de Vincennes to be propaganda for French colonialism, the Surrealists publish a scathing leaflet headlined "Do not Visit the Colonial Exhibition!" and dispose of their own collections of "primitive" objects at auction.
- **November:** Foujita visits Latin America with his new partner, the model Mady Lequeux.
- **Autumn:** the Italian painter Alberto Magnelli moves permanently to Paris.
- Succeeding the groups Cercle et Carré and Art Concret, Abstraction-Création brings together numerous representatives of the different kinds of abstract art practised in Paris, for the most part by foreign artists.
- Invited by Ambroise Vollard to illustrate the Bible, Chagall visits Palestine.
- France has 2.7 million foreign inhabitants, 6.6 per cent of the total population, comprised of 800,000 Italians, 500,000 Poles, 350,000 Spaniards, 150,000 Belgians, 100,000 Swiss and 82,900 Russian exiles.

1938

- **March:** German troops enter Austria. The *Anschluss* results in 6,000–8,000 Austrians seeking refuge in Paris.
- **June:** in order to assist Otto Freundlich, gallerist Jeanne Bucher opens a subscription to fund the purchase of one of his paintings for the Musée du Jeu de Paume; many foreign artists contribute, including Picasso, Miró and Kandinsky.

1939

- **April:** the end of the civil war in Spain prompts a great exodus of 500,000 Spanish refugees to France.
- **Spring:** Foujita and his new partner, Kimiyo, decide to return to France; they move to Rue Ordener in Montmartre.
- **September:** Great Britain and France declare war on Germany. Start of the Second World War. Considered "suspect, dangerous or undesirable", many German artists who had found refuge in France are interned in the south of the country.
- Kisling leaves Paris for Sanary-sur-Mer in the Var region of France.
- Zadkine and Mondrian leave France for New York.

1940

- **May:** after staying some time in Toulouse, Lipchitz moves to the United States.
- **14 June:** Paris is occupied by German forces.
- **18 June:** from London, General Charles de Gaulle makes a radio appeal for continuing resistance against the German occupier, rallying together what will become the Free French Forces.
- The Musée du Jeu de Paume is requisitioned by the Nazis for the storage of works of art confiscated from Jewish collectors.
- Threatened by the German occupation, Brassaï leaves for Cannes, in the south of France; the Delaunays leave Paris for Châtel-Guyon in Auvergne, before moving to Mougins in the Alpes-Maritimes; Foujita returns to Japan; Hayden settles in the Auvergne; Kars finds refuge in Lyon, then in Switzerland; Kollar moves to Poitiers; Krull leaves for Brazil and enters the service of Free France; Marcoussis retreats to Cusset, near Vichy; Orloff leaves Paris for Saujon, near Royan, but returns to Paris in the face of the German advance; while Ilse Bing, interned in the Pyrenees mountains, manages to escape and leaves France for New York.

BIOGRAPHIES

Christian Briend,
Nathalie Ernoult,
Inès Lassale
and Anne Lemonnier

ALEXANDER ARCHIPENKO
Kiev (Ukraine), 1887–New York (USA), 1964

Alexander Archipenko first trained at the Kiev School of Fine Art before pursuing his studies in Moscow. In 1908, he arrived in Paris, where he had a studio in La Ruche. Finding the teaching at the École Nationale des Beaux-Arts too conservative, he preferred to study Antiquity independently at the Louvre. In 1910, he exhibited for the first time at the Salon des Indépendants, and then again the following year at the Salon d'Automne. This early recognition enabled him to arrange a series of solo exhibitions across Europe, the first of which was in Hagen, Germany. He continued to experiment, creating his first assemblages, which were noticed by Apollinaire. During the First World War, Archipenko left Paris and moved to Nice. In 1918, he moved to Berlin, where he opened an art school, before moving once more to settle in New York in 1923. There, he set up his own art school and also taught at the Woodstock summer school. He was soon integrated into society, obtaining US citizenship in 1928.

CAT. 27
Head of a Woman and Table, 1916
Painted cement and plaster, 33.7 × 34.5 × 20.5 cm
Signed bottom left
Paris, Centre Pompidou – Musée National d'Art Moderne. Gift of Alexina Duchamp and Pierre Jullien, 1978
Inv. AM 1977-583

MAX BECKMANN
Leipzig (Germany), 1884–New York (USA), 1950

Trained at the Weimar Academy, Max Beckmann went to Paris for the first time in 1903. Then residing in Berlin, he showed at the Berlin Secession's 1906 exhibition, won a scholarship to study in Florence and again spent a few months in Paris. During the First World War he served as a medical orderly in the German army. The experience transformed his hitherto conventional pictorial language, his new "expressionist" distortions being marked by an atypical objectivity. Returning to civilian life following a nervous breakdown, he settled in Frankfurt in 1915 – taking a teaching appointment in 1925 – while continuing to regularly spend time in Paris. Dismissed from his post when the Nazis came to power, he moved to Berlin in 1933 and then to Amsterdam four years later. In 1947, Beckmann left for the USA, where he taught in Washington and Brooklyn.

CAT. 83
Portrait of a Frenchman, 1933
Oil on canvas, 70 × 60 cm
Signed and dated bottom right
Paris, Centre Pompidou – Musée National d'Art Moderne. Purchased with the support of the Fonds du Patrimoine, 2006. Inv. AM 2006-32

ILSE BING
Frankfurt-am-Main (Germany), 1899–New York (USA), 1998

After studying mathematics and then history in Frankfurt and Vienna, Ilse Bing turned to photography in 1923. In 1930 she moved to Paris, where she photographed urban landscapes structured by the geometrical forms that would soon turn her into a Parisian representative of the New Vision. Her use of a light, compact Leica camera enabled her to take spontaneous shots. She experimented with different techniques, including night photography, and contributed to a new, modernist and humanist interpretation of the city. As a pioneer of photojournalism, her work was published in many magazines, notably *Arts et métiers graphiques* and *L'Art vivant*, and appeared in the first exhibition on modern photography held at the Musée des Arts Décoratifs, Paris, in 1936. In 1937, she spent time in New York, where she took part in the exhibition "Photography 1839–1937" at the Museum of Modern Art. In 1940, having returned to France, she was interned as a German Jew in the camp at Gurs, but obtained a visa for the United States the following year. In 1957, she took her first colour photographs. Two years later, she gave up professional photography to concentrate on writing and drawing. Rediscovered in the 1970s, she published her first book of photographs in 1982, with a preface by her colleague Gisèle Freund.

CAT. 67
Paris, Three Men on Steps, 1931
Silver gelatin print (print, 1983), 27.8 × 35.5 cm
Signed and dated bottom right
Paris, Centre Pompidou – Musée National d'Art Moderne. Purchased with the assistance of Yves Rocher, 2011, former collection of Christian Bouqueret. Inv. AM 2012-2061

MARIA BLANCHARD
(born María Gutierrez Cueto)
Santander (Spain), 1881–Paris, 1932

Born into a cultured bourgeois family, Maria Blanchard studied with academic painters in Madrid. In 1908, a bursary from the city of Santander enabled her to go to Paris, where she enrolled at both the Vitti and Vassilieff academies in Montparnasse. Returning to Spain in 1913, she secured a chair in drawing at Salamanca, but did not succeed in making her mark. In 1916, she went back to Paris, where she met Pablo Picasso and saw Juan Gris, whose work influenced her a great deal. At this time Blanchard was living in severe poverty. In 1919, she was supported by Léonce Rosenberg, who had just opened his gallery L'Effort Moderne. Blanchard took part in the Salon des Indépendants for the first time in 1920. The following year, having taken in her sister and three children, she worked tirelessly to provide for them all. The death of Gris in 1927 affected her deeply and she withdrew into herself, turning to religion.

CAT. 21
Child with a Hoop, 1917
Oil on canvas, 140 × 85 cm
Monogram bottom left
Paris, Centre Pompidou – Musée National d'Art Moderne. Purchase, 1951. Inv. AM 3096 P

CONSTANTIN BRANCUSI
Pestisani (Romania), 1876–Paris, 1957

Constantin Brancusi was born into a peasant family living at the foot of the Carpathians. In 1893, he enrolled at Craiova School of Arts and Crafts, before going on to the Bucharest School of Fine Art in 1898. He arrived in Paris in July 1904 and attended the studio of the sculptor Antonin Mercié. In 1907, Brancusi spent a few months working in Rodin's studio, but soon left to practise direct carving on his own. In 1910, he exhibited for the first time at the Salon des Indépendants, where he subsequently became a regular participant. In 1916, he moved to Impasse Ronsin, where his studio soon drew all the major figures of the Paris art scene. John Quinn became his main collector and, in 1922, exhibited his work in New York. Brancusi travelled there on several occasions. As a result of a Romanian commission, he made a monumental ensemble in Targu Jiu comprising *The Endless Column*, *Gate of the Kiss* and *Table of Silence*. Brancusi obtained French citizenship in 1952 and bequeathed his studio to the French state in 1956.

CAT. 47
Brancusi Working at Night in his Studio, Impasse Ronsin, 1920
Silver gelatin print, 29.9 × 23.8 cm
Paris, Centre Pompidou – Musée National d'Art Moderne. Bequest of Constantin Brancusi, 1957
Inv. PH 827 D

CAT. 48
Sculptures in the Studio, Impasse Ronsin, 1920
Silver gelatin print, 39.8 × 29.8 cm
Paris, Centre Pompidou – Musée National d'Art Moderne. Bequest of Constantin Brancusi, 1957
Inv. PH 608 D

The Studio Impasse Ronsin, 1926

Silver gelatin print, 29.7 × 23.7 cm
Paris, Centre Pompidou – Musée National d'Art
Moderne. Bequest of Constantin Brancusi, 1957
Inv. PH 72 A

CAT. 50

The Cockerel, 1935

Polished bronze, limestone (?), wood,
103.4 × 12.1 × 29.9 cm (with plinths: 253.4 cm)
Paris, Centre Pompidou – Musée National d'Art
Moderne. Acquisition, 1947
Inv. AM 817 S

BRASSAÏ (born Gyula Halász)
Braşov (Romania), 1899–Paris, 1984

The young Gyula Halász (later Brassaï) first came
to Paris when his father obtained a year's leave
in the city in 1903. As a young man, he served
in the Austro-Hungarian army 1917–18, before
enrolling at Budapest Academy of Fine Art, where
he studied painting. He continued his training in
Berlin, intending to become a painter, and moved
to Paris in 1924, where he made his living as a
journalist. He became a friend of the Hungarian
photographer André Kertész, who invited Brassaï
to work with him. Brassaï travelled all around
Paris and, in 1929, took the first photographs of
his series *Paris de nuit* (*Paris by Night*), published
in 1932. His photographs of life in Paris express
a humanist vision focusing on working-class
people. In the same year, Brassaï also met Picasso,
whose sculptures he photographed, publishing his
Conversations with the artist in 1964. In 1933, he
embarked on his series on graffiti, which brought
him immediate recognition when it was published
in the 1960s.

CAT. 63

Lamplighter, Place de la Concorde, c. 1930

Silver gelatin print, 29.7 × 23.5 cm
Paris, Centre Pompidou – Musée National d'Art
Moderne. Dation, 2011. Inv. AM 2012-166

CAT. 64

Moulin Rouge, 1932

Silver gelatin print (printed by the artist),
30 × 24 cm
Paris, Centre Pompidou – Musée National d'Art
Moderne. Gift of Gilberte Brassaï, 2002
Inv. AM 2003-5 (8)

CAT. 65

The Pont-Neuf at Night, c. 1932

Silver gelatin print (printed by the artist),
30 × 22 cm
Paris, Centre Pompidou – Musée National d'Art
Moderne. Gift of Gilberte Brassaï, 2002
Inv. AM 2003-5 (20)

CAT. 66

*The Quatre Saisons Bal Musette, Rue de
Lappe, c.* 1932

Silver gelatin print, 29 × 22 cm
Paris, Centre Pompidou – Musée National d'Art
Moderne. Purchased with the assistance of Yves
Rocher, 2011, former collection of Christian
Bouqueret . Inv. AM 2012-2704

MARIANNE BRESLAUER
Berlin (Germany), 1909–Zurich
(Switzerland), 2001

Born into the intellectual bourgeoisie of Berlin,
Marianne Breslauer discovered photography when
she visited an exhibition by Frieda Riess. She then
attended classes given by Riess at the Lette-Haus,
from 1927–29, in the "Portrait Photography"
section. At the end of her training, having taken
part in the exhibition "Film und Foto" in Stuttgart
in 1929, Breslauer went to Paris and captured snapshots of life in the city. Upon her return to Berlin
in 1930, she was hired as a photojournalist by the
Ullstein publishing house. In 1931, she travelled
to Palestine and then on to Spain, where she took
many portraits of passers-by. Feeling that she
did not really have the makings of a reporter,
Breslauer left Ullstein in 1932 and went back to
Paris, working as an independent photographer
in fashion and advertising. The Nazis' rise to
power drove her to leave Berlin for Amsterdam
in 1936, where she married an art dealer. In 1939,
she settled in Zurich and ended her career as an
artist to concentrate on the art market.

CAT. 61

La Rotonde Seen from Above, 1929

Silver gelatin print, 23.7 × 17.8 cm, 23.3 × 17.6 cm
(without margins)
Paris, Centre Pompidou – Musée National d'Art
Moderne. Purchased with the assistance of Yves
Rocher, 2011, former collection of Christian
Bouqueret. Inv. AM 2012-2728

CAT. 62

Quays of the Seine, 1929

Silver gelatin print, 22.7 × 29.5 cm
Paris, Centre Pompidou – Musée National d'Art
Moderne. Purchased with the assistance of Yves
Rocher, 2011, former collection of Christian
Bouqueret. Inv. AM 2012-2725

MARC CHAGALL
Vitebsk (Byelorussia), 1887–Saint-
Paul-de-Vence (France), 1985

Marc Chagall showed a talent for drawing at an
early age and was still young when he joined the
studio of Yehuda (Yuri) Pen in Vitebsk, before
moving on to the school of the Imperial Society for
the Encouragement of the Arts in St Petersburg.

He arrived in Paris in late 1910, moved into La
Ruche the following year and exhibited at the Salon
des Indépendants for the first time in 1912. His
paintings showed scenes that were imbued with
his religious education and drew extensively on
his memories of Vitebsk. In 1914, Chagall went to
Moscow. In 1918, during the Russian Revolution, he
was appointed people's superintendant for fine art
in the Vitebsk region, and soon afterwards founded
an academy of art and a museum in his home city.
In 1920, he was required to leave his academy and
he lived in Moscow until 1922, before moving to
Berlin, and then to Paris, where he had many solo
exhibitions. Chagall received commissions for
engravings from the art dealer Ambroise Vollard,
including a series of illustrations for the Bible,
for which he travelled to Palestine. He became a
French citizen in 1927. During the Second World
War, Chagall was in New York. He returned to
France in 1950, creating many painted decors,
mosaics and works in stained glass.

CAT. 24

The Father, 1911

Oil on canvas, 80 × 44.2 cm
Signed and dated on the reverse
Paris, Centre Pompidou – Musée National d'Art
Moderne. Dation, 1988. Inv. AM 1988-55
On long-term loan to the Musée d'Art et d'Histoire
du Judaïsme, Paris

CAT. 25

To Russia, Asses and Others, 1911

Oil on canvas, 157 × 122 cm
Signed and dated bottom centre
Paris, Centre Pompidou – Musée National d'Art
Moderne. Gift of the artist, 1953. Inv. AM 2925 P

CAT. 23

Mazin, the Poet, 1911–12

Oil on canvas, 73 × 54 cm
Signed bottom right
Paris, Centre Pompidou – Musée National d'Art
Moderne. Gift of Ida Chagall, 1984
Inv. AM 1984-120

JOSEPH CSÁKY
Szeged (Hungary), 1888–Paris, 1971

Joseph Csáky had little interest in classical art
training and learned direct carving techiques
on his own. In 1908, he left Hungary for Paris,
where he moved into La Ruche. In 1911, he took part
in the Salon d'Automne, where he subsequently
became a regular exhibitor, and in the Salon des
Indépendants from 1913. When the First World
War broke out he enlisted in the Foreign Legion.
After the war Csáky went back to making art,
exploring geometrical forms and moving towards
Art Deco. In 1921, the gallery owner Léonce
Rosenberg offered him a three-year contract and

invited him to take part in the exhibition "Les Maîtres du cubisme" ("The Masters of Cubism"). In 1922, Csáky obtained French citizenship. From 1928, he became more interested in portraying the human body, a direction reinforced by his trip to Greece in 1935. During the Second World War he moved to Valence. Rosenberg's death in 1947 left Csáky alone and in serious financial difficulties, until his meeting with Pierre Levy, who became a patron.

CAT. 26

Head, 1914

Stone, 39 × 20 × 21.5 cm
Signed and dated on the reverse
Paris, Centre Pompidou – Musée National d'Art
Moderne. Purchase, 1977. Inv. AM 1977-1

GIORGIO DE CHIRICO
Volos (Greece), 1888–Rome (Italy), 1978

Giorgio de Chirico was born in Greece to Italian parents. After studying painting and drawing at the Athens Polytechnic, De Chirico continued his artistic education at the Munich Academy of Fine Arts, which he attended from 1905 to 1909. It was there that he made Classical Antiquity and German philosophy the cornerstones of his work. After residing for a time in Florence, he lived in Paris between 1911 and 1914; there he met Guillaume Apollinaire and Paul Guillaume, the latter becoming his dealer. At the Paris salons, he showed his first *Piazza d'Italia* paintings, dream-like compositions featuring arcaded squares filled with antique sculptures. Back in Italy during the First World War, he inspired the formation of the Metaphysical School of painting, considered by André Breton to be a forerunner of Surrealism. In 1919, however, De Chirico joined the Valori Plastici group, returning to a deliberately traditional style in a fierce rejection of the "modern spirit". After spending some years in Rome, he returned to Paris from 1924 to 1931, enjoying many solo shows there under the banner of the "return to order", thus making an enemy of the Surrealists. In Italy, the decorative projects of the Mussolini regime offered him the opportunity to paint large-scale murals inspired by Antiquity. In the 1940s, he recycled, not without irony, elements of his "metaphysical interiors" of the 1910s.

CAT. 16

Premonitory Portrait of Guillaume Apollinaire, spring 1914

Oil and charcoal on canvas, 81.5 × 65 cm
Signed and dated bottom right
Paris, Centre Pompidou – Musée National d'Art
Moderne. Purchased 1975. Inv. AM 1975-52

SONIA DELAUNAY
(born Sarah Sophie Stern Terk) Gradyzk (Ukraine), 1885–Paris, 1979

Having studied drawing in Germany 1903–5, Ukrainian Sonia Terk moved to Paris in 1906 and enrolled at the La Palette academy. She quickly developed an interest in the study of colour, light and movement. In 1907, she took part in the first group exhibition held by Wilhelm Uhde at Galerie Notre-Dame-des-Champs, and had her first solo show there the following year. After a marriage of convenience with Uhde in 1908, she married Robert Delaunay in 1910. She first exhibited at the Salon des Indépendants in 1914. Upon the outbreak of war in August, the Delaunays decided to stay in Spain and then went to Portugal. They returned to Paris in 1921. In 1924, Sonia opened a "simultaneous" textiles studio whereby her geometric forms were applied to fabrics for clothes. In 1940, the Delaunays left Paris for Châtel-Guyon, before settling in Mougins. After Robert's death in 1941, Sonia went to join the Arps in Grasse. In January 1945, she returned to Paris, where she was a key figure in geometric abstraction until her death.

CAT. 3

Young Girl Sleeping, 1907

Oil on canvas mounted on wood panel, 46 × 55 cm
Paris, Centre Pompidou – Musée National d'Art
Moderne. Gift of Sonia Delaunay and Charles
Delaunay, 1964. Inv. AM 4086 P

CAT. 4

Philomena, 1907

Oil on canvas, 92 × 54.5 cm
Signed and dated bottom right
Paris, Centre Pompidou – Musée National d'Art
Moderne. Purchased from the artist by the state,
1974; attribution, 1976. Inv. AM 1976-947
On long-term loan to the Musée Fabre, Montpellier

CAT. 8

Simultaneous Contrasts, 1912

Oil on canvas, 46 × 55 cm
Signed and dated bottom left
Paris, Centre Pompidou – Musée National d'Art
Moderne. Gift of Sonia Delaunay and Charles
Delaunay, 1964. Inv. AM 4090 P

SERGE FÉRAT
(born Serge Jastrebzoff) Moscow (Russia), 1881–Paris, 1958

Serge Férat was born into a bourgeois family and attended the Kiev School of Fine Art. In 1899, social unrest in Russia led him to leave the country with his cousin Hélène d'Oettingen. After spending time in Florence, they settled in Paris in 1900, where Férat attended the Académie Julian. In 1905, he exhibited for the first time at the Salon des Indépendants under the name Serge Roudnieff. In 1910, he discovered the work of Picasso and became friendly with Apollinaire, with whom he ran the magazine *Les Soirées de Paris* from 1912 until the outbreak of war. At this time Férat was a Cubist painter, whose still lifes were inspired by those of Braque and Picasso. During the First World War he worked as a nurse at the Italian government hospital, where he treated Apollinaire, who had been wounded at the front. His first solo exhibition was held in 1917 at Galerie Percier. In the same year, Férat created the sets and costumes for Apollinaire's play *Les Mamelles de Tirésias*, illustrating the published version of 1918. During the 1920s, his style evolved towards poetic realism, often featuring figures from the *commedia dell'arte*.

CAT. 15

Glass, Pipe and Bottle, 1914–15

Oil and sand on card, 45 × 55 cm
Signed bottom right
Paris, Centre Pompidou – Musée National
d'Art Moderne. Purchased by the state, 1955;
attribution, 1956. Inv. AM 3401 P

LÉONARD FOUJITA (born Tsuguharu Foujita), Tokyo (Japan), 1886–Zurich (Switzerland), 1968

In 1900, a drawing by the young Tsuguharu Foujita was selected for the World's Fair in Paris. Deciding on a career as an artist, Foujita studied at the Tokyo School of Fine Arts before leaving Japan for the French capital in 1913. There, he took a studio in the Cité Falguière, in Montparnasse, alongside Modigliani and Soutine; his paintings soon brought him great success. In 1916, during the war, he left for London; returning to Paris the following year, he showed at the Salon d'Automne of 1919 and then at the Salon des Indépendants of 1920. In 1929, Foujita visited Japan with his wife Youki. After an extensive tour of South America, he settled in Tokyo in 1933. Having come back to Paris in 1939, he returned again to Japan in May 1940, just before the German invasion. There, he worked as a war artist, featuring in many exhibitions staged by the army. In 1949, he obtained an American visa and settled in New York. Back in France, in 1950, he was commissioned to decorate the chapel of Notre-Dame-de-la-Paix in Reims, where he is buried.

CAT. 45

My Interior (Still Life with Alarm Clock), 1921

Oil on canvas stuck on wood panel, 130 × 97 cm
Signed, titled and dated bottom left
Paris, Centre Pompidou – Musée National d'Art
Moderne. Gift of the artist, 1951. Inv. AM 3057 P

CAT. 46

Portrait of the Artist, 1928

Oil and gouache on canvas, 35 × 27 cm
Signed and dated on right
Paris, Centre Pompidou – Musée National d'Art
Moderne. French government purchase, 1937;
allocated 1937. Inv. JP 848 P

JUAN GRIS (born Jose Victoriano Gonzales Perez), Madrid (Spain), 1887–Boulogne-Billancourt (France), 1927

After training at the Escuela de Artes y Manufacturas, Madrid, Juan Gris attended the studio of the academic painter José Maria Carbonero. In 1906, he moved to Paris, where he worked for satirical magazines such as *L'Assiette au beurre* and *Le Charivari*. In 1912, he exhibited for the first time at the Salon des Indépendants with a Cubist portrait of Picasso. He introduced himself to the dealer Daniel-Henry Kahnweiler, with whom he signed a contract the following year and who also became his biographer. Gris was one of the gallery's main artists, alongside Picasso, Braque and Léger. Caught unawares by the outbreak of war while staying in the Pyrenees, he decided to remain in France throughout the conflict. As Kahnweiler had fled to Switzerland, Gris' work was handled by the art dealer Léonce Rosenberg. In 1920, Gris' health deteriorated, but he continued to paint still lifes, pierrots and harlequins. In 1923, he was again exhibited by Kahnweiler, this time at the dealer's Galerie Simon. In 1924, he created sets and costumes for the Ballets Russes. On his death at the age of forty, Gris left an important body of work reflecting his enduring loyalty to Cubist aesthetics.

CAT. 19

Still Life on a Chair, April 1917

Oil on wood panel, 100 × 73 cm
Paris, Centre Pompidou – Musée National d'Art
Moderne. Gift of Raoul La Roche, 1953
Inv. AM 3169 P

CAT. 20

Man from Touraine, September 1918

Oil on canvas, 100 × 65 cm
Signed and dated bottom left
Paris, Centre Pompidou – Musée National d'Art
Moderne. Gift of M. and Mme André Lefèvre, 1952
Inv. AM 3976 P

HENRI HAYDEN
Warsaw (Poland), 1883–Paris, 1970

After enrolling as an engineering student at the Warsaw Polytechnic, Henri Hayden simultaneously attended the School of Fine Art. On graduating in 1907, he moved to Paris, took a studio in the Boulevard Saint-Michel and enrolled at La Palette academy. He spent the summer of 1908 on the trail of Gauguin in Pont-Aven, a period that was an important source of inspiration for him. In 1909, Hayden exhibited at the Salon d'Automne and then, in 1910, at the Salon des Indépendants. His first solo show was at Galerie Druet the following year. The influence of Cézanne led him to adopt the Cubist style early on, before the outbreak of the First World War. His style sparked the interest of the dealer Léonce Rosenberg, with whom he signed an exclusive contract. This was followed by a period of intense work, reflected in his most ambitious painting, *Les Trois Musiciens* (*Three Musicians*), shown at the Salon des Indépendants in 1921 (Paris, Centre Pompidou, Musée National d'Art Moderne, on loan to the Musée des Beaux-Arts, Lyon). However, the following year, Hayden turned away from Cubism. After the Second World War he settled in the town of Reuil-en-Brie, east of Paris. In its bucolic atmosphere, he painted many still lifes and landcapes reflecting essential views with refined colours.

CAT. 13

Parisian Woman with a Fan, 1912

Oil on canvas, 92 × 65 cm
Signed and dated bottom right
Paris, Centre Pompidou – Musée National
d'Art Moderne. Purchased by the state, 1963;
attribution, 1965. Inv. AM 4287 P
On long-term loan to the Musée d'Art et d'Histoire
du Judaïsme, Paris

FLORENCE HENRI
New York (USA), 1893–Compiègne (France), 1982

Florence Henri was born to a French father and German mother, whom she lost at an early age. She first studied painting in Britain, and then music in Germany. During the First World War she lived in Berlin, where she played piano accompaniments for silent films. In 1919, she abandoned her music career and enrolled at the Berlin Academy of Art. In 1924, she moved to Paris and joined the Montparnasse academies, where André Lhote and Fernand Léger were teachers. A visit to the Dessau Bauhaus in 1927 pursuaded her to change medium and take up photography. At first she took self-portraits and still lifes. In 1929, she opened her own studio in Paris and developed a new increasingly abstract approach to photography, joining the New Vision, which was then developing in Germany, where she regularly exhibited. Her first solo show was at Studio 28 in Paris in 1930. After the Second World War, she gave up photography in favour of abstract painting.

CAT. 58

Shop Windows, c. 1930

Silver gelatin print (1977), 24.8 × 22.3 cm
Paris, Centre Pompidou – Musée National d'Art
Moderne. Gift of of Galleria Martini & Ronchetti
with the artist's agreement, 1978
Inv. AM 1978-490

CAT. 59

Bridge over the Canal Saint-Martin, c. 1930–35

Silver gelatin print (1977), 23 × 23 cm
Paris, Centre Pompidou – Musée National d'Art
Moderne. Gift of of Galleria Martini & Ronchetti
with the artist's agreement, 1978
Inv. AM 1978-498

CAT. 60

Barges on the Seine, c. 1930–35

Silver gelatin print (1977), 24.6 × 23.9 cm
Paris, Centre Pompidou – Musée National d'Art
Moderne. Gift of of Galleria Martini & Ronchetti
with the artist's agreement, 1978
Inv. AM 1978-497

GEORGES KARS (born Georges Karpeles), Kralupy (Czech Republic), 1882–Geneva (Switzerland), 1945

In the years 1899–1905, Georges Kars trained at the Academy of Art in Munich, while also studying history of art at the university. He travelled to Spain and stayed in Madrid, where he met Juan Gris in 1905, before continuing on to Portugal. In 1908, he settled in the Montmartre district of Paris. Kars exhibited at the Salon d'Automne for the first time in 1909. During the First World War he went to Belgium and then to Prague. In 1919, he returned to France and had his first solo exhibition at Galerie La Licorne in 1922. He took part in the first Salon des Tuileries the following year. Although the influence of Cubism led him to simplify his forms, Kars remained a realist in his nudes and synthetic portraits. In 1932, Galerie Berthe Weill offered him a solo exhibition. The Second World War obliged him to flee to Geneva and, at the Liberation, a few days before a planned return to Paris, he took his own life.

CAT. 77

Woman with a Grey Shawl, 1930

Oil on canvas, 100 × 81 cm
Signed and dated bottom right
Paris, Centre Pompidou – Musée National d'Art
Moderne. Entered in 1933
Inv. JP 670 P

André Kertész (born Andor Kertész), Budapest (Hungary), 1894–New York (USA), 1985

André Kertész was born into a wealthy family and attended business school in Budapest. Having obtained a post at the stock exchange, he spent his first month's salary on a camera and taught himself photography by taking pictures of his everyday surroundings and experimenting with different techniques. He was drafted in 1914, but did not abandon photography, taking snapshots at the front. In 1925, he moved to Paris and, in 1928, bought a Leica, a small, light and compact camera suited to spontaneous snapshots. He took views of Paris and many portraits. The weekly magazine *Vu* launched in the same year, showcasing the work of photographers, and Kertész became one of its main contributors. In 1936, he signed a contract with the American Keystone agency and left Paris for New York. His first retrospective was held in 1964 at the Museum of Modern Art, New York.

CAT. 52

Boulevard Malesherbes at Midday, 1925

Silver gelatin print (1977), 25.2 × 20.3 cm
Paris, Centre Pompidou – Musée National d'Art
Moderne. Gift of the artist, 1978. Inv. AM 1978-70 (1)

CAT. 51

On the Quays, Paris, 1926

Silver gelatin print (1977), 25.3 × 20.4cm
Paris, Centre Pompidou – Musée National d'Art
Moderne. Gift of the artist, 1978. Inv. AM 1978-85 (1)

CAT. 53

Bal Musette, Paris, 1926

Silver gelatin print (1977), 20.3 × 25.3 cm
Paris, Centre Pompidou – Musée National d'Art
Moderne. Gift of the artist, 1978. Inv. AM 1978-82 (1)

CAT. 55

Shadow of the Eiffel Tower, 1929

Silver gelatin print (1977), 20.4 × 25.3 cm
Paris, Centre Pompidou – Musée National d'Art
Moderne. Gift of the artist, 1978. Inv. AM 1978-109 (1)

CAT. 56

Fishing, Paris, 1929

Silver gelatin print (1977), 25.3 × 20.3 cm
Paris, Centre Pompidou – Musée National d'Art
Moderne. Gift of the artist, 1978. Inv. AM 1978-111 (1)

CAT. 54

Dubo, Dubon, Dubonnet, 1934

Silver gelatin print (1977), 25.3 × 20.3 cm
Paris, Centre Pompidou – Musée National d'Art
Moderne. Gift of the artist, 1978. Inv. AM 1978-151 (1)

Michel Kikoïne
Gomel (Byelorussia) 1892–Paris, 1968

Michel Kikoïne attended a school of painting in Minsk, training alongside Chaïm Soutine. In 1908, both artists enrolled at the Vilnius Academy of Fine Art, graduating in 1911. While there, they met another painter, Pinchus Kremegne, with whom Kikoïne travelled to Paris in 1912. Kikoïne attended then attended the École Nationale des Beaux-Arts and exhibited at the Salon des Indépendants for the first time in 1914. When war broke out, he enlisted in the French army. His first solo exhibition was at Galerie Chéron, Paris, in 1919. In 1922, he and Soutine went to Cagnes, where Kikoïne painted landscapes. In 1926, he exhibited at the Salon des Tuileries for the first time and moved to Montrouge in the following year. In 1939, he joined the military reserve near Soissons, where he made several gouaches of garrison life. After the Liberation, he returned to Paris and embarked on a series of trips to Israel for exhibitions. At the end of his life, he often went to the South of France, where he painted marine landscapes.

CAT. 32

The Pont-Neuf, 1918

Oil on canvas, 60 × 73 cm
Signed bottom right
Paris, Centre Pompidou – Musée National d'Art
Moderne. Gift of Claire Maratier and Jacques
Yankel, 1978. Inv. AM 1978-759

CAT. 33

Portrait of Claire, 1927

Oil on canvas, 73 × 60 cm
Signed bottom right
Paris, Centre Pompidou – Musée National d'Art
Moderne. Gift of Claire Maratier and Jacques
Yankel, 1978. Inv. AM 1978-760

Kisling (born Moïse Kisling)
Krakow (Poland), 1891 – Sanary-sur-Mer (France), 1953

After training at the Kraków School of Fine Art, Moïse Kisling arrived in Paris in 1910. He briefly attended the École Nationale des Beaux-Arts and moved into a studio in Montparnasse. In 1912, he signed a contract with gallery owner Adolphe Basler. Kisling exhibited for the first time at the Salon des Indépendants in 1913, where he showed figurative works in a highly personal style. He spent the summer of 1914 in the Netherlands, but returned to France when war broke out and joined the Foreign Legion. Having been wounded and discharged in 1915, he returned to Paris and then travelled to Spain. In 1919, Galerie Druet hosted his first solo exhibition. Kisling took part in the first Salon des Tuileries in 1923. In 1939, he left Paris for Sanary-sur-Mer and subsequently lived in New York, where his work found great favour. In 1946, Kisling returned to France, where he continued to paint until his death.

CAT. 44

Woman with a Polish Shawl, 1928

Oil on canvas, 100 × 72.5 cm
Signed bottom left
Paris, Centre Pompidou – Musée National d'Art
Moderne. Purchased from the artist by the state,
1934; attribution, 1934. Inv. AM 2006 P
On long-term loan to the Musée d'Art et d'Histoire
du Judaïsme, Paris

François Kollar
Senec (Slovakia), 1904–Créteil (France), 1979

After starting out as a railway worker in Bratislava, Slovak François Kollar moved to Paris in 1924. He had no money and took a job as a turner at the Renault car factory. In 1927, Kollar joined the Studio Draeger and took his first pictures. After taking part in the international photography exhibition in Munich in 1930, he opened his own studio in Paris, working for advertising agencies and in fashion, while also experimenting with different techniques. During this period he received a commission from the publisher Horizons de France for a photoreportage entitled *La France travaille* (*France at Work*), a huge study of the labour world in urban, rural and industrial areas. This project, completed in 1934, helped to establish him professionally. After the Second World War, which he spent in the Poitou-Charentes region, Kollar opened a new studio in Paris and practised both experimental and commercial photography.

CAT. 69

The Eiffel Tower, c. 1930

Silver gelatin print, 28.2 × 21.7 cm
Paris, Centre Pompidou – Musée National d'Art
Moderne. Purchased with the assistance of Yves
Rocher, 2011, former collection of Christian
Bouqueret. Inv. AM 2012-3429

CAT. 70

Detail of the Structure of the Eiffel Tower, 1935

Silver gelatin print, 27.9 × 21.8 cm
Paris, Centre Pompidou – Musée National d'Art
Moderne. Purchased with the assistance of Yves
Rocher, 2011, former collection of Christian
Bouqueret. Inv. AM 2012-3357

Germaine Krull
Poznan (Germany), 1897–Wetzlar (Germany), 1985

In her youth, Germaine Krull travelled throughout Europe and regularly stayed in Paris. She studied photography in Munich, where she opened her own studio in 1919, specialising in portraits. In 1920, she opened another studio in Berlin, before moving to the Netherlands. In 1926, Krull moved to Paris and worked as a freelance photographer for various magazines. She explored many different genres, notably portraiture and urban landscapes, which she elevated through her sensitive images. In 1931, she once again began travelling all over Europe for various exhibitions. In 1940, she fled the German Occupation, going first to Brazil and then to Brazzaville, at that time the capital of French Equatorial Africa, where she headed the propaganda photography department of the Free French government-in-exile. She returned to France in 1944. Two years later, she went to Indochina for a reportage and continued to travel all over South-East Asia until 1983, when she finally returned to Germany a few years before her death.

CAT. 57

Traffic in front of the Louvre, Paris, 1926

Silver gelatin print, 16 × 11.6 cm
Paris, Centre Pompidou – Musée National d'Art
Moderne. Purchase, 1995. Inv. AM 1995-87

FRANTIŠEK KUPKA
Opocno (Czech Republic), 1871– Puteaux (France), 1957

After studying at the Prague Academy of Fine Arts, where he enrolled in 1889, František Kupka moved on to the Vienna Academy before eventually settling in Paris, in 1896, where he painted in a Symbolist manner. He also made a career as an illustrator, publishing drawings in the satirical press, notably *L'Assiette au beurre*. In 1910, he moved to Puteaux, not far from Jacques Villon. Close to the Section d'Or group, in 1912, he exhibited three canvases at the Salon des Indépendants, illustrating his explorations in modelling by means of tonal planes, and two non-figurative paintings entitled *Amorpha* at the Salon d'Automne. After the First World War, in which he served at the front, on the Somme, he returned to his investigation of colour and movement and took up a teaching post in Prague. In 1921, Galerie Jacques Povolozky in Paris hosted his first solo show. Between 1931 and 1934, he was a member of the Abstraction-Création group. He featured in the exhibition "Cubism and Abstract Art" at the Museum of Modern Art, New York, in 1936. Ten years later, he had a major retrospective in Prague.

CAT. 5

The Yellow Scale, 1907

Oil on canvas, 79 × 79 cm
Signed and dated bottom right
Paris, Centre Pompidou – Musée National d'Art
Moderne. Gift of Eugénie Kupka, 1963
Inv. AM 4165 P

CAT. 6

The Archaic, 1910

Oil on canvas, 110 × 90 cm
Signed and dated bottom right
Paris, Centre Pompidou – Musée National d'Art
Moderne. Gift of Eugénie Kupka, 1963
Inv. AM 4169 P

CAT. 9

Study for Amorpha,
Fugue in Two Colours, 1911–12

Oil on canvas, 66 × 66.5 cm
Signed and dated bottom right
Paris, Centre Pompidou – Musée National d'Art
Moderne. Purchased 1957. Inv. AM 3563 P

CAT. 10

Disks of Newton: Study for
Fugue in Two Colours, 1911–12

Oil on canvas, 49.5 × 65 cm
Signed, titled and dated bottom right
Paris, Centre Pompidou – Musée National d'Art
Moderne. Gift of Eugénie Kupka, 1959
Inv. AM 3635 P

ERGY LANDAU
Budapest (Hungary), 1896–Paris, 1967

Having joined the studio of Austrian photographer Franz Xaver Setzer in Vienna in 1918, Ergy Landau then moved to Rudolph Dührkopp's studio in Berlin. Upon her return to Hungary, she opened her own studio in Budapest, and became friendly with the Moholy-Nagys. In 1923, she moved to Paris, where she opened the Studio Landau on Rue Lauriston the following year. She photographed female nudes and portraits of children and the Parisian celebrities who came to sit for her. In 1927, she shed the pictorialist influences that still characterised her portraits and joined the modernist photographers of the New Vision. In 1929, she took part in the "Film und Foto" exhibition in Stuttgart and, in 1933, became one of the founders of the Rapho agency. After the Second World War, Landau also worked in photoreportage, developing a humanist vision.

CAT. 68

Saint-Lazare Railway Station, 1934

Silver gelatin print, 29 × 22.8 cm
Stamp bottom right
Paris, Centre Pompidou – Musée National d'Art
Moderne. Purchase, 1989. Inv. AM 1989-76

TAMARA DE LEMPICKA (born Tamara Gorska), Warsaw (Poland), 1898– Cuernavaca (Mexico), 1980

Tamara de Lempicka trained at the Academy of Fine Arts in St Petersburg. Forced to leave Russia by the Bolshevik Revolution of 1917, she first went to Copenhagen and then to Paris, where she studied under Maurice Denis and André Lhote at the Académie de la Grande Chaumière. She showed at the Salon d'Automne of 1922 and had her first solo show at the Galeria Bottega di Poesia, Milan, in 1925. her distinctive style combining Italian Mannerism and neo-Cubism, coupled with her eccentric personality made her famous. She became one of the most fashionable portraitists – not only of bohemians, but also of the French and Italian aristocracy, her risqué portrayals more than once provoking scandal. On the outbreak of the Second World War, she moved to the USA.

CAT. 81

Girl in a Green Dress, 1927–30

Oil on wood, 61.5 × 45.5 cm
Signed, top right
Paris, Centre Pompidou – Musée National d'Art
Moderne. Purchased 1932
Inv. JP 557 P

CAT. 82

Thadeus Lempicki, 1928

Oil on canvas, 130 × 80.5 cm
Paris, Centre Pompidou – Musée National d'Art
Moderne. Gift of the artist, 1976
Inv. AM 1976-912
On long-term loan to the Musée des Années 30,
Boulogne-Billancourt

JACQUES LIPCHITZ
Druskininkai (Lithuania), 1891– Capri (Italy), 1973

After studying business in his home country, Jacques Lipchitz arrived in Paris in 1909, attending the École Nationale des Beaux-Arts and then the Académie Julian. In 1913, he exhibited for the first time at the Salon d'Automne. In 1914, he visited Majorca with Diego Rivera, then went on to Madrid when war broke out. Lipchitz returned to Paris in 1915 and took over Brancusi's former studio in Montparnasse. The gallery owner Léonce Rosenberg gave him a contract in 1916 and hosted his first solo exhibition at at his gallery, L'Effort Moderne, in 1920. The following year, Lipchitz exhibited at the Salon des Indépendants. The American patron Albert C. Barnes bought some of Lipchitz's sculptures and commissioned him to make bas-reliefs for his foundation. After spending time in Toulouse in May 1940, Lipchitz left for the USA, and met with great success in New York. In 1960, he returned to France, living in Savoie before moving to Italy, where he worked on monumental sculptures. During this period he also made several trips to Israel for exhibitions.

CAT. 29

Sailor with Guitar, 1917

Stone, 90 × 38 × 34 cm
Signed and dated on the reverse
Paris, Centre Pompidou – Musée National d'Art
Moderne. Purchase, 1979. Inv. AM 1978-736

MANÉ-KATZ (born Mane Katz)
Kremenchug (Ukraine), 1894–Tel Aviv (Israel), 1962

Born into a devout Orthodox Jewish milieu, Mané-Katz learned to draw in secret. He first attended the Vilnius School of Art, then the School of Decorative Art in Myrhorod and in the Kiev School of Art, where he first properly encountered mainstream European culture. In 1913, at the age of nineteen, he travelled to Paris, where he studied under Fernand Cormon at the École Nationale des Beaux-Arts, becoming friends with Chaïm Soutine and Marc Chagall. Upon the outbreak of the First World War, he sought to enlist in the French Foreign Legion but was rejected on the grounds of being too short. In 1916–17, he lived in Petrograd (Saint Petersburg), where he documented Jewish life. He then returned to the Ukraine, where he gave drawing lessons and had his first exhibition in Kharkiv in 1919. Having returned to Paris in 1921, the following year he exhibited works inspired by traditional Eastern European Jewish themes at Galerie Percier. In 1937, the French government bought one of his paintings, while Galerie Charpentier held a retrospective of his work. Following the German invasion of France in 1939, he was arrested by enemy troops, but managed to escape and travelled to the United States. After the war, he returned to live in Paris, making regular visits to Israel, where there is now a Mané-Katz Museum in Haifa.

CAT. 34

Two Rabbis, 1930

Oil on canvas, 92 × 72 cm
Signed and dated bottom right
Paris, Centre Pompidou – Musée National d'Art
Moderne. Gift of Jean Cassou. Inv. AM 5015 P

LOUIS MARCOUSSIS
(born Ludwik Kazimierz Markus)
Warsaw (Poland), 1878–Cusset (France), 1941

Born into a family of rich industrialists, Louis Marcoussis studied law in Warsaw before enrolling at the School of Fine Art in Kraków. In 1903, he moved to Paris, where he was based near Montmartre, attended the Académie Julian and contributed illustrations to many satirical magazines. He exhibited for the first time at the Salon d'Automne in 1905, and then at the Salon des Indépendants the following year. He also exhibited engravings at the Salon de la Section d'Or in 1912. In July 1913, Marcoussis married a Polish student at the Académie Ranson, the painter Alice Halicka. At the Salon des Indépendants of 1914, Marcoussis showed a painting featuring a musician, his most ambitious work of that period. During the war he enlisted in the Foreign Legion and obtained French citizenship. In 1919, he returned to Paris and continued to paint in a Cubist style that he did not fundamentally question for the rest of his career. In addition to reverse painting on glass (1919–28), he produced a great many engravings linked to his sustained interest in literature and poetry, reflected in 1934 in his collection after Guillaume Apollinaire, *Eaux-fortes pour Alcools* (*Alcohol-inspired etchings*). In 1925, he had his first solo exhibition at Galerie Pierre Chareau, Paris.

CAT. 12

Still Life with Chessboard, 1912

Oil on canvas, 143 × 97 cm
Signed and dated bottom right
Paris, Centre Pompidou – Musée National d'Art
Moderne. Purchase, 1950. Inv. AM 2988 P

AMEDEO MODIGLIANI
Livorno (Italy), 1884–Paris, 1920

Amedeo Modigliani studied at the Scuola Libera di Nudo in Florence and then at Venice's Academy of Fine Arts. In 1906, he moved to Paris, settling in Montmartre, close to the Bateau-Lavoir. In 1909, he became friends with Constantin Brancusi and moved to Montparnasse, where he sculpted in stone. He later took a studio at La Ruche, returning to painting with an extensive series of portraits featuring painter friends and other regulars of Montparnasse. In 1916, he was taken under the wing of dealer Leopold Zborowski, on whose initiative he was given his first solo show at Galerie Berthe Weill the following year. The nudes he presented caused a scandal. Despite a spell in the South of France in 1918–19, the artist's health continued to decline, and he died in January 1920.

CAT. 36

Woman's Head, 1911–13

Stone, 47 × 27 × 31 cm
Paris, Centre Pompidou – Musée National d'Art
Moderne. Purchased 1950. Inv. AM 903 S

CAT. 35

Woman's Head, 1912

Stone, 58 × 12 × 16 cm
Signed in the hair
Paris, Centre Pompidou – Musée National d'Art
Moderne. Purchase, 1949. Inv. AM 876 S

CAT. 37

Lolotte, June 1917

Oil on canvas, 55 × 35.5 cm
Signed top right
Paris, Centre Pompidou – Musée National d'Art
Moderne. Purchased 1932. Inv. JP 558 P
On long-term loan to the Musée d'Art et d'Histoire
du Judaïsme, Paris

CAT. 38

Gaston Modot, 1918

Oil on canvas, 92.7 × 53.6 cm
Signed top right
Paris, Centre Pompidou – Musée National d'Art
Moderne. Acceptance in lieu of tax, estate of Alex
Maguy-Glass, 2002. Inv. AM 2002-128

CAT. 39

Portrait of Dédie (Odette Hayden), 1918

Oil on canvas, 92 × 60 cm
Signed top left
Paris, Centre Pompidou – Musée National d'Art
Moderne. M. and Mme André Lefèvre, donation,
1952. Inv. AM 3974 P

CAT. 40

The Young Apprentice, 1918–19

Oil on canvas, 100 × 65 cm
Signed top left
Paris, Musée de l'Orangerie, collection of Jean
Walter and Paul Guillaume
Inv. RF 1963-71

MELA MUTER
(born Marie-Melania Klingsland)
Warsaw (Poland) 1876–Paris, 1967

Born into a cultured Jewish family, Mela Muter studied in Warsaw under Milosz Kotarbinski in classes reserved for women at the School of Painting and Drawing. In 1901, she moved to Paris with her socialist journalist husband and became one of the first artists of the Polish diaspora in Paris, attending the Colarossi and Grande-Chaumière academies. In 1905, she exhibited for the first time at the Salon des Indépendants and then at the Salon d'Automne. During these years, she frequently stayed at Concarneau in Brittany, and became familiar with the works of the Pont-Aven school, which influenced her for a time. In 1914, she went to Avignon, only returning to Paris at the end of the war. Her first solo exhibition was held in 1918 at Galerie Chéron. Exhibiting for the first time at the Salon des Tuileries in 1924, Muter became known for her many portraits in a highly personal style, depicting the celebrities, politicians, writers, artists and musicians she knew. However, she was a politically active artist whose paintings also depicted the disadvantaged.

The Sculptor François Pompon, 1924

Oil on canvas, 146 × 114 cm
Signed and dated top right
Paris, Centre Pompidou – Musée National
d'Art Moderne. Purchased by the state, 1933;
attribution, 1937. Inv. AM 2289 P
On long-term loan to the Musée des Beaux-Arts,
Dijon

CHANA ORLOFF
Starokostyantyniv (Ukraine), 1888–Tel Aviv (Israel), 1968

Chana Orloff's family fled the pogroms in Ukraine
and sought refuge in Palestine in 1905. In 1910,
Orloff moved to Paris and attended the École
des Arts Décoratifs and the Académie Vassilieff,
where she made her first sculptures. In 1912, she
met Modigliani and exhibited for the first time at
the Salon d'Automne in 1913. In the early 1920s,
she gained a reputation as a portrait artist in the
modern, synthetic style, which brought her a great
many commissions. In 1922, she had her first solo
exhibition at Galerie Povolozky. In 1926, Orloff
commissioned her own studio in Villa Seurat
from the architect Auguste Perret. She obtained
French citizenship in 1926 and made her first
trip to the USA in 1928. In 1940, Orloff moved to
Switzerland, where she worked until the end of the
war. On returning to Paris, she found her studio
ransacked. In 1949, she travelled to Israel, where
she continued to make sculptures and received
many commissions.

CAT. 42

Daniel O. Widhopff, 1923

Bronze (cast by Alexis Rudier, Paris),
106 × 61 × 54 cm
Signed on the reverse, bottom right
Paris, Centre Pompidou – Musée National
d'Art Moderne. Purchased by the state, 1946;
attribution, 1947. Inv. AM 827 S

JULES PASCIN
(born Julius Mordecai Pincas)
Vidin (Bulgaria), 1885–Paris, 1930

After art training in Budapest and Vienna, Jules
Pascin went to Munich, where he enrolled at the
Academy of Art in 1903. At this time, he published
drawings in the satirical magazine *Simplicissimus*.
In 1905, he moved to Paris, taking a studio in
Montparnasse. In 1908, he exhibited for the first
time at the Salon d'Automne, and in 1910 at the
Salon des Indépendants. Pascin mainly painted
portraits and female nudes. When war broke out,
he moved to the USA. Returning to Paris in 1920,
he became an important figure in Montparnasse
and held his first solo exhibition at Galerie Pierre
Loeb in 1924. The following year, Pascin exhibited

at the Salon des Tuileries before embarking on
a series of trips to Italy and then Palestine. He
returned to New York and continued his travels in
Spain and Portugal. In 1929, he signed a contract
with Galerie Bernheim-Jeune. On 2 June 1930,
suffering from depression and alcoholism, Pascin
took his own life.

CAT. 41

Hermine David, 1918

Oil on canvas, 51 × 43 cm
Paris, Centre Pompidou – Musée National d'Art
Moderne. Gift of Hermine David and Lucy Krohg,
1936. Inv. JP 783 BIS P
On long-term loan to the Musée Richard Anacréon,
Granville

CAT. 78

Alfred Flechtheim Dressed as a Toreador,
1925

Oil on canvas, 104 × 80 cm
Signed top right
Paris, Centre Pompidou – Musée National d'Art
Moderne. Bequest of Alfred Flechtheim, 1938
Inv. JP 871 P

PABLO PICASSO
Málaga (Spain), 1881–Mougins (France), 1973

Pablo Picasso trained in Madrid and Barcelona,
where he was part of the Els Quatre Gats circle, and
arrived in Paris in 1901. His "blue period" began
at the Bateau-Lavoir, followed, after 1905, by his
"rose period". In 1907, influenced by the work of
Cézanne and by African and Oceanian art, Picasso
painted *Les Demoiselles d'Avignon* (New York,
The Museum of Modern Art), a work that helped
give rise to Cubism, which he conceived with
Georges Braque. During the First World War,
while Picasso was working on designs for the
ballet *Parade*, he returned to a more traditional
figuration. In the 1920s and 1930s, he produced
autobiographical paintings and sculptures with
aggressive forms, akin to Surrealism. In 1937, he
painted *Guernica* for the Spanish pavilion at the
international exhibition in Paris (Madrid, Museo
Nacional Centro de Arte Reina Sofía). After the
Liberation, he settled on the Riviera, where he
produced work in many different forms, characterised by a capacity for invention that makes him
one of the 20th century's greatest artists.

CAT. 1

Gustave Coquiot, 1901

Oil on canvas, 100 × 81 cm
Signed bottom right
Paris, Centre Pompidou – Musée National d'Art
Moderne. Purchased by the Musées Nationaux,
1933. Inv. JP 652 P. On long-term loan to the Musée
National Picasso, Paris

CAT. 11

Woman Seated in an Armchair, spring
1910

Oil on canvas, 100 × 73 cm
Paris, Centre Pompidou – Musée National d'Art
Moderne. Bequest of Georges Salles, 1967
Inv. AM 4391 P

CAT. 22

Young Girl with a Hoop, spring 1919

Oil and sand on canvas, 142.5 × 79 cm
Signed and dated top right
Paris, Centre Pompidou – Musée National d'Art
Moderne. Bequest of Baroness Eva Gourgaud, 1965
Inv. AM 4312 P

ALFRED RETH
Budapest (Hungary), 1884–Paris, 1966

After training at art school in Budapest, Alfred
Reth spent time in Italy before moving to Paris
in 1905, where he lived in Montparnasse and
attended the studio of Jacques-Émile Blanche.
After a second stay in Italy, Reth returned to Paris
in 1907. He discovered Hindu and Khmer art and
also took an interest in the works by Cézanne
exhibited that year at the Salon d'Automne. He
rubbed shoulders with the Cubists, whose artistic
pursuits he shared, as reflected in the works he
sent to the Salon des Indépendants and Salon
d'Automne from 1911. His first solo exhibition
was at Galerie Berthe Weill in 1914. During the
war, Reth was interned as a "citizen of an enemy
country of France". In the 1930s, Reth became
a convert to abstraction and a member of the
group Abstraction-Création, founded in 1931.
The period after the Second World War saw the
establishment of the Salon des Réalités Nouvelles,
where Reth exhibited abstract paintings featuring
different textures and materials.

CAT. 14

The Hubin Restaurant, 1913

Oil on canvas, 130 × 97 cm
Signed bottom left
Paris, Centre Pompidou – Musée National
d'Art Moderne. Purchased by the state, 1955;
attribution, 1955. Inv. AM 3358 P

GINO SEVERINI
Cortona (Italy), 1883–Paris, 1966

Having met Umberto Boccioni and Giacomo
Balla in Rome in 1901, Gino Severini adopted
the divisionist technique used by Seurat. In
1906, he moved to Paris, near Montmartre, and
made contact with the artistic community. He
exhibited at the Salon d'Automne of 1907 and
the Salon des Indépendants of 1908. In 1910,
he was a signatory of the *Manifesto of Futurist*

Painters and, in 1912, was part of the exhibition at Galerie Bernheim-Jeune that launched Futurism in Paris. The following year, Severini married the daughter of Paul Fort, "prince of poets". Although the First World War inspired him to paint many more Futurist paintings, he soon converted to a Cubist style, influenced by Juan Gris. In 1919, he signed a contract with the gallery owner Léonce Rosenberg, who gave him a solo exhibition in the same year. In 1921, he published the treatise *Du cubisme au classicisme* (*From Cubisim to Clacissism*), which marked his return to traditional figuration. He then began creating murals, notably featuring figures based on the *commedia dell'arte* and also religious subjects. In Italy, during the 1930s, he received several commissions from the regime of Benito Mussolini. After 1945, Severini pursued a style between abstraction and figuration.

CAT. 17

Portrait of Paul Fort, 1915

Oil, chalk, charcoal, Indian ink and objects on paper glued on canvas, 81 × 65 cm
Signature and dedication bottom right
Paris, Centre Pompidou – Musée National d'Art Moderne. Gift of Mme Severini and her daughters, 1967. Inv. AM 4414 P

CHAÏM SOUTINE
Smilavichy (Byelorussia), 1893– Paris, 1943

Chaïm Soutine displayed a talent for drawing at an early age. As his family followed the Judaic rule forbidding all forms of representation, he left home to study drawing in Minsk and Riga in 1907. In 1913, he moved to Paris, where he attended the École Nationale des Beaux-Arts and copied works in the Louvre. He was one of the Russian artists at La Ruche. In 1915, Soutine met Modigliani, who introduced him to his own art dealer, Léopold Zborowski. Soutine signed his first contract with Zborowski in 1918 and then, at the dealer's invitation, spent time in the South of France, in Céret and Cagnes, where he painted many landscapes. During this time, the American collector Alfred C. Barnes was in Paris and bought a large number of Soutine's paintings. On his return to the city in 1925, Soutine painted his series of flayed oxen, inspired by Rembrandt, and many portraits. His first solo exhibition was at Galerie Bing in 1927. The following year, Soutine met Marcellin and Madeleine Castaing, who became his patrons and supporters. Soutine suffered from poor health and died during the Second World War, having remained in France and been obliged to flee anti-Jewish persecution.

CAT. 30

Still Life with Pipe, 1916

Oil on canvas, 54 × 73.4 cm
Signed bottom right
Paris, Centre Pompidou – Musée National d'Art Moderne. Dation, 1988. Inv. AM 1988-756
On long-term loan to the Musée d'Art Moderne, Troyes

CAT. 72

The Sculptor Oscar Mieštchaninoff, 1923–24

Oil on canvas, 83 × 65 cm

Signed top right
Paris, Centre Pompidou – Musée National d'Art Moderne. Bequest of Mme Miestchaninoff, 1972 Inv. AM 1972-30

CAT. 73

The Best Man, 1924–25

Oil on canvas, 100 × 81 cm
Signed bottom right
Paris, Musée de l'Orangerie, collection of Jean Walter and Paul Guillaume. Inv. RF 1960–48

CAT. 31

The Hanging Chicken, 1925

Oil on wood panel, 125 × 80 cm
Paris, Centre Pompidou – Musée National d'Art Moderne
Siezed from the former collection of Baron Kojiro Matsukata and assigned to the Musée National d'Art Moderne in 1959, under the terms of the peace treaty with Japan. Inv. AM 3612 P

CAT. 74

The Head Altar Boy, 1925

Oil on canvas, 100 × 55.9 cm
Paris, Centre Pompidou – Musée National d'Art Moderne. Dation, 1995. Inv. AM 1995-207
On long-term loan to the Musée des Beaux-Arts, Chartres

CAT. 75

The Young English Girl, c. 1934

Oil on canvas, 46 × 65 cm
Paris, Musée de l'Orangerie, collection of Jean Walter and Paul Guillaume. Inv. RF 1963-97

AMADEO DE SOUZA-CARDOSO
Amarante (Portugal), 1887–Espinho (Portugal), 1918

Born into a bourgeois family in northern Portugal, Amadeo de Souza-Cardoso showed a talent for drawing at a young age. In accordance with his father's wishes, he enrolled at the School of Fine Art in Lisbon in 1905, intending to become an architect. However, the academic teaching did not suit the young artist, who moved to Paris the following year, where he published caricatures. He became a painter and, in 1911, held an exhibition of his work in his own studio with Modigliani. In the same year, he began sending paintings in a linear, primitivist style to the Salon des Indépendants, and then to the Salon d'Automne in 1912, the year in which he published his album of *XX Dessins*, revealing the originality of his decorative style. He was friendly with Robert and Sonia Delaunay and experimented with a style akin to Cubism, being drawn to abstraction. War broke out when De Souza-Cardoso was in Barceona, from where he returned to Portugal. There he created many compositions reflecting a highly coloured synthetic Cubism, influenced by the aesthetics of collage. In 1918, De Souza-Cardoso fell victim to the Spanish flu.

CAT. 7

Riders, 1913

Oil on canvas, 100 × 100 cm
Signed bottom right
Paris, Centre Pompidou – Musée National d'Art Moderne. Purchased 1959. Inv. AM 3636 P
On long-term loan to the Musée Fabre, Montpellier

LÉOPOLD SURVAGE
(born Leopold Freder Sturzwage) Moscow (Russia), 1879–Paris, 1968

Léopold Survage initially took over the family piano-building business, before studying at the art school in Moscow and then moving to Paris in August 1909. There, he enrolled at the Matisse and Colarossi academies. He exhibited at the Salon d'Automne in 1911, and at the Salon des Indépendants in 1913 with early Cubist paintings. His *Rythmes colorés* series was painted in the years 1912–14 and comprises the elements of a highly innovative abstract film. The project met with enthusiasm from Apollinaire, but was never made. Survage was exempted from military service due to poor health and moved to Nice. In 1917, Apollinaire organised Survage's first solo exhibition, linked to the magazine *Les Soirées de Paris*. Survage's painting is characterised by contrasting perspectives, which led the artist to collaborate notably with the Ballets Russes (*Mavra*, comic opera by Igor Stravinsky, 1922). He was one of the artists who relaunched the Salon de la Section d'Or, and was supported at that time by Léonce Rosenberg's gallery, L'Effort Moderne. Although Survage returned to a stylised figuration in the late 1920s, Cubism remained a major source of inspiration throughout his long career. This can be seen in the set designs he made for the International Exposition of Art and Technology in Modern Life, held in Paris in 1937.

CAT. 18

The Baroness Hélène d'Oettingen, 1917

Oil on canvas, 200 × 235 cm
Paris, Centre Pompidou – Musée National d'Art Moderne. Purchased by the state, 1964; attribution, 1964. Inv. AM 4277 P

KEES VAN DONGEN

(born Cornelis Théodorus Marie van Dongen), Delfshaven (Netherlands), 1877–Monaco (Principality of Monaco), 1968

After attending the Academy of Fine Art in Rotterdam, Kees van Dongen first spent time in Paris in 1897, making his living by publishing drawings in satirical magazines. In 1904, he exhibited at the Salon des Indépendants and Salon d'Automne, while the dealer Ambroise Vollard organised his first solo exhibition. The following year, his work appeared in the "Fauve cage" at the Salon d'Automne of 1905. In 1906, Van Dongen moved to the Bateau-Lavoir in Montmartre. He exhibited at Galerie Daniel-Henry Kahnweiler, but soon signed a contract with Galerie Bernheim-Jeune. His subjects of choice were portraits, nudes, the cabarets of Montmartre and fairground scenes in brilliant colours. In the 1910s, he travelled to Spain, Morocco and Egypt, bringing back paintings in a smoother, more orientalist style. Before the First World War, he had some *succès de scandale,* while rubbing shoulders with the smart set in Paris, for whom he became the portrait artist of choice in the 1920s. He obtained French citizenship in 1929. During the Second World War, Van Dongen agreed to be part of a group of French artists travelling to the Germany of the Third Reich, a decision for which he was much criticised.

CAT. 2

Nini, Dancer at the Folies-Bergère, c. 1909

Oil on canvas, 130 × 97 cm
Signed bottom left
Paris, Centre Pompidou – Musée National d'Art Moderne. Gift of Jean Aron, 1948
Inv. AM 2834 P

CAT. 80

Jasmy Jacob, 1920

Oil on canvas, 195 × 131.5 cm
Signed bottom centre
Paris, Centre Pompidou – Musée National d'Art Moderne. Bequest of Jasmy Alvin, 1946
Inv. AM 2699 P

CAT. 79

Billy, c. 1920

Oil on canvas, 100 × 81 cm
Signed bottom centre
Paris, Centre Pompidou – Musée National d'Art Moderne. Bequest of Annette Wolfers-Denner, 2009. Inv. AM 2009-138
On long-term loan to the Musée de Grenoble

WOLS

(born Alfred Otto Wolfgang Schulze) Berlin (Germany), 1913–Paris, 1951

Raised in Dresden, where he trained both as a violinist and as a photographer, Wols briefly attended the Bauhaus in Dessau. In 1932, he moved to Paris, where he established himself as a photographer and mixed with the Surrealists. At the start of the Second World War, his German origins led to his being interned at the camp at Les Milles, near Aix-en-Provence, where he made many drawings in a detailed style, some of which reflect the conditions in which he was detained. Eventually freed, he moved to Cassis and then Dieulefit, where he began painting in small formats. In 1945, he returned to Paris, where he exhibited his graphic works at Galerie René Drouin and became friendly with the writer Jean-Paul Sartre. Drouin assisted him financially, enabling him to return to oil painting, which he exhibited in 1947. He became an important figure in action painting and matter painting. He died prematurely as a result of his alcoholism.

CAT. 71

Doll on the Cobbles, 1938–39

Silver gelatin print, 23 × 17 cm
Paris, Centre Pompidou – Musée National d'Art Moderne. Purchase, 2004. Inv. AM 2004-13

OSSIP ZADKINE

Vitebsk (Byelorussia), 1888–Paris, 1967

Byelorussian Ossip Zadkine showed a talent for drawing and modelling at a young age. In 1905, he was sent to stay with a family in Britain, where he attended art school and learned to sculpt in wood. After first returning home to his family, he moved to Paris in 1910 and enrolled at the École Nationale des Beaux-Arts. He had a studio in La Ruche and exhibited for the first time in 1911 at the Salon des Indépendants and Salon d'Automne, with directly carved sculptures influenced by primitivism. When war broke out, Zadkine enlisted in the first foreign regiment of the French army. Having been gassed and discharged in 1917, he returned to Paris, where he met Modigliani. In the 1920s, Zadkine obtained his first solo exhibition, showing work that reflected an expressive Cubism, soon to be influenced by Greek mythology. He spent the years 1941–45 in exile in New York and Arizona. On his return, his reputation grew. He received monumental commissions such as *The Destroyed City* for the city of Rotterdam in 1950.

CAT. 28

Woman with a Fan, 1920

Bronze (numbered 2/5), 85 × 34 × 27 cm
Signed and dated, bottom left
Paris, Centre Pompidou – Musée National d'Art Moderne. Purchased by the state, 1962; attribution, 1962. Inv. AM 1319 S

EUGÈNE ZAK

Mogilno (Poland), 1884–Paris, 1926

Eugène Zak arrived in Paris from Poland in 1902, and initially studied under the academic painter Jean-Léon Gérôme at the École Nationale des Beaux-Arts, before attending the Académie Colarossi. In 1903, he went to Italy, where he was profoundly influenced by the art of the Renaissance, and then he visited Munich. Like many of his contemporaries, Zak was influenced by the work of Cézanne. On his return to Paris, he exhibited at the Salon d'Automne from 1904 and at the Salon des Indépendants from 1906. His first solo exhibition was organised in 1911 by Galerie Druet. When the First World War broke out, Zak went to Nice and then to Vence. In 1916, he moved to Poland and then to Germany, finally settling in France in 1921. There, he refined his style, midway between the classical tradition and a desire for formal stylisation. In 1924, Zak exhibited at the Salon des Tuileries. He died of a heart attack at the age of 42.

CAT. 43

The Toy, 1924

Signed bottom left
Paris, Centre Pompidou – Musée National d'Art Moderne. Gift of Hedwige Zak, 1937
Inv. AM 2140 P

BIBLIOGRAPHY

Entries in order of date of publication.

Warnod, 1925
André Warnod, *Les Berceaux de la jeune peinture. L'École de Paris*, Paris, Albin Michel, 1925.

Kiki, 1929
Kiki, *Souvenirs*, with preface by Foujita, Paris, Henri Broca, 1929.

Carco, 1953
Francis Carco, *L'Ami des peintres. Bohème d'artistes*, Paris, Gallimard, 1953.

Chagall, 1960
Marc Chagall, *My Life*, trans. from the French of *Ma Vie* by E. Abbott, New York, Orion Press, 1960.

Nacenta, 1960
Raymond Nacenta, *École de Paris. Son histoire, son époque*, Neuchâtel, Ides et Calendes, 1960.

Dorival, 1961
Bernard Dorival, *L'École de Paris au Musée national d'art moderne*, Paris, Aimery Somogy, 1961.

Crespelle, 1962
Jean-Paul Crespelle, *Montparnasse vivant*, Paris, Hachette, 1962.

Zadkine, 1968
Ossip Zadkine, *Le Maillet et le Ciseau. Souvenirs de ma vie*, Paris, Albin Michel, 1968.

Crespelle, 1976
Jean-Paul Crespelle, *La Vie quotidienne à Montparnasse à la grande époque, 1905-1930*, Paris, Hachette, 1976.

Warnod, 1978
Jeanine Warnod, *La Ruche & Montparnasse*, Paris and Geneva, Weber, 1978.

Cohen, 1985
Arthur A. Cohen, "From Eastern Europe to Paris and Beyond", in exh. cat., New York, 1985, pp. 61–66.

Golan, 1985
Romy Golan, "*The École Française vs. the École de Paris*: The Debate About the Status of Jewish Artists in Paris between the Wars", in exh. cat., New York, 1985, pp. 81–87.

Klüver and Martin, 1985
Billy Klüver and Julie Martin, "Carrefour Vavin", in exh. cat., New York, 1985, pp. 69–79.

Silver, 1985
Kenneth E. Silver, "The Circle of Montparnasse: Jewish Artists in Paris, 1905–1945", in exh. cat., New York, 1985, pp. 13–59.

Green, 1987
Christopher Green, *Cubism and Its Enemies: Modern Movements and Reaction in French Art, 1916–1928*, New Haven and London, Yale University Press, 1987.

Warnod, 1988
Jeanine Warnod, *Les Artistes de Montparnasse*, Paris, Mayer-Van Wilder, 1988.

Kaspi and Marès, 1989
André Kaspi and Antoine Marès, eds, *Le Paris des étrangers depuis un siècle*, Paris, Imprimerie nationale, 1989.

Klüver and Martin, 1989
Billy Klüver and Julie Martin, *Kiki et Montparnasse, 1900-1930*, Paris, Flammarion, 1989.

Silver, 1989
Kenneth E. Silver, *Esprit de corps: The Art of the Parisian Avant-Garde and the First World War, 1914–1925*, Princeton, NJ, Princeton University Press, 1989.

Gee, 1991
Malcolm Gee, "Art Patrons of the 1920s", in exh. cat., Montreal, 1991, p. 404–15.

Golan, 1991
Romy Golan, "Modes of Escape: The Representation of Paris in the Twenties", in exh. cat., Montreal, 1991, pp. 336–75.

Klüver and Martin, 1991
Billy Klüver and Julie Martin, "Paris, the Artists' City", in exh. cat., Montreal, 1991, pp. 378–90.

Chevrefils Desbiolles, 1993
Yves Chevrefils Desbiolles, *Les Revues d'art à Paris, 1905-1940*, Paris, Éditions Ent'revues, 1993.

Marès and Milza, 1994
Antoine Marès and Pierre Milza, eds, *Le Paris des étrangers depuis 1945*, Paris, Publications de la Sorbonne, 1994.

Monnier and Vovelle, 1994
Gérard Monnier and José Vovelle, eds, *Un art sans frontières. L'internationalisation des arts en Europe, 1900-1950*, Paris, Publications de la Sorbonne, 1994.

Bertrand Dorléac, 1995-96
Laurence Bertrand Dorléac, "L'École de Paris, un problème de définition", *Revista de História da Arte e Arqueologia*, 1995-96.

Bouqueret, 1997
Christian Bouqueret, *Des Années folles aux années noires. La Nouvelle Vision photographique en France, 1920-1940*, Paris, Marval, 1997.

Delaperrière and Marès, 1997
Maria Delaperrière and Antoine Marès, eds, *Paris, capitale culturelle de l'Europe centrale ? Les échanges intellectuels entre la France et les pays de l'Europe médiane, 1918-1939*, Paris, Institut d'études slaves, 1997.

Nahon, 1998
Pierre Nahon, *Les Marchands d'art en France, XIXe et XXe siècles*, Paris, Éditions de la Différence, 1998.

Rotily, 1998
Jocelyne Rotily, *Artistes américains à Paris, 1914-1939*, Paris, L'Harmattan, 1998.

Andral and Krebs, 2000
Jean-Louis Andral and Sophie Krebs, eds, *L'École de Paris. L'atelier cosmopolite*, Paris, Gallimard/Paris-Musées, 2000.

Bertrand Dorléac, 2000
Laurence Bertrand Dorléac, "L'École de Paris, suites", in exh. cat., Paris, 2000, pp. 148–57.

Fabre, 2000
Gladys Fabre, "Qu'est ce que l'École de Paris ?", in exh. cat., Paris, 2000, pp. 25–40.

Fischer, 2000
Yona Fischer, "Le désir de Paris", in exh. cat., Paris, 2000, pp. 103–13.

Gee, 2000
Malcolm Gee, "Le réseau économique", in exh. cat., Paris, 2000, pp. 127–37.

Green, 2000
Christopher Green, "Les cubismes de 'l'École de Paris'", in exh. cat., Paris, 2000, pp. 58–70.

Marès, 2000
Antoine Marès, "Pourquoi des étrangers à Paris ?", in exh. cat., Paris, 2000, pp. 138–47.

Molderings, 2000
Herbert Molderings, "Nouvelles images de Paris", in exh. cat., Paris, 2000, pp. 71–84.

Nieszawer, Boyé and Fogel, 2000
Nadine Nieszawer, Marie Boyé and Paul Fogel, *Peintres juifs à Paris, 1905-1939. École de Paris*, Paris, Denoël, 2000.

Silver, 2000
Kenneth E. Silver, "Made in Paris", in exh. cat., Paris, 2000, pp. 41–57.

Fraquelli, 2002
Simoneta Fraquelli, "Montparnasse and the Right Bank: Myth and Reality", in exh. cat., London/Bilbao, 2002, pp. 106–17.

Warnod, 2004
Jeanine Warnod, *L'École de Paris. Dans l'intimité de Chagall, Foujita, Pascin, Cendrars, Carco, Mac Orlan, à Montmartre et à Montparnasse*, Paris, Arcadia Éditions/Musée du Montparnasse, 2004.

Warnod, 2008
Jeanine Warnod, *Chez la baronne d'Oettingen. Paris russe et avant-gardes (1913–1935)*, Paris, Éditions de Conti, 2008.

Renault, 2013
Olivier Renault, *Montparnasse. Les lieux de légende. Ateliers, cafés mythiques, académies, cité d'artistes*, Paris, Parigramme, 2013.

Nieszawer and Princ, 2015
Nadine Nieszawer and Déborah Princ, eds, *Jewish Artists of the School of Paris, 1905–1939*, Paris, Somogy, 2015.

Yagil, 2015
Limore Yagil, *Au nom de l'art, 1933-1945. Exils, solidarités et engagements*, Paris, Fayard, 2015.

Chagall, 2017
Marc Chagall, *Mon univers. Autobiographie*, translated from Yiddish by Chantal Ringuet and Pierre Anctil, Montreal, Fidès, 2017.

Joyeux-Prunel, 2017
Béatrice Joyeux-Prunel, *Les Avant-Gardes artistiques, 1918-1945. Une histoire transnationale*, Paris, Gallimard, "Folio histoire", 2017.

EXHIBITIONS

Geneva, 1973
L'École de Paris et la belle époque de Montparnasse, Geneva, Musée du Petit Palais, 1973 (curated by Georges Peillex).

New York, 1985
The Circle of Montparnasse. Jewish Artists in Paris, 1905–1945, New York, The Jewish Museum, October 1985–February 1986 (curated by Kenneth E. Silver and Romy Golan).

Montréal, 1991
Les Années 20. L'âge des métropoles / The 1920s: Age of the Metropolis, Montreal, Musée des Beaux-Arts de Montréal, 20 June–10 November 1991 (curated by Jean Clair).

Lausanne, 1994
Les Peintres de Zborowski. Modigliani, Utrillo, Soutine et leurs amis, Lausanne, Fondation de l'Hermitage, 24 June–23 October 1994 (curated by Marc Restellini and Joachim Pissarro).

Paris, 1995
Les Heures chaudes de Montparnasse, Paris, Espace Electra, 15 May–23 July 1995 (curated by Jean-Marie Drot).

Paris, 1996
Autour de Bourdelle. Paris et les artistes polonais, 1900-1918, Paris, Musée Bourdelle, 23 October 1996–19 January 1997 (curated by Elsbieta Grabska).

New York, 2000
Painters in Paris, 1895–1950, New York, The Metropolitan Museum of Art, 8 March–31 December 2000 (curated by William Liebermann).

Paris, 2000
L'École de Paris, 1904-1929, la part de l'Autre, Paris, Musée d'Art Moderne de la Ville de Paris, 30 November 2000–11 March 2001 (curated by Jean-Louis Andral and Sophie Krebs).

London/Bilbao, 2002
Paris, Capital of the Arts, 1900–1968, London, Royal Academy of Arts, 26 January–19 April 2002; Bilbao, Guggenheim Museum, 21 May–3 September 2002 (curated by Ann Dumas, Gladys Fabre, Norman Rosenthal and Sarah Wilson).

Budapest, 2003
Modigliani, Soutine és Montparnasse-i barátaik / Modigliani, Soutine and Their Friends from Montparnasse, Budapest, Hungarian Jewish Museum, 23 July–19 October 2003 (curated by László Beke).

Paris, 2005
Montparnasse déporté, Paris, Musée du Montparnasse, 12 May–2 October 2005 (curated by Sylvie Buisson).

Okazaki, 2006
L'École de Paris: Between Primitivism and Nostalgia, Okazaki, Okazaki City Museum, 30 June–30 July 2006; Kumamoto, Kumamoto Prefectural Museum of Art, 4 August–9 October 2006; Kobe, Hyogo Prefectural Museum of Art, 18 October–17 December 2006 (curated by Sophie Krebs).

Martigny, 2013
Modigliani et l'École de Paris, Martigny, Fondation Pierre Gianadda, 21 June–24 November 2013 (curated by Catherine Grenier).

Turin, 2015
Modigliani et la bohème di Parigi, Turin, Galleria Civica d'Arte Moderna e Contemporanea, 14 March–19 July 2015 (curated by Jean-Michel Bouhours).

RENDEZVOUS IN PARIS
PICASSO, CHAGALL, MODIGLIANI & CO.
(1900–1939)

Edited by
Christian Briend
assisted by Anna Hiddleston-Galloni

Graphic design:
-scope Ateliers, Beirut
Photogravure :
-scope Ateliers, Beirut
English translation:
Dafydd Rees Roberts
English copy-editor:
Ros Schwartz
Ros Schwartz Translations, London

Printed in July 2019 by
Grammlich Offsetdruckerei
Pliezhausen, Germany

ISBN 978-614-8035-33-3
(English edition)

COVER IMAGE
Pablo Picasso (1881-1973)
Young Girl with a Hoop (detail), spring 1919
Oil and sand on canvas, 142.5 × 79 cm
Paris, Centre Pompidou – Musée National d'Art Moderne.
Bequest of Baroness Eva Gourgaud, 1965
Inv. AM 4312 P

Published by

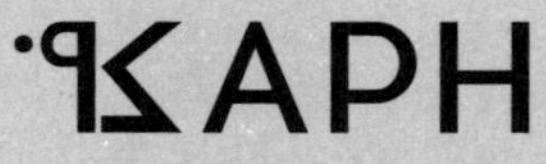

Gouraud street, Gemmayze
Renno building, 3rd floor
Beirut
Lebanon
Tel. +961 3 601 123
Fax. +961 1 999 068
www.kaphbooks.com

Our books are distributed

Les Presses du Réel
(France, Belgium, Switzerland and Luxemburg)
www.lespressesdureel.com

Idea Books (rest of the world)
www.ideabooks.nl